IN VITRO PHARMACOLOGICAL STUDY PROTOCOLS: ETHICAL AND PRACTICAL GUIDE FOR BUDGET–CONSCIOUS LAB

A practical guide for biotechnology, microbiology, pharmaceutical chemistry and pharmacy researchers seeking cost-effective, ethically sound in vitro experimental models for pharmacological studies

Mayank Tenguria
and
Prabhat Kumar Jain

Disclaimer or Author's Note

The protocols and methods described in this book are designed as generalized guidelines to aid researchers, scholars, and students in conducting their studies. While every effort has been made to ensure accuracy and applicability, users are encouraged to adapt or modify these protocols as necessary based on the specific requirements of their research setting. This includes, but is not limited to, adjusting stock concentrations of reagents, substrates, enzymes, or samples to accommodate variations in laboratory equipment, wavelengths, chemical brands, order of reagent addition and local conditions.

Such modifications should be made thoughtfully to optimize outcomes and ensure the reliability of results. The flexibility inherent in these protocols is intended to maximize their utility across diverse research environments. Feedback and suggestions for improvements are always welcome to refine and enhance the methods further.

Contents

Chapter 1

Introduction to Ethical *In Vitro* Pharmacological Studies of Phytochemicals

Pharmacology explores the effects of drugs on biological systems through *in vitro*, *in vivo*, and clinical trial studies. ***In vitro* studies** involve controlled testing on cells or tissues in laboratory settings, providing a fast, ethical, and precise way to screen compounds for therapeutic potential. ***In vivo* studies**, conducted in animal models, further explore drug safety, pharmacokinetics, and therapeutic potential, bridging *in vitro* results with more complex biological interactions providing essential insights before human trials. **Clinical trials** are conducted on humans to evaluate safety, efficacy, and optimal dosing, ultimately paving the way for regulatory approval and public availability.

In vitro methods, however, are increasingly favoured in early-stage drug discovery for being cost-effective and ethically sound. Assays like cell viability and enzyme inhibition are efficient for early-stage drug discovery, offer accessible, reproducible platforms, making *in vitro* approaches invaluable for rapidly identifying promising drug leads for further development.

1.1 Scope of *In Vitro* Studies in Phytochemistry

Phytochemistry, the study of bioactive compounds in plants, has drawn significant attention due to the medicinal, therapeutic, and nutritional benefits these compounds offer. Traditionally, plant-based compounds have been integral to folk medicine, but scientific advancements now allow for a more structured, scientific approach to studying these phytochemicals. This surge in interest is fueled by the quest to identify new drug candidates from natural sources, particularly those that can be synthesized or used as lead compounds for drug development.

In vitro studies offer a controlled environment to investigate how phytochemicals interact with various biological systems. This scope is extensive, encompassing cytotoxicity, antimicrobial activity, anti-inflammatory effects, and enzyme inhibition. Moreover, *in vitro* studies serve as an essential screening step in the drug discovery pipeline, allowing for an assessment of a compound's pharmacological potential before moving to more complex *in vivo* studies or clinical trials. These methods significantly minimize the use of animal models, thereby aligning with the current push for ethically responsible research. Consequently, *in vitro* methodologies have become indispensable in phytochemical research, providing an ethical, efficient, and cost-effective platform to assess bioactive compounds from plants.

1.2 Importance and Applications in Drug Discovery

Drug discovery relies heavily on *in vitro* studies to investigate the efficacy, potency, and mechanisms of novel compounds. Phytochemicals serve as valuable resources, offering a variety of chemical structures that exhibit pharmacological activity. In the early stages of drug discovery, *in vitro* methods enable researchers to isolate and characterize specific plant-derived compounds, such as flavonoids, alkaloids, terpenoids, and polyphenols. These compounds often exhibit antioxidant, antimicrobial, anticancer, and anti-inflammatory properties, which can be harnessed in designing new therapeutic drugs.

Beyond efficacy screening, *in vitro* methods allow for the examination of toxicity, drug metabolism, and pharmacokinetics, critical elements in drug discovery. The use of cell cultures, enzyme assays, and various biochemical methods enables detailed assessments without animal testing. For example, cancer cell lines are widely used in screening for anticancer activity, while microbial assays help evaluate antimicrobial properties. With the development of more sophisticated *in vitro* methods, such as 3D cell culture and microfluidic systems, researchers are able to mimic physiological conditions more accurately. This contributes to the refinement of lead compounds before advancing to *in vivo* models, accelerating the drug development process while reducing the ethical concerns associated with traditional pharmacology research.

1.3 Overview of Bioactive Phytochemicals

Phytochemicals are non-nutritive, biologically active compounds found in plants. They play a protective role in plants and contribute to plant resilience against pathogens, herbivores, and environmental stressors. Phytochemicals can be broadly categorized into various classes, including alkaloids, flavonoids, tannins, saponins, glycosides, and terpenoids, each exhibiting unique chemical structures and biological activities.

Each class of phytochemicals possesses specific pharmacological properties. For instance, flavonoids are renowned for their antioxidant activity, making them effective in neutralizing free radicals and protecting cells from oxidative stress. Alkaloids exhibit diverse biological effects and are known for their analgesic, anti-malarial, and anticancer properties. Terpenoids, which include compounds like limonene and menthol, possess anti-inflammatory and antimicrobial properties. The diversity of these compounds makes phytochemicals attractive candidates for drug discovery, with potential applications in treating diseases ranging from infections to cancer and neurodegenerative disorders.

The bioactivity of these phytochemicals in human health is well-documented, and their safety and efficacy can be rigorously assessed through *in vitro* studies. By understanding the mechanisms of action and bioavailability of these compounds, researchers can harness the potential of phytochemicals in developing natural, safe, and effective therapeutic agents.

1.4 Overview of Ethical Considerations in Pharmacology

Ethics in pharmacology is paramount, particularly as it relates to animal welfare, human rights, and environmental impact. With the adoption of the 3Rs principle (Replacement, Reduction, Refinement), there is a push towards minimizing animal use in research. The replacement principle encourages the use of non-animal models, like cell cultures and computational methods, wherever feasible. Reduction focuses on minimizing the number of animals used, and refinement seeks to alleviate any potential pain or distress experienced by animals during experiments.

In vitro methods align with these ethical standards by reducing or eliminating the need for animal testing. They also afford a higher degree of control and repeatability, which can enhance data quality and reliability. Furthermore, *in vitro* pharmacological studies provide ethical advantages by reducing the environmental impact associated with traditional drug testing and development. For instance, plant-based *in vitro* studies can be conducted sustainably, using only the necessary quantities of plant material and limiting waste generation.

Ethical considerations also extend to the sources of the plants themselves. For sustainable phytochemical research, sourcing practices should ensure that plant material is harvested responsibly and does not endanger species or disrupt ecosystems. By integrating ethical considerations into phytochemical research, scientists contribute to a more responsible and sustainable approach to drug discovery and development.

1.5 Advantages of Using Easy and Ethically Sound *In Vitro* Methods

The appeal of *in vitro* methods lies in their accessibility, cost-effectiveness, and ethical soundness. Many *in vitro* pharmacological assays require minimal equipment, making them accessible to laboratories with limited resources. Techniques such as cell viability assays, enzyme inhibition assays, and antimicrobial susceptibility tests can be performed using affordable reagents and basic lab infrastructure. This simplicity is particularly beneficial for early-stage drug discovery, as it allows for high-throughput screening of phytochemicals, expediting the identification of potential drug candidates.

From an ethical standpoint, *in vitro* methods reduce the reliance on animal models, minimizing the ethical dilemmas associated with animal research. These methods also allow for controlled testing conditions, providing a reproducible environment to study specific pharmacological effects without external interferences. Furthermore, *in vitro* methods facilitate customization of assays to focus on particular biological pathways or cell types, contributing to precision in pharmacological studies.

In addition, these ethically sound methods support the development of cruelty-free products, particularly in the cosmetics and nutraceuticals industries, where consumer demand for ethically sourced and cruelty-free products is high. Therefore, using *in vitro* methodologies aligns with both ethical standards and societal expectations, making it a sustainable choice for phytochemical research.

1.6 Applications of Phytochemicals in Ethically Responsible Research

Ethically responsible research has become increasingly important in modern science, where researchers are expected to balance scientific innovation with social and environmental responsibilities. *In vitro* pharmacological studies provide an ethical pathway for studying phytochemicals, as they reduce the ecological footprint of research activities and promote the responsible use of resources. By focusing on plant-based compounds, researchers contribute to a natural and sustainable approach to drug discovery, which is especially relevant in light of global concerns about environmental preservation and resource depletion.

Phytochemicals have a wide range of applications in ethically responsible research, from studying potential therapeutic agents to developing natural pesticides and food preservatives. In antimicrobial studies, for instance, plant-derived compounds provide promising alternatives to synthetic chemicals, with the added benefit of being environmentally friendly and sustainable. Anti-inflammatory and anticancer assays are also commonly conducted with phytochemicals, given their diverse mechanisms of action and low toxicity profiles.

Moreover, *in vitro* studies on phytochemicals can be tailored to assess interactions with human cell lines, providing valuable insights into the compounds' potential effects on human health without the ethical complexities associated with human testing. Through these applications, phytochemicals offer a bridge between scientific innovation and ethical responsibility, contributing to a future where research is both effective and ethically grounded.

Final Thoughts

In vitro pharmacological studies of phytochemicals represent a crucial intersection of scientific innovation and ethical responsibility. These studies harness the potential of plant-derived compounds to develop therapeutic agents while adhering to principles that prioritize human and animal welfare, environmental sustainability, and resource conservation. Through their accessible, cost-effective, and ethically sound approach, *in vitro* methods have opened new pathways for drug discovery, allowing researchers to explore the pharmacological potential of phytochemicals in a controlled and responsible manner. As the demand for ethical and sustainable research practices grows, *in vitro* studies of phytochemicals offer a model for future scientific endeavours that seek to balance innovation with respect for life and the environment.

Chapter 2

Preparation and Standardization of Plant Extracts

To study the biological and pharmacological activity of phytochemicals, selecting and collecting suitable plant material is essential. Proper selection ensures the presence of desired bioactive compounds, enhancing the study's relevance and effectiveness. For laboratories with minimal infrastructure, simple extraction methods, such as maceration, decoction, or Soxhlet extraction, offer effective yet accessible means to obtain phytochemical-rich extracts. These methods, which require basic equipment, allow researchers to prepare extracts efficiently while maintaining bioactivity. Implementing such approaches enables the exploration of plant compounds' potential benefits even in resource-limited settings, supporting diverse scientific and therapeutic research applications.

2.1 Guidelines for Selecting Plant Material

The selection of appropriate plant material is crucial in the preparation of plant extracts for research and therapeutic applications. Several factors must be considered to ensure that the chosen plant species are suitable for extraction:

1. **Botanical Source**: It is vital to choose plants that are well-documented for their medicinal properties. Herbal texts, pharmacopoeias, and ethnobotanical studies can provide valuable information about the efficacy and traditional uses of various plants. However, some unknown or undocumented plant can also be chosen for novel instigation point of view.

2. **Plant Part**: Different parts of the plant (leaves, roots, flowers, seeds, bark) may contain varying concentrations of active compounds. The selection should be based on the part known to have the highest yield of the desired bioactive components. However, random selection of plant parts can also be done from research point of view.

3. **Harvesting Time**: The time of year, season, and time of day when the plant is harvested can significantly affect the concentration of active compounds. For example, certain phytochemicals may peak in concentration during specific flowering or fruiting stages. Some of the phytochemicals may remain in higher concentration in particular seasons like summer, rainy or winters, which should be kept in mind to plan the research. However, random harvesting time would also do to have preliminary idea from research point of view.

4. **Growing Conditions**: Environmental factors, such as soil type, altitude, and climate, can influence the phytochemical profile of a plant. Collecting samples from consistent environments can reduce variability. For instance, *Asparagus racemosus* (Shatavari), *Terminalia chebula* (Haritika), *Withania somnifera* (Ashwagandha) would have differences in phytochemical profiles when collected from

Himalayan ranges and Plains of India. So, this should be kept in mind or one can collect plants from any random places depending on their research or learning objectives.

5. **Health of the Plant**: The selected plant should be healthy, free from disease, and collected from clean, pollution-free areas to ensure the absence of contaminants.

2.2 Collection, Botanical Authentication, and Taxonomy

Once suitable plant material is selected, proper collection and identification processes must be undertaken:

1. **Collection**: Plants should be harvested sustainably, taking care not to deplete natural populations. This often involves collecting small amounts of plant material from multiple individuals of the species.
2. **Botanical Authentication**: Accurate identification is crucial. This can be achieved by comparing samples against herbarium specimens, consulting local botanists, or using identification keys and guides. Accurate labeling with details such as the collection date, location, and collector's name is essential. This can be documented in suitable table formats.
3. **Taxonomy**: Understanding the taxonomy of the selected plant helps in recognizing its family, genus, and species, which can indicate the potential for bioactive compounds. Genetic analysis may also be used for verification, especially for closely related species. One can do this depending upon the availability of the facilities and specialization.

2.3 Simple Extraction Methods Suitable for Lab-Scale Studies

Once the plant material has been collected and authenticated, the next step involves the extraction of bioactive compounds. The general flow of work involves; the processing of plant material, defatting of plant material, extraction of phytochemical, concentration of phytochemical extract, preparation of working stock solution, phytochemical profiling and biological or pharmacological studies.

2.3.1 Processing of plant material

The initial step in preparing plant material for phytochemical extraction involves collection, cleaning, drying, and grinding. Fresh plant material is collected during the appropriate season and growth stage to ensure maximum bioactive compound concentration. After collection, the material is rinsed thoroughly to remove any soil, dust, and contaminants. Once clean, the plant material is dried—air or shade drying is typically preferred to avoid degradation of heat-sensitive compounds. For a quicker drying process, an oven can be used at a controlled temperature (not exceeding 40–50°C) to prevent the loss of volatile compounds. Once dry, the material is ground into a fine powder using a mill or grinder. This grinding step increases surface area, which significantly improves the extraction efficiency of phytochemicals.

2.3.2 Defatting of Plant Material

Defatting is an essential pre-extraction step, particularly when the plant material contains lipids, waxes, or chlorophyll, as these can interfere with the isolation of the target phytochemicals. The process begins with selecting a nonpolar solvent, such as n-hexane or petroleum ether, which dissolves fats and oils without affecting other components. Typically, the defatting process is performed using a Soxhlet apparatus, where the plant powder is extracted with the chosen solvent over 6–8 hours. Alternatively, a maceration technique can be applied by soaking the plant powder in the solvent for 24 hours, stirring occasionally in a beaker or wide mouth glass bottle with lid. Once defatting is complete, the mixture is filtered, and the solvent is discarded. This leaves behind defatted plant material, which is now ready for further extraction steps with solvents suitable for isolating specific phytochemicals.

2.3.3 Phytochemical Extraction

Following defatting, phytochemical extraction is conducted using solvents chosen according to the polarity of the desired compounds—methanol or ethanol for polar compounds, and chloroform or ethyl acetate for semi-polar compounds. Several simple extraction methods are suitable for lab-scale studies. With minimal lab facilities and to keep the process simple, we will outline the following three easy extraction approaches;

1. **Maceration**: This is a straightforward technique where the plant material is immersed in a solvent (such as water, ethanol, or methanol) at room temperature for a specified period, typically ranging from several hours (24–72 hours) to a few days (3 to 5 days) with occasional shaking to enhance compound dissolution in a covered beaker or a wide mouth closed lid glass bottle. The mixture is then strained to separate the liquid extract from the solid residue. The maceration process is simple, cost-effective, and suitable for extracting delicate compounds, as it operates at room temperature, preserving heat-sensitive phytochemicals. Its prolonged soaking allows efficient extraction of polar and semi-polar compounds without specialized equipment, making it ideal for small-scale and resource-limited labs conducting phytochemical studies.
2. **Decoction**: Suitable for tougher plant parts such as roots, bark, and seeds, decoction involves boiling the plant material in water for a set duration. The plant material is first coarsely ground, then added to boiling water and simmered for 15–60 minutes, depending on the plant type or process goes on till the initial volume of water reduces to half. The boiling process helps to break down the cell walls, facilitating the release of soluble compounds. The resulting mixture is then cooled, strained, and stored. Decoction is beneficial for extracting compounds that are stable at higher temperatures, such as tannins, glycosides, and alkaloids. Water is the most common solvent, but alcohol-water mixtures can also be used for better solubility of specific phytochemicals, enhancing extraction efficiency and yield.
3. **Soxhlet Extraction**: Soxhlet extraction, or Soxhlation, is a continuous extraction process ideal for isolating compounds from plant material with moderate to high polarity. This technique is often used for more efficient extraction of lipophilic compounds. The Soxhlet apparatus allows for continuous extraction, where the solvent is heated and vaporized, then condensed back into the extraction chamber containing the plant material. The cycle continues until the desired extraction efficiency is reached. This method is more complex and requires specific laboratory equipment but yields concentrated extracts.

In this process, finely ground plant material is placed in a porous thimble or wrapped in filter paper within the extractor (middle) part of Soxhlet apparatus. A suitable solvent is heated in the round bottom flask below, and as it evaporates, it passes through the plant material, dissolving target compounds. The solvent containing the extract condenses in the condenser above, then drips back into the flask, cycling through multiple times until maximum extraction is achieved. Afterward, the solvent is evaporated, leaving behind a concentrated extract.

Soxhlation is highly efficient and uses minimal solvent compared to traditional maceration, making it ideal for larger-scale extractions with enhanced yield. Suitable solvents include ethanol, methanol, chloroform, and hexane, chosen based on the polarity of the target compounds. This method is particularly beneficial for extracting thermally stable bioactives in a resource- and time-efficient manner.

2.3.4 Concentration of Extracts

Concentrating extracts after extraction is an essential step to obtain a potent, residue-free sample. While a rotary evaporator is the most efficient and widely used tool for solvent removal, but sometimes, it may not be accessible in all laboratories. The rotary evaporator works by applying reduced pressure and gentle heat to evaporate the solvent at lower temperatures, preserving heat-sensitive compounds and concentrating the extract efficiently.

In resource-limited laboratory settings, cost-effective alternatives include drying at room temperature or using a water bath. Room temperature drying is suitable for volatile solvents like ethanol, which gradually evaporate over several days. This method requires good ventilation to prevent the buildup of solvent fumes. Alternatively, a water bath at low temperatures (around 40–50°C) can be used to gently heat the extract, accelerating solvent evaporation without significant risk to the compounds. For this the liquid extract obtained after extraction is taken in a beaker of suitable size and placed in water bath at 40–50°C and allowed to evaporate the residual solvent till the slurry, past or crystals of extract are obtained. This solvent free extract is then collected by scraping it from the beaker weighed and stored in a container at room temperature or at 4–5°C in a refrigerator for further studies. This approach is effective for water, alcohol based or any polar solvent based extracts, though it requires careful monitoring to avoid overheating and degradation of sensitive phytochemicals.

2.4 Standardization Techniques to Ensure Reproducibility

Standardization is essential to ensure that plant extracts are reproducible and reliable. Several techniques can be employed:

1. **Phytochemical Screening**: Preliminary qualitative tests can be conducted to identify the presence of major classes of compounds (alkaloids, flavonoids, tannins, etc.) in the extracts. This provides a baseline understanding of the extract's composition.
2. **Quantitative Analysis**: Techniques such as High-Performance Liquid Chromatography (HPLC) and Gas Chromatography-Mass Spectrometry (GC-MS) can be used for quantitative analysis of specific phytochemicals. This helps in determining the concentration of active ingredients in the extracts.

3. **Bioassays**: Conducting biological assays (antioxidant, antimicrobial, etc.) using standardized extracts can help assess their efficacy. Comparing these results across batches ensures consistency in biological activity.

4. **Quality Control**: Implementing quality control measures, such as checking for contaminants (microbial or chemical) and ensuring that the extract meets specified criteria for purity and potency, is crucial for standardization.

5. **Documentation**: Keeping detailed records of extraction methods, conditions, and results is vital for reproducibility. This documentation can serve as a reference for future studies and for regulatory purposes.

2.4.1 Cost Effective Qualitative and Quantitative Analysis

Phytochemical analysis is essential for identifying and quantifying bioactive compounds in plant extracts, categorized into qualitative and quantitative methods. **Qualitative analysis** involves preliminary phytochemical screening, which detects major bioactive groups such as alkaloids, flavonoids, tannins, saponins, terpenoids, and glycosides through simple chemical tests. For example, Mayer's test indicates the presence of alkaloids, while ferric chloride tests identify phenolic compounds. Additionally, Thin-Layer Chromatography (TLC) is employed to separate and visualize compounds, providing insight into the extract's complexity and confirming the presence of specific phytochemicals.

Quantitative analysis aims to determine the concentration of key phytochemicals using various techniques. The Folin-Ciocalteu assay measures Total Phenolic Content (TPC), while the aluminum chloride method quantifies Total Flavonoid Content (TFC). Total Alkaloid Content (TAC) and Total Tannin Content can be assessed through colorimetric methods, with results expressed in relevant equivalents. These cost-effective methods enable comprehensive analysis of phytochemicals in laboratories with basic infrastructure.

Comprehensive Overview of Phytochemical Constituents in Extracts

Phytochemical extracts are rich in diverse bioactive compounds, each contributing to the therapeutic potential of the plant. Here is a comprehensive overview of the major phytochemical groups:

Alkaloids:

Alkaloids are a diverse group of naturally occurring organic compounds that contain nitrogen atoms. They are found primarily in plants and have significant pharmacological effects, including analgesic, antimalarial, and antitumor properties. Common alkaloids include morphine, quinine, and caffeine. Alkaloids typically have bitter tastes and are used in medicine for their potent biological activities.

Flavonoids:

Flavonoids are a large family of polyphenolic compounds found in fruits, vegetables, and certain beverages. They are known for their antioxidant properties, which help in protecting cells from oxidative stress. Flavonoids also exhibit anti-inflammatory, antiviral, and anticancer activities. Examples include quercetin, kaempferol, and catechins, which contribute to the health benefits of a diet rich in fruits and vegetables.

Tannins:

Tannins are polyphenolic compounds that are abundant in a wide range of plants. They have astringent properties, which make them useful in treating burns and wounds. Tannins also exhibit antioxidant, antimicrobial, and anti-inflammatory activities. They are found in high concentrations in tea, wine, and certain fruits. The presence of tannins is often associated with a bitter or astringent taste.

Terpenoids:

Terpenoids, also known as isoprenoids, are a diverse class of organic chemicals derived from five-carbon isoprene units. They are found in all classes of living organisms and are particularly abundant in plants, where they play roles in growth, development, and defence. Terpenoids have various medicinal properties, including antimicrobial, anticancer, and anti-inflammatory effects. Examples include menthol, camphor, and artemisinin.

Saponins:

Saponins are glycosides with a distinctive foaming characteristic when mixed with water. They are found in many plants, including beans and legumes, and have various health benefits. Saponins exhibit antimicrobial, anti-inflammatory, and immune-boosting properties. They also have potential cholesterol-lowering effects by binding to bile acids. The presence of saponins is often detected by their ability to produce froth in aqueous solutions.

Glycosides:

Glycosides are compounds in which a sugar is bound to a non-carbohydrate moiety, usually a small organic molecule. They play a crucial role in plant defence and have significant medicinal properties. Cardiac glycosides, like digoxin, are used to treat heart conditions, while other glycosides have anticancer, antimicrobial, and anti-inflammatory effects. Glycosides are widely distributed in the plant kingdom and contribute to the pharmacological effects of many medicinal plants.

Anthraquinones:

Anthraquinones are aromatic organic compounds found in several plant species, particularly in the Rhamnaceae, Polygonaceae, and Fabaceae families. They are known for their laxative properties, making them useful in treating constipation. Anthraquinones also exhibit antimicrobial, antiviral, and anticancer activities. They are often identified by their characteristic colour reactions and are used in traditional and modern medicine for their therapeutic properties.

These phytochemical groups contribute significantly to the medicinal value of plants, offering a wide range of therapeutic benefits.

2.5 Storing and Handling Extracts to Preserve Bioactivity

Proper storage and handling of plant extracts are essential to maintain their bioactivity over time. Several strategies should be implemented:

1. **Storage Conditions**: Extracts should be stored in airtight containers, preferably amber glass bottles, to protect them from light and moisture. Cool, dark, and dry environments are ideal for minimizing degradation. Refrigeration can further extend the shelf life of heat-sensitive extracts.
2. **Avoiding Contamination**: Using clean utensils and avoiding direct contact with hands during handling can help prevent contamination. It's also important to minimize the number of times an extract is opened to reduce exposure to air and humidity.
3. **Regular Testing**: Periodically testing the extracts for their bioactivity can help monitor changes in potency over time. This can be done through repeated bioassays or analytical methods.
4. **Labeling**: Clearly labeling storage containers with the date of extraction, type of extract, and storage conditions helps maintain organization and track the age of each extract.

Overall, the preparation and standardization of plant extracts are multifaceted processes that require careful attention to detail. From the selection of plant material to extraction methods, standardization techniques, and storage practices, each step plays a critical role in ensuring that the resulting extracts are effective, reproducible, and safe for use in research and therapeutic applications. By adhering to these guidelines, researchers can harness the full potential of plant-derived compounds in their studies.

Chapter 3

Phytochemical Screening and Characterization

3.1 Quick Tests for Various Phytoconstituents

Phytochemical analysis is a fundamental step in exploring the medicinal potential of plants, aimed at identifying and quantifying bioactive compounds within extracts. Phytochemical screening uses simple, rapid tests to identify the presence of key phytoconstituents in plant extracts. Each class of compound reacts with specific reagents, producing colour changes or precipitates that indicate their presence. Below are some common quick tests for various phytoconstituents:

3.1.1 Preliminary Phytochemical Analysis

Preliminary screening provides an affordable way to identify major phytochemical groups that require minimal reagents and equipment, providing an initial qualitative insight into the phytochemical profile. The following test protocols and method that provide clear and reliable visible reactions that we can depend on;

Organoleptic property of extract

When evaluating the organoleptic properties of a phytochemical extract that is concentrated, dried, and devoid of any traces of solvent, the process remains fundamentally similar, with some modifications to account for the physical state of the extract. Here's how to approach this evaluation:

1. **Preparation of Sample**
   - **Concentration and Drying**: Ensure the extract have been properly concentrated and dried, free from any solvent residues.
   - **Sample Size**: Use a consistent sample size for evaluation.
2. **Appearance**
   - **Visual Inspection**: Observe the dry extract under both natural and artificial light.
     - **Form**: Note whether the extract is in powder, crystalline, or any other solid form.
     - **Colour**: Compare the colour to a standard chart or reference sample, documenting the shade and intensity.
     - **Homogeneity**: Check for uniformity and absence of clumping or unevenness.
3. **Odor**
   - **Smell Evaluation**: Gently sniff the dried extract.

- **Intensity**: Rate the strength of the odour (e.g., faint, mild, strong).
- **Character**: Describe the nature of the odour (e.g., earthy, floral, spicy).

4. Colour of extract

- Dissolve small amount of extract in distilled water as necessary to achieve a uniform slurry.
- Using a glass rod take just a small amount of slurry and rub it on a filter paper in a line to make strip of about 0.5 mm to 10 mm thick allow it to dry.
- Observe the colour in natural daylight, which provides the most accurate colour representation.
- Compare the observed colour with a colour reference chart such as the Munsell Colour Chart or Pantone Colour Guide.
- Match the extract's colour to the closest shade on the chart, and record the corresponding colour code.
- Note the exact colour description, including any specific nuances such as "light green," "dark brown," "amber," etc.
- Take a photograph of the sample against the white background for visual records, ensuring consistent lighting and angle.

5. Taste (We are not recommending this)

- **Taste Test (If Applicable)**: For safety, ensure the extract is non-toxic and suitable for tasting.
  - **Flavour Profile**: Dissolve a small amount in a suitable medium (e.g., water) and taste.
  - **Aftertaste**: Note any lingering flavours or sensations after tasting.

6. Texture

- **Tactile Sensation**: Feel the dried extract between your fingers.
  - **Consistency**: Describe the texture (e.g., fine, coarse, sticky, free-flowing).
  - **Flow Properties**: Assess if the extract is free-flowing or has a tendency to clump.

7. Reconstitution (Optional)

- **Reconstitution**: Dissolve the extract in a suitable solvent (e.g., water or ethanol) to observe changes in organoleptic properties.
  - **Solubility**: Note how easily the extract dissolves.
  - **Changes in Properties**: Reassess colour, odour, and taste in the reconstituted form.

8. Documentation

- **Record Observations**: Use sensory evaluation forms to systematically document all findings.
- **Descriptive Analysis**: Provide detailed descriptions for each evaluated property.

9. **Comparison with Standards**

- **Benchmarking**: Compare observations with known standards or previous batches to ensure consistency.
- **Quality Control**: Use the data for quality assurance purposes.

10. **Safety Considerations**

- **Ethical Practices**: Ensure the dried extract is safe for sensory evaluation, particularly for taste tests.
- **Training:** Sensory evaluators should be trained to recognize and report any adverse reactions.

Evaluating the organoleptic properties of a dried and solvent-free phytochemical extract is essential for quality control and ensuring product consistency. By following a detailed and systematic approach, researchers can accurately assess sensory attributes, which are crucial for consumer acceptance and therapeutic efficacy.

3.1.2 Stock preparation of tests

Before testing phytochemical extracts for various chemical constituents, it is essential to prepare a working stock solution. For water-soluble extracts, sterile distilled water is typically used. However, for extracts that do not dissolve easily in water, a 1-2% solution of DMSO can be employed to prepare the working stock solution. Generally, a stock solution of 100 mg/mL is preferred for studies. To prepare this, 1 gram of the phytochemical extract is placed in a watch glass or petri dish, and a small amount of water is added to dissolve the extract using a glass rod. Once a homogeneous solution is achieved, the final volume is adjusted to 10 mL, resulting in a 100 mg/mL stock solution. This stock can then be further diluted according to the specific requirements of the experiments.

3.1.3 Phytochemical Tests

A small portion of the stock extract is diluted and then subjected to phytochemical testing using the methods outlined by Harbourne (1983) to evaluate the presence of various phytochemical constituents described below;

Test for alkaloids: About 100 μL of stock is taken in china dish and diluted with distilled water. Now few drops of Dragendorff's reagent are added, orange red precipitate indicates the presence of alkaloids.

Test for flavonoids: About 100 μL of stock is diluted with distilled water then 2-3 drops of 10% lead acetate are added. A creamy white dirty precipitate indicates the presence of flavonoids.

Test for Tannins: Small quantity of extract is mixed with water, heated, filtered and 2-3 drops of ferric chloride solution are added. A dark green solution indicates the presence of tannins.

Test for glycosides: Benedict reagent is used to check the presence of glycosides in diluted extract. The diluted extract is first warmed then 2-3 drops of Benedict's reagent are added to the reaction tube. The appearance of yellow or orange precipitate indicates the presence of glycoside in extract.

Test for saponins: About 100 μL of stock is diluted with 5 ml of distilled then warmed a little, then shaken vigorously which if results into frothing (appearance of creamy mix of small bubbles) shows the presence of saponins which must last for at least 1 to 5 minutes.

Test for terpenoids: About 100 μL of stock is diluted with distilled water followed by mixing with 2 ml chloroform ($CHCl_3$) and concentrated H_2SO_4 (3ml) will be carefully added to form a layer. A reddish-brown coloration or ring at the interface indicates the presence of terpenoids.

Anthraquinone Test: About 100 μL of stock of extract is taken in a test tube then slightly warmed and 2 ml of chloroform is added into it. This is followed by adding equal volume of 10% ammonia solution. The appearance of purple colour/tint or purple ring at the junction will be the indication of presence of anthraquinone in the test extract.

NOTE: The amount of stock extract for testing can be taken in range of 100 μL to 1 ml volume according the intensity of reaction or experimental requirement.

3.2 Thin-Layer Chromatography (TLC) Analysis

TLC is a low-cost method for separating and identifying compounds in plant extracts. Using silica or alumina-coated plates, the sample is applied and developed in a solvent system. Different compounds migrate at varying rates, producing distinct bands that can be visualized with UV light or stains. TLC provides valuable qualitative insights into the presence and diversity of compounds such as alkaloids, flavonoids, and terpenoids. Generally, the presence of quercetin or rutin equivalent flavonoids and gallic acid equivalent polyphenols are routinely assessed on TLC. However, any other specific chemical constituent could also be tried to detect in phytochemical extracts like colchicine, curcumin etc.

3.2.1 Methodology for detection of Quercetin by TLC Analysis

Thin Layer Chromatography (TLC) is an effective technique for the qualitative analysis of phytochemicals such as quercetin. Below is a detailed methodology, including the requirements for the experiment.

Requirements

1. **Materials and Equipment:**
   - **Quercetin Standard**: Pure quercetin for reference.
   - **Plant Extract**: The sample containing quercetin.
   - **TLC Plates**: Silica gel or alumina plates (typically 0.2 mm thick).
   - **Developing Solvent**: A suitable solvent system (e.g., Ethyl acetate: Methanol: Water in a ratio of 10:1:1 or as needed).
   - **Capillary Tubes**: For spotting the samples.
   - **Glassware**: Beakers, a TLC chamber, and a watch glass.

- **UV-Vis TLC Visualizer**: For visualizing quercetin (254 nm or 365 nm).
- **Pencil**: For marking on the TLC plate.
- **Ruler**: To measure distances accurately.

Methodology

1. **Preparation of the TLC Plate:**
   - **TLC Plates:** Thin layer silica gel 60G F254 DC Kieselgel 60 plates cut into 5×7 cm size is generally preferred for analysis that gives good results
   - **Marking**: Using a pencil, lightly mark a baseline about 1 cm from the bottom of the TLC plate. This is where the samples will be spotted.
   - **Spotting the Samples**: Using a capillary tube, apply small spots of the quercetin standard (known concentration) and the plant extract onto the marked baseline. Ensure that the spots do not touch each other and allow adequate space for development. Allow them to dry properly.
2. **Preparation of the Developing Chamber:**
   - **Solvent System**: Prepare the developing solvent in a clean beaker according to the chosen solvent ratio.
   - **Saturation**: Place a piece of filter paper in the TLC chamber and pour in enough solvent to saturate the chamber without touching the TLC plate. Cover the chamber with a watch glass.
3. **Developing the TLC Plate:**
   - **Placement**: Carefully place the spotted TLC plate in the saturated chamber, ensuring that the baseline is above the solvent level.
   - **Development**: Allow the solvent to ascend the plate by capillary action until it reaches about 1 cm from the top. This usually takes around 10-30 minutes.
4. **Visualization:**
   - **Drying**: Remove the plate from the chamber and allow it to dry in the air.
   - **UV Visualization**: Place the dried plate under a UV chamber at 254 nm or 365 nm to visualize quercetin as a spot on the plate.
5. **Analysis:**
   - **Retention Factor (R_f) Calculation**: Measure the distance travelled by the quercetin spot and the solvent front. Calculate the R_f value using the formula:

$$R_f = \frac{\text{Distance travelled by the compound}}{\text{Distance travelled by the solvent}}$$

- **Comparison**: Compare the R_f values and appearance of the sample spots with those of the quercetin standard to confirm the presence of quercetin.

Notes:

- Ensure that all glassware and equipment are clean and free from contaminants to avoid interference in the results.
- Proper safety measures should be taken while handling solvents and working in the fume hood.
- Document all observations, including R_f values and any notable characteristics of the spots for further analysis.

This methodology outlines a systematic approach to using TLC for the detection of quercetin in plant extracts, providing a reliable means of qualitative analysis in phytochemical studies.

3.3 Quantitative Analysis of Phytochemical Groups

Quantitative analysis of phytochemical groups involves measuring specific classes of bioactive compounds present in plant extracts. Commonly analysed groups include Total Phenolic Content (TPC), Total Flavonoid Content (TFC), Total Alkaloidal Content (TAC), Total Tannin Content, Total Terpenoid Content, and Total Glycoside Content. Each group represents compounds with unique biological properties, such as antioxidant, anti-inflammatory, antimicrobial, and cytotoxic activities, which contribute to the therapeutic potential of the plant. Quantifying these groups provides insight into the plant's potency and consistency in active constituents, helping to standardize extracts for both research and potential therapeutic applications. Using colorimetric assays, spectrophotometry, or chromatography, researchers can accurately measure these groups to better understand the plant's pharmacological profile.

3.3.1 Estimation of Total Polyphenolic Content

The **total phenolic content** of the extracts can be determined using Folin-Ciocalteu method with suitable modification. Here extracts are suitably diluted with their respective solvents and oxidized with Folin-Ciocalteu reagent, and the reaction was neutralized with sodium carbonate. The absorbance of the resulting blue colour is measured at ***650 nm.***

Requirements

1. **Materials:**
   - Plant extract (prepared in methanol or ethanol)
   - Gallic acid (standard phenolic compound)
   - Folin-Ciocalteu reagent
   - Sodium carbonate (Na_2CO_3) solution (20% w/v)
   - Distilled water

2. **Equipment:**
    - UV-Vis spectrophotometer
    - Cuvettes (preferably 1 cm path length)
    - Pipettes and micropipettes
    - Volumetric flasks or test tubes (10 mL, 50 mL, and 100 mL)

Procedure

1. **Preparation of Gallic Acid Standard Solution:**
    - Prepare a stock solution of gallic acid by dissolving 50 mg standard Gallic acid in 50 ml methanol (70%), it will give 1 mg/ml stock solution of standard polyphenol gallic acid.
    - Now prepare various aliquots of 10–50μg/ml in methanol (or aliquots of suitable dilutions) or we can serially dilute the stock solution to get 1000 μg/ml, 500 μg/ml, 250 μg/ml 125 μg/ml, 62.5 μg/ml, 31.25 μg/ml.

    Or

    - ***Alternatively,*** make a 10–fold dilution of 1000 μg/ml, to get 100 μg/ml and make serial dilution of this solution to get aliquots of 100 μg/ml, 50 μg/ml, 25 μg/ml 12.5 μg/ml and 6.25 μg/ml gallic acid in 70% methanol.
2. **Preparation of Sample Extract Solution:**
    - The 100 mg/ml stock concentration of phytochemical extract or any sample is suitably diluted in methanol to prepare a 1 mg/mL solution or as per sample requirements then filtered for estimation of polyphenols ***(*One must aware of the dilution factor of sample diluted).***
3. **Preparation of Standard Curve Plot:**
    - Take 5 test tubes and put 100 μL each gallic acid standard concentration aliquot in separate tubes and make up the volume 2 ml with distilled water, mixed thoroughly with 100 μl of Folin–Ciocalteu reagent for 3 min, which is followed by addition of 1 ml of 20% (w/v) sodium carbonate. Now incubate the reaction mixture in waterbath at 60°C for 30 minutes.
    - The mixture was allowed to stand for a further 20 minutes in the dark, and absorbance of each reaction in different test tubes is measured at 650 nm using pre-set spectrophotometer. Using these standard concentrations of gallic acid and their respective absorbance prepare the standard curve plot on MS-Excel.
4. **Estimation of TPC in Sample:**
    - Take 100 μl of crude extract (1 mg/mL) in a test tube and add 2 ml distilled water, mix thoroughly with 100 μl of Folin–Ciocalteu reagent for 3 min, which is followed by addition of 1 ml of 20% (w/v) sodium carbonate.

- Now incubate the reaction mixture in waterbath at 60°C for 30 minutes. The mixture was allowed to stand for a further 20 minutes in the dark and absorbance of each reaction in different test tubes is measured at 650 nm or 700 nm using pre-set spectrophotometer. After this compare the absorbance reading with plotted standard curve to illustrate the TPC in sample.

5. **Calculation of Total Phenolic Content:**
   - Use the calibration curve to determine the concentration of phenolic compounds in the plant extract.
   - Express the results as milligrams of gallic acid equivalent per gram of extract (mg GAE/g extract).

Note: If the absorbance reading doesn't fit between the minimum and maximum absorbance values of standard plot, repeat the experiment with diluted sample. It would be much better to do experiments with at least 3 dilutions of samples also from beginning. The reaction can also be performed without the addition of sodium carbonate minding that the reaction mixture must be alkaline.

Notes:

- Ensure all glassware and reagents are clean and free of contaminants.
- Run all samples and standards in triplicate to enhance result reliability.
- Protect samples from light to prevent degradation of phenolic compounds.

This method provides a consistent and reproducible way to estimate the total phenolic content in phytochemical extracts, aiding in the assessment of their antioxidant and therapeutic potential.

3.3.2 Estimation of Total Flavonoidal Content

The Aluminium Chloride colorimetric assay is widely used for the quantitative estimation of flavonoids in plant extracts based on the complex formation between flavonoids and $AlCl_3$. When flavonoids, especially flavonols and flavones, react with aluminium chloride, they form a stable yellow complex that can be measured spectrophotometrically at 415 to 420 nm. This reaction is selective for flavonoids, allowing their quantification in the presence of other phenolic compounds. The absorbance intensity is directly proportional to the concentration of flavonoids in the sample, providing a reliable estimation of the Total Flavonoid Content (TFC).

Requirements

1. **Materials:**
   - Plant extract (prepared in methanol or ethanol)
   - Quercetin (or rutin) standard solution
   - Aluminium chloride ($AlCl_3$) solution (2% w/v)
   - Sodium hydroxide (NaOH) solution (1 M)
   - Methanol (for preparing solutions)

2. **Equipment:**
   - UV-Vis spectrophotometer
   - Cuvettes (preferably 1 cm path length)
   - Pipettes and micropipettes
   - Volumetric flasks or test tubes (10 mL, 50 mL, and 100 mL)

Procedure

1. **Preparation of Standard Quercetin Solution:**
   - Prepare a stock solution of quercetin by dissolving 50 mg of quercetin in 50 mL of methanol to obtain a 1 mg/mL solution.
   - From this, prepare a series of dilutions (e.g., 10, 20, 40, 60, 80, and 100 μg/mL) to generate a standard calibration curve.
2. **Preparation of Sample Extract Solution:**
   - Prepare the plant extract solution by dissolving 1 gm of dried powder of drug was extracted with 100 ml methanol, filter, and make up the volume up to 100 ml. One ml (1mg/ml) of this extract will be used for the estimation of flavonoid or as per sample requirements.
3. **Reagent Addition:**
   - Pipette 1 ml of test sample or standard and 4 ml of distilled water will be added to a 10 ml volumetric flask or test tube.
   - Add 1 mL of 2% $AlCl_3$ solution and let it stand for 5 minutes.
   - Finally, add 1 mL of 1 M NaOH solution and bring the total volume to 10 mL with distilled water. Mix thoroughly.
4. **Incubation and Measurement:**
   - Allow the reaction mixture to stand for 30 to 60 minutes at room temperature for full colour development.
   - Measure the absorbance at 420 nm using a UV-Vis spectrophotometer against a blank prepared using the same reagents but without the sample or standard. Or you can also use the distilled water or methanol as blank.
5. **Preparation of Calibration Curve:**
   - Plot the absorbance values of the quercetin standards at 420 nm against their concentrations to obtain a calibration curve.

6. **Calculation of Total Flavonoid Content:**
   - Use the calibration curve to determine the concentration of flavonoids in the plant extract.
   - Express the results as milligrams of quercetin equivalent per gram of extract (mg QE/g extract).

Notes:

- Ensure that all glassware and reagents are clean and free of contaminants.
- Run all samples and standards in triplicate to ensure accuracy.
- Use methanol as a blank for setting the baseline of the spectrophotometer.
- This method is a reliable way to estimate flavonoid content and is commonly used in phytochemical analysis to assess the antioxidant potential and therapeutic properties of plant extracts.

3.3.3 Estimation of Total Tannin Content

The Folin-Denis method is commonly employed for the quantitative estimation of tannins in plant extracts. This spectrophotometric method is based on the reduction of phosphotungstomolybdic acid in the Folin-Denis reagent by tannin-like compounds in an alkaline medium, forming a blue colour. The intensity of the colour, which is proportional to the tannin concentration, is measured at 700 nm.

Requirements

1. **Materials:**
   - Plant extract (prepared in methanol or ethanol)
   - Tannic acid (standard for calibration)
   - Folin-Denis reagent
   - Sodium carbonate (Na_2CO_3) solution (7% w/v)
   - Distilled water
2. **Equipment:**
   - UV-Vis spectrophotometer
   - Cuvettes (preferably 1 cm path length)
   - Pipettes and micropipettes
   - Volumetric flasks (10 mL, 50 mL, and 100 mL)

Procedure

1. **Preparation of Tannic Acid Standard Solution:**
   - Prepare a stock solution of tannic acid by dissolving 10 mg of tannic acid in 10 mL of distilled water to obtain a 1 mg/mL solution.
   - Prepare a series of dilutions (e.g., 10, 20, 30, 40, and 50 μg/mL) to create a standard calibration curve.
2. **Preparation of Sample Extract Solution:**
   - Prepare the plant extract solution by dissolving an appropriate amount of extract in distilled water (e.g., 1 mg/mL) or as per sample requirements.
3. **Reagent Addition:**
   - Pipette 1 mL of the standard or sample extract solution into a test tube.
   - Add distilled water to make up the volume to 7.5 mL.
   - Add 0.5 mL of Folin-Denis reagent, followed by 1 mL of 7% Na_2CO_3 solution.
   - Make up the total volume to 10 mL with distilled water and mix thoroughly.
4. **Incubation and Measurement:**
   - Allow the reaction mixture to stand at room temperature for 30 minutes to develop colour.
   - Measure the absorbance at 700 nm using a UV-Vis spectrophotometer against a blank prepared with the same reagents but without the sample or standard.
5. **Preparation of Calibration Curve:**
   - Plot the absorbance values of the tannic acid standards at 700 nm against their concentrations to obtain a calibration curve.
6. **Calculation of Total Tannin Content:**
   - Use the calibration curve to determine the tannin concentration in the plant extract.
   - Express the results as micrograms of tannic acid equivalent per 100 μg/mL of extract (μg TAE/100 μg extract).

Notes:

- Ensure that all glassware and reagents are clean and free of contaminants.
- Run all samples and standards in triplicate to improve result accuracy.
- Use distilled water as a blank for setting the spectrophotometer baseline.

This method is a standard approach to determine tannin content in plant extracts, providing insight into the potential antioxidant and astringent properties of the sample.

3.3.4 Estimation of Total Alkaloidal Content

This method, adapted from Shamsa et al. (2008) with modifications, enables the quantitative estimation of alkaloids in plant extracts. The assay is based on the formation of a yellow complex between alkaloids and bromocresol green (BCG), which can then be measured spectrophotometrically at 470 nm.

Requirements

1. **Materials:**
   - Plant extract (1 mg/mL concentration in 2N HCl)
   - Atropine (standard alkaloid for calibration)
   - Bromocresol green (BCG) solution
   - Phosphate buffer solution (pH 7)
   - Chloroform
   - 2N HCl solution
2. **Equipment:**
   - UV-Vis spectrophotometer
   - Cuvettes (preferably 1 cm path length)
   - Pipettes and micropipettes
   - Volumetric flasks (10 mL, 50 mL, and 100 mL)

Procedure

1. **Preparation of Atropine Standard Solution:**
   - Prepare a stock solution of atropine by dissolving 10 mg of atropine in 10 mL of 2N HCl.
   - Prepare a series of dilutions to obtain concentrations of 10, 20, 40, 60, 80, and 100 μg/mL.
2. **Preparation of Sample Extract Solution:**
   - Dissolve 1 mg of the plant extract in 1 mL of 2N HCl.
   - Filter the solution and dilute it appropriately to achieve a concentration of 100 μg/mL.
3. **Reagent Addition:**
   - Prepare a phosphate buffer solution with a neutral pH of 7.
   - In a large test tube, add 1 mL of the sample or standard solution.
   - Add 5 mL of BCG solution and 5 mL of phosphate buffer to the tube.
   - Shake the mixture well to form the yellow complex.

4. **Extraction with Chloroform:**
   - Add 5 mL of chloroform to the tube containing the reaction mixture.
   - Shake vigorously to extract the BCG-alkaloid complex into the chloroform layer.
   - Carefully collect the chloroform layer in a clean tube and dilute it to a final volume of 10 mL with chloroform.
5. **Measurement of Absorbance:**
   - Measure the absorbance of the chloroform solution at 470 nm using a UV-Vis spectrophotometer.
   - Prepare a reagent blank by following the same steps but without the plant extract.
6. **Preparation of Calibration Curve:**
   - Plot the absorbance values of the atropine standards against their concentrations to create a calibration curve.
7. **Calculation of Total Alkaloidal Content:**
   - Determine the concentration of alkaloids in the plant extract by comparing the absorbance of the sample with the standard calibration curve.
   - Express the results as micrograms of atropine equivalent per 100 μg/mL of extract (μg AE/100 μg extract).

Notes:

- Ensure all glassware and reagents are free from contaminants.
- Run all samples and standards in triplicate to enhance accuracy.
- Use a blank for setting the spectrophotometer baseline.

This BCG-based method provides a reliable way to measure the total alkaloidal content in phytochemical extracts, which can contribute to understanding the pharmacological potential of the sample.

3.3.5 Total Alkaloid Content Estimation by Harborne's Method

This alternate standard method for total alkaloid content estimation is adapted from Harborne (1973). In this procedure, alkaloids are precipitated from the extract by the addition of ammonia, and the precipitate is dried and weighed to quantify the alkaloidal content.

Requirements

1. **Materials:**
   - Phytochemical extract (2.5 g)
   - Methanol (CH_3OH)

- 10% acetic acid in methanol (10% CH_3COOH solution)
- Concentrated ammonium hydroxide (NH_4OH)
- 0.1 M ammonium hydroxide solution (NH_4OH)

2. Equipment:

- Beaker (250 mL)
- Filtration setup (filter paper, funnel)
- Oven
- Weighing balance

Procedure

1. Extraction of Alkaloids:

- Place 2.5 g of the phytochemical extract in a 250 mL beaker.
- Add 200 mL of 10% CH_3COOH in methanol to the beaker and stir the mixture.
- Allow the mixture to incubate for 4 hours at room temperature to enable alkaloid extraction.

2. Precipitation of Alkaloids:

- After 4 hours, add concentrated NH_4OH dropwise to the mixture until alkaloids are completely precipitated. Continue adding NH_4OH until no further precipitation occurs.
- Allow the solution to settle, then carefully decant or filter to remove the supernatant.

3. Washing and Collection of Precipitate:

- Wash the precipitate by adding 20 mL of 0.1 M NH_4OH to remove any remaining impurities.
- Filter out the precipitate and collect the residue on filter paper.

4. Drying and Weighing:

- Transfer the filter paper with the alkaloid precipitate to an oven.
- Dry the precipitate at a suitable temperature (e.g., 60°C) until a constant weight is obtained.
- Weigh the dried precipitate to determine the alkaloid content.

5. Calculation of Total Alkaloid Content:

- Calculate the total alkaloid content in terms of percentage by comparing the weight of the dried alkaloid precipitate with the initial weight of the extract used. Following formulae is useful;

$$\text{Percent alkaloid} = \text{Weight of alkaloid} / \text{Weight of sample} \times 100$$

Notes:

- Make sure to add NH_4OH slowly to avoid excessive precipitation that might be difficult to filter.
- Perform the drying step carefully to avoid decomposition of alkaloids.

This method, based on Harborne's (1973) procedure, provides an efficient way to quantify alkaloid content by precipitating and isolating alkaloids from plant extracts, useful in phytochemical and pharmacological studies.

3.3.6 Estimation of Total Terpenoidal Content

The estimation of total terpenoidal content (TTC) is typically done using a spectrophotometric method that involves extraction with organic solvents, followed by colorimetric analysis to quantify terpenoids in the extract.

Principle of the Method:

The vanillin-sulfuric acid method relies on the reaction between terpenoids and vanillin in an acidic environment, producing a coloured complex that can be measured spectrophotometrically. This assay is sensitive to terpenoids, as vanillin reacts with the terpenoid structure to yield a stable colour, which correlates with the terpenoid content in the extract.

Requirements

1. **Materials:**
    - Plant extract (typically methanolic or ethanolic)
    - Standard terpenoid (linalool or lupeol)
    - Petroleum ether (for extraction)
    - Vanillin reagent (5% in acetic acid)
    - Sulfuric acid (H_2SO_4, concentrated)
2. **Equipment:**
    - UV-Vis spectrophotometer
    - Cuvettes (1 cm path length)
    - Pipettes and micropipettes
    - Volumetric flasks and test tubes
    - Ice bath (optional, for handling sulfuric acid)

Procedure

1. **Extraction of Terpenoids:**
   - Dissolve 1 g of the plant extract in 10 mL of petroleum ether.
   - Allow the mixture to stand for 30 minutes to enable terpenoids to partition into the petroleum ether phase.
   - Separate the petroleum ether layer, which contains the terpenoids.
2. **Reaction with Vanillin Reagent:**
   - Transfer 0.5 mL of the petroleum ether extract to a clean test tube.
   - Add 1.5 mL of vanillin reagent (5% vanillin in acetic acid) to the tube.
   - Carefully add 2.5 mL of concentrated sulfuric acid to the mixture. (Handle with care; use an ice bath if necessary.)
   - Mix the solution thoroughly and incubate it at room temperature for 30 minutes to allow colour development.
3. **Measurement of Absorbance:**
   - Measure the absorbance of the resulting solution at 538 nm using a UV-Vis spectrophotometer.
   - Prepare a reagent blank by following the same steps without adding the extract.
4. **Preparation of Standard Calibration Curve:**
   - Prepare a standard solution of a known terpenoid compound (e.g., linalool or lupeol) in petroleum ether.
   - Create a series of dilutions of the standard solution and treat them as described above.
   - Measure absorbance values at 538 nm and plot a standard curve of absorbance versus concentration.
5. **Calculation of Total Terpenoidal Content:**
   - Compare the absorbance of the sample solution with the standard curve to calculate the concentration of terpenoids in the extract.
   - Express the results as micrograms of terpenoid equivalent per gram of extract (e.g., μg TE/g extract).

Notes:

- Ensure careful handling of sulfuric acid and vanillin reagent, as these are highly reactive chemicals.
- All samples and standards should be prepared in duplicate or triplicate to ensure accuracy.
- Use fresh reagents to achieve consistent colour development.

This protocol provides an effective approach for quantifying terpenoids in plant extracts, which is valuable in phytochemical profiling and for understanding the pharmacological potential of the studied plant material.

3.3.7 Estimation of Total Glycosidal Content

The estimation of total glycosidal content is commonly performed using a colorimetric assay with Baljet's reagent, which reacts with glycosides to produce a measurable colour change. This method allows quantification based on the intensity of the colour formed.

Principle of the Method:

Baljet's reagent reacts with glycosides to form a coloured complex, which can be measured spectrophotometrically. The intensity of the colour produced is proportional to the glycoside concentration in the extract, allowing quantification of total glycosidal content. This method is widely used for screening glycosides in various plant extracts, providing a rapid and efficient way to estimate their concentration.

Requirements

1. **Materials:**
    - Plant extract (typically methanolic or ethanolic)
    - Baljet's reagent (95 mL of 1% picric acid solution and 5 mL of 10% NaOH)
    - Standard glycoside solution (e.g., digitoxin or salicin for calibration)
2. **Equipment:**
    - UV-Vis spectrophotometer
    - Cuvettes (1 cm path length)
    - Pipettes and micropipettes
    - Test tubes and volumetric flasks

Procedure

1. **Preparation of Baljet's Reagent:**
    - Mix 95 mL of 1% picric acid solution with 5 mL of 10% NaOH to prepare Baljet's reagent.
    - Store the reagent in an amber bottle to protect it from light, as picric acid is light-sensitive.
2. **Preparation of Extract Solution:**
    - Dissolve an appropriate amount of the plant extract in methanol or ethanol to obtain a concentration of 1 mg/mL.
3. **Reaction with Baljet's Reagent:**
    - Transfer 1 mL of the extract solution into a clean test tube.
    - Add 1 mL of Baljet's reagent to the tube, and mix thoroughly.
    - Incubate the mixture at room temperature for 30 minutes to allow the colour to develop.

4. **Measurement of Absorbance:**
   - After the incubation period, measure the absorbance of the solution at 495 nm using a UV-Vis spectrophotometer.
   - Prepare a blank solution by following the same steps without the plant extract.
5. **Preparation of Standard Calibration Curve:**
   - Prepare standard solutions of a known glycoside (e.g., digitoxin or salicin) in methanol.
   - Follow the same steps as described above to react the standards with Baljet's reagent.
   - Measure the absorbance values of the standard solutions and plot a standard curve of absorbance versus concentration.
6. **Calculation of Total Glycosidal Content:**
   - Calculate the glycosidal content in the sample by comparing its absorbance to the standard curve.
   - Express the results as micrograms of glycoside equivalent per gram of extract (e.g., μg GE/g extract).

Notes:

- Handle picric acid carefully, as it is highly reactive and potentially explosive in dry form.
- All samples and standards should be prepared in duplicate or triplicate for accuracy.
- Ensure all reagents are freshly prepared to achieve consistent colour development.

This method provides a straightforward approach to estimating glycosidal content in phytochemical extracts, supporting studies on plants with medicinal or pharmacological relevance.

3.4 Advanced Techniques for Structural Elucidation

Structural elucidation of compounds is a cornerstone of scientific research, enabling researchers to identify the composition, structure, and functionality of molecules. Advanced analytical techniques such as **High-Performance Liquid Chromatography (HPLC)**, **Fourier Transform Infrared Spectroscopy (FTIR)**, **Nuclear Magnetic Resonance (NMR)**, and **Mass Spectrometry (MS)** are indispensable tools in modern research. However, the availability of these instruments and the technical skills required to operate them remain significant challenges, particularly in resource-limited laboratories.

High-Performance Liquid Chromatography (HPLC)

HPLC is a versatile technique for separating, identifying, and quantifying compounds in complex mixtures. It is extensively used in pharmacology, environmental analysis, and natural product research. HPLC provides precise information about compound purity and concentration. However, the instrument is expensive, requires regular maintenance, and needs skilled personnel for operation and data interpretation.

Fourier Transform Infrared Spectroscopy (FTIR)

FTIR is employed to identify functional groups and study molecular interactions. It is particularly useful in identifying chemical bonds in a sample by measuring the absorption of infrared light. FTIR instruments are relatively more accessible but require technical expertise to prepare samples correctly and analyze the spectra effectively.

Nuclear Magnetic Resonance (NMR)

NMR spectroscopy offers detailed information about the molecular structure, stereochemistry, and dynamics of compounds. It is a gold standard for structural elucidation in organic chemistry. However, NMR instruments are highly sophisticated, expensive, and demand a deep understanding of theory and practical skills to operate and interpret data, making them less accessible to resource-limited labs.

Mass Spectrometry (MS)

Mass spectrometry determines the molecular mass and provides insights into the molecular formula and structure. It is frequently used in conjunction with other techniques like gas chromatography (GC-MS) or liquid chromatography (LC-MS) for comprehensive analysis. The equipment cost and the need for advanced software for data analysis pose additional barriers to its use in underfunded laboratories.

3.4.1 Challenges in Resource-Limited Laboratories

Many laboratories, especially in developing regions, lack access to these sophisticated tools due to high procurement and operational costs. Additionally, the absence of trained personnel to handle and maintain such instruments limits their usage. These challenges can lead to delays and inaccuracies in research, impeding scientific progress.

The Importance of Collaboration and Outsourcing

In situations where these facilities are unavailable or technical expertise is lacking, **collaboration with established research institutions** or **outsourcing sample analysis** to accredited laboratories is a pragmatic approach. Collaborations allow access to state-of-the-art instruments and expertise, fostering more reliable and efficient research. Outsourcing, though it incurs additional costs, ensures high-quality data without the need for in-house resources. In resource-limited settings, forging collaborations with the national institutes or outsourcing analyses to startups and colleges with adequate facilities is a practical alternative.

National programs like **FIST (Fund for Improvement of S&T Infrastructure)** and **RUSA (Rashtriya Uchchatar Shiksha Abhiyan)** have also empowered colleges and universities to develop advanced labs, offering affordable services for researchers.

National Institutes Offering Analytical Facilities in India

Several government-supported research institutes in India provide analytical services or collaborate on research:

1. **Indian Institute of Science (IISc), Bengaluru**
   - Offers services for NMR, MS, and FTIR analyses.
   - Supports academic and industry collaborations.
2. **Council of Scientific and Industrial Research (CSIR) Labs**
   - Examples: CSIR-Indian Institute of Chemical Technology (IICT), Hyderabad; CSIR-National Chemical Laboratory (NCL), Pune.
   - Provide high-end instrumentation for structural elucidation.
3. **Indian Institute of Technology (IITs)**
   - IITs like Delhi, Bombay, Kanpur, and Madras have advanced central instrumentation facilities.
   - They often accept samples for analysis on a service or collaborative basis.
4. **National Institute of Pharmaceutical Education and Research (NIPERs)**
   - Located in Mohali, Hyderabad, and other locations.
   - Specialized in pharmaceutical and biochemical analyses.
5. **Sophisticated Analytical Instrumentation Facilities (SAIF)**
   - Supported by the Department of Science and Technology (DST).
   - SAIF centers are located in institutions like IIT Bombay, Panjab University, and CDRI Lucknow.

Support from Startups and Colleges

1. **Startups and Private Laboratories**
   - Startups like SciGenom Labs (Cochin), Sartorius Analytical Lab (Bengaluru), and others offer contract research and testing services. In central India, Molmet Biotech Research Pvt. Ltd., CMBR Biotech Pvt. Ltd and Scan Research Lab are the one of the renowned startups engaged in contract research and testing services.
   - They are flexible with sample sizes and provide tailored analysis.
2. **Colleges and Universities with Advanced Facilities**
   - Institutions like Vellore Institute of Technology (VIT) and SRM University offer testing services to external researchers.
   - Some colleges collaborate with industries to provide cost-effective solutions for HPLC, MS, and FTIR analyses.

Advanced analytical techniques like HPLC, FTIR, NMR, and MS are pivotal for structural elucidation and essential for research; however, their accessibility is often constrained in resource-limited laboratories due to financial and technical limitations. In such cases, collaborations with national institutes, startups, and universities offering analytical services, as well as outsourcing, are strategic alternatives to achieve research goals effectively. By leveraging the expertise and infrastructure of capable institutions, researchers can ensure the reliability of their findings while optimizing resources and avoiding the prohibitive costs of establishing in-house facilities.

Chapter 4

Introduction to *In Vitro* Pharmacological Assays

In vitro pharmacological assays are essential tools in drug discovery and natural product research, providing a controlled environment to study the effects of chemical compounds, plant extracts, or isolated phytochemicals on cellular models. The term "*in vitro*" translates to "within glass," referring to experiments conducted outside a living organism, typically within test tubes, petri dishes, or multi-well plates. These methodologies allow researchers to evaluate the biological activity, efficacy, and safety of compounds without the complexity of a whole-organism system. This chapter delves into an overview of *in vitro* methodologies, their importance in pharmacological research, and introduces the various pharmacological activities that can be assessed through these methods.

4.1 Overview of *In Vitro* Methodologies and Their Importance

In vitro assays are crucial for initial stages in drug development and are favoured for their cost-effectiveness, control, and reproducibility. Compared to *in vivo* studies, where testing is done within a living organism, *in vitro* systems allow precise manipulation of the experimental environment. This capability lets researchers isolate specific cellular responses, assess dosage impacts with accuracy, and reduce variability caused by external factors. Additionally, *in vitro* assays are indispensable for studying pharmacological effects on human cell lines or tissue models, providing more reliable insights before moving on to animal studies or clinical trials.

These methodologies play a critical role in screening potential drug candidates, toxicity testing, and understanding mechanisms of action. They serve as a bridge between theoretical or molecular studies and more complex *in vivo* investigations. Furthermore, *in vitro* assays contribute to ethical research practices by reducing reliance on animal testing. Researchers can efficiently and ethically test hundreds of compounds, determine suitable dosages, and narrow down promising candidates for further testing. Advances in cell line models and 3D cell cultures have enhanced the relevance and accuracy of *in vitro* assays, making them an integral part of modern pharmacological research.

4.2 Importance of *In Vitro* Methods in Drug Discovery and Pharmacology

In vitro methods play an essential role in the early stages of drug discovery and pharmacological research. These methods enable the high-throughput screening of hundreds or even thousands of compounds to identify potential therapeutic candidates. **This is particularly important in drug discovery, where the initial stages focus on screening large compound libraries for specific biological activity.** By assessing these compounds at a cellular level, researchers can rapidly identify candidates that show promise, allowing them to narrow down their focus for further development. **This approach saves both time and resources, enabling more efficient and cost-effective drug discovery.** In many cases, understanding the molecular mechanism of action can inform dosing, delivery methods, and potential side effects, thereby contributing to safer and more effective treatments.

4.2.1 Applications of *In Vitro* Methodologies in Pharmacological Testing

In vitro assays are versatile and can be tailored to study a wide range of pharmacological activities, making them essential for evaluating compounds with therapeutic potential. Below are some of the key pharmacological activities that can be assessed:

1. **Cytotoxicity Assays**

   Cytotoxicity assays are widely used in pharmacology to assess the potential toxicity of compounds to cells. These assays measure cell viability after exposure to a compound, providing essential information about the compound's safety and therapeutic window. Commonly used methods include the MTT, MTS, and LDH assays, which are colorimetric assays that detect cell metabolic activity or membrane integrity. These methods are crucial in cancer pharmacology, where cytotoxicity helps in determining the ability of a drug to selectively target and kill cancer cells.

2. **Receptor Binding and Enzyme Inhibition Assays**

   Understanding how a drug interacts with specific receptors or enzymes is critical in pharmacology. *In vitro* receptor-binding assays allow researchers to quantify the affinity of a drug for a particular receptor, providing insights into its potency and potential therapeutic effects. Enzyme inhibition assays, on the other hand, help determine a drug's ability to block or reduce enzyme activity, which is useful in treating diseases where enzyme activity is implicated, such as cardiac, hypertension, cancer, neural, kidney, or hepatic disorders,

3. **Absorption and Metabolism Studies**

   In vitro methodologies also allow for the examination of drug absorption and metabolism, which are crucial for understanding bioavailability and pharmacokinetics. Caco-2 cell models, for example, are often used to predict intestinal absorption, while liver microsomes or hepatocytes are used to study metabolic stability. These studies allow researchers to predict how a drug will be absorbed, distributed, metabolized, and excreted in the body, contributing to dose optimization and reducing the risk of adverse effects.

4. **Anti-inflammatory and Antioxidant Assays**

   Many drugs and natural products aim to modulate inflammatory or oxidative processes. *In vitro* anti-inflammatory assays, such as those measuring COX enzyme inhibition or cytokine release, allow researchers to evaluate a compound's potential to treat conditions like arthritis or asthma. Antioxidant assays, such as the DPPH and ABTS assays, assess a compound's ability to scavenge free radicals. These methods are widely used in pharmacology to identify compounds that may protect cells from oxidative damage linked to aging, cardiovascular diseases, and neurodegenerative disorders.

5. **Apoptosis and Cell Cycle Analysis**

   In cancer pharmacology, the ability of a compound to induce apoptosis (programmed cell death) or alter the cell cycle is crucial. *In vitro* assays that measure DNA fragmentation, caspase activity, or cell cycle phases using flow cytometry are instrumental in evaluating how a drug impacts cancer cells. These assays provide valuable information on how a compound influences cell proliferation, making them indispensable for assessing anti-cancer potential.

6. ***In Vitro* Models for Drug-Drug Interactions**

Drug-drug interactions (DDIs) are a significant concern in pharmacology, as concurrent administration of multiple drugs can alter their effects or increase toxicity. *In vitro* assays allow researchers to study these interactions at the cellular level, particularly with regard to cytochrome P450 enzymes responsible for drug metabolism. These assays can predict potential adverse interactions, informing safer medication regimens and reducing the risk of harmful side effects.

7. ***In Vitro* Antimicrobial Studies**

In vitro antimicrobial studies are fundamental to testing the efficacy of compounds against various pathogens, such as bacteria, fungi, and viruses. Techniques like the agar well diffusion, broth microdilution, and disk diffusion assays measure the inhibition zone or minimum inhibitory concentration (MIC) of a compound. These studies are essential for identifying potential natural or synthetic antimicrobial agents, providing insight into compound potency and spectrum against pathogens, and helping to mitigate antibiotic resistance by screening for new therapeutic agents.

8. **Antidiabetic Activity**

In antidiabetic assays, yeast models are a simple and effective method for screening compounds that influence glucose metabolism. Yeast cells can serve as a model for insulin-independent glucose uptake and metabolism, allowing researchers to measure how phytochemicals affect glucose utilization. Additionally, enzyme inhibition models that focus on α-amylase and α-glucosidase inhibition are common in antidiabetic research, as these enzymes are involved in carbohydrate breakdown. Inhibiting their activity slows glucose absorption, offering a potential mechanism for managing blood sugar levels in diabetic patients.

9. **Yeast Cell Models for *In Vitro* Studies**

The yeast model is a valuable tool for studying diabetes and hepatoprotective effects due to its simplicity, cost-effectiveness, and relevance to key metabolic and stress-response pathways shared with human cells. In diabetes research, yeast, like *Saccharomyces cerevisiae*, helps screen compounds for glucose uptake and metabolism effects, offering insights into potential anti-hyperglycemic actions. For hepatoprotection, yeast models enable observation of oxidative stress responses by simulating liver-like cellular damage through agents like hydrogen peroxide, assessing the protective or antioxidant effects of test compounds. This model thus provides an efficient and insightful method for preliminary evaluation of phytochemicals with potential antidiabetic and hepatoprotective benefits.

10. **Anthelmintic and Anti-Parasitic Activity Assays**

Anthelmintic assays commonly use *Pheretima posthuma* (earthworm) models due to their similarities to human intestinal parasites. In this model, compounds are tested for their efficacy in paralyzing or killing the worms, simulating their anthelmintic potential. The assay observes the mortality or paralysis time, indicating the compound's potency against parasitic organisms. This model is inexpensive and reliable for primary screening, helping to identify effective anthelmintic agents that could later be adapted for human parasitic infections.

4.3 Ethical and Practical Advantages

In vitro methodologies have notable ethical advantages. By using cellular and molecular systems rather than animal models, these methods reduce the need for animal testing, addressing ethical concerns and supporting the principles of the 3Rs (Replace, Reduce, Refine) in animal research. Moreover, *in vitro* methods are often more practical, requiring fewer resources, simpler infrastructure, and shorter study times compared to *in vivo* studies. This increased efficiency makes *in vitro* methodologies accessible to smaller research laboratories and supports preliminary research that can justify more extensive *in vivo* studies later.

Through these various *in vitro* pharmacological activities, researchers gain critical insights into the therapeutic potential and safety profile of compounds. While each assay focuses on different biological functions, collectively, these studies help form a complete picture of a compound's pharmacological properties. This chapter provides a foundation for understanding the relevance of each type of activity and how these assays support the pathway from initial discovery to potential therapeutic application.

4.4 Overview of Upcoming Chapters

In the following chapters, we present streamlined, cost-effective protocols and Standard Operating Procedures (SOPs) for essential *in vitro* assays critical to early-stage drug development, designed for laboratories with limited resources. Emphasis is placed on affordable, accessible methods for assessing pharmacological activities, such as antioxidant, antimicrobial, anti-inflammatory, and organ-protective effects. Each assay is chosen for reliability and simplicity, enabling implementation with basic laboratory infrastructure. Key methodologies include enzyme inhibition models, spectrophotometric assays, and budget-friendly culture methods, all of which provide foundational insights without requiring extensive equipment.

The chapters explore assays like DPPH and ABTS for antioxidant potential, COX and LOX inhibition for anti-inflammatory assessment, and accessible models, such as yeast for antidiabetic studies and *Pheretima posthuma* for anthelmintic testing. These protocols also extend to inexpensive models for neuroprotective, anti-aging, and cytotoxicity studies, offering essential data to aid drug discovery and therapeutic research. This collection offers a practical toolkit for laboratories operating on limited budgets, helping researchers to generate meaningful preliminary data across pharmacological areas and contribute efficiently to advancements in drug development.

Chapter 5

In Vitro Antioxidant and Free Radical Scavenging Assays

5.1 Overview of Oxidative Stress and Its Relevance

5.1.1 Introduction to Oxidative Stress

Oxidative stress is a physiological condition resulting from an imbalance between the production of reactive oxygen species (ROS) and the biological system's ability to detoxify these reactive intermediates or repair the damage they cause. ROS, which include free radicals like superoxide anion (O_2^-) and hydroxyl radical (OH•), as well as non-radical molecules like hydrogen peroxide (H_2O_2), are highly reactive and can damage cells by modifying proteins, lipids, and DNA. Oxidative stress is implicated in aging and a broad spectrum of diseases, making it a central topic in medical research.

5.1.2 Sources of Reactive Oxygen Species

ROS are generated both endogenously and exogenously. Endogenously, they are primarily byproducts of cellular respiration within mitochondria. Enzymatic activities in peroxisomes, phagocytic immune cells, and cellular responses to inflammation also contribute to ROS production. Exogenous sources of ROS include environmental pollutants, tobacco smoke, radiation, certain medications, and heavy metals. Prolonged exposure to these sources can overwhelm antioxidant defences, leading to sustained oxidative stress.

Free Radicals: Free radicals are part of normal metabolites for many organisms, and a complex system of endogenous and exogenous antioxidant sources in the body are employed to mitigate the potential damage from free radicals. When the body is in a state of aging or stress, these highly reactive chemical species are produced excessively, and structural abnormalities and dysfunction of the cell and mitochondrial membranes can arise. Excessive free radicals affect animal performance, even resulting in the development of diseases. Improving the antioxidant status of living animals or individuals is one of the primary methods for improving their performance and health.

5.1.3 Antioxidant Defence Mechanisms

The body has developed a comprehensive antioxidant system to counteract oxidative stress. This system includes enzymatic antioxidants, like superoxide dismutase (SOD), catalase (CAT), and glutathione peroxidase (GPx), which neutralize ROS and reduce their damaging potential. Additionally, non-enzymatic antioxidants, including vitamins C and E, glutathione, and polyphenolic compounds found in plants, play a role in scavenging free radicals. When the balance between ROS production and antioxidant defences is disrupted, oxidative stress occurs, leading to potential cellular and tissue damage.

5.1.4 Cellular Impact of Oxidative Stress

Oxidative stress can induce a range of harmful cellular effects. Lipid peroxidation, where ROS attack cell membranes, can result in loss of cell integrity and function. DNA damage from ROS can lead to mutations, contributing to cancer development. ROS also affect proteins by modifying their structure and function, potentially disrupting enzymatic activities, cell signalling, and protein-protein interactions. These effects cumulatively contribute to aging and the progression of various diseases.

5.1.5 Role of Oxidative Stress in Diseases

Oxidative stress is a major factor in the pathogenesis of numerous diseases:

- **Neurodegenerative Diseases**: In conditions like Alzheimer's, Parkinson's, and Huntington's disease, oxidative stress contributes to neuronal damage and death. Accumulation of ROS in neurons exacerbates protein aggregation, mitochondrial dysfunction, and inflammatory responses.
- **Cardiovascular Diseases**: Oxidative stress plays a role in atherosclerosis, hypertension, and heart failure. ROS promote endothelial dysfunction, inflammation, and lipid oxidation, all of which contribute to cardiovascular pathology.
- **Cancer**: By causing DNA mutations, oxidative stress is linked to cancer initiation and progression. ROS also activate pathways that promote cancer cell survival and proliferation.
- **Diabetes**: Oxidative stress contributes to pancreatic β-cell dysfunction, insulin resistance, and complications such as neuropathy and retinopathy in diabetes.

5.1.6 Therapeutic Approaches and Future Directions

Efforts to manage oxidative stress involve enhancing antioxidant intake through diet, supplements, and pharmaceuticals. Dietary antioxidants like polyphenols, vitamins, and minerals have shown potential in combating oxidative stress-related conditions. Emerging research focuses on developing drugs that target oxidative stress pathways more specifically and enhancing endogenous antioxidant mechanisms. Additionally, lifestyle changes, such as reducing exposure to environmental ROS sources and improving diet, can help mitigate oxidative stress.

Antioxidants

Antioxidants are compounds that inhibit oxidation, a chemical reaction that can produce free radicals and chain reactions that may damage the cells of organisms. Antioxidants such as thiols or ascorbic acid may act to inhibit these reactions.

Antioxidants are substances that can prevent or slow damage to cells caused by free radicals, unstable molecules that the body produces as a reaction to environmental and other pressures. Antioxidants have the ability to scavenge free radicals in the human body and have been suggested to contribute to the protective effect of plant-based foods on diseases such as cardiovascular disease (CVD), cancer, and type-2 diabetes.

Antioxidants can be divided into three groups based on their mechanism:

1. Primary antioxidants, which function essentially as free radical terminators (scavengers);
2. Secondary antioxidants, which are important preventive antioxidants that function by retarding chain initiation; and
3. Tertiary antioxidants, which are concerned with the repair of damaged biomolecules.

Antioxidants from Natural Resources

Medicinal plants are traditionally used in folk medicine as natural healing remedies with therapeutic effects such as prevention of cardiovascular diseases, inflammation disorders, or reducing the risk of cancer. In addition, pharmacological industry utilizes medicinal plants due to the presence of active chemical substances as agents for drug synthesis. They are valuable also for food and cosmetic industry as additives, due to their preservative effects because of the presence of antioxidants and antimicrobial constituents.

The antioxidant properties of plants, such as medicinal plants, herbs, and spices, and their constituent compounds have been widely studied. The research in this area has been led at least partially by several branches of industry seeking for natural protecting compounds.

Extracts from natural plant materials are mixtures of many components. In many research studies concerning determination of antioxidant activity, the correlation between antioxidant capacity results and phenolics concentration was observed. The results also depend on the chemical nature and structure of the phenolic compounds present in the extracts. In many assays, extracts with higher total phenolic contents were noticeable in antioxidant activity.

Antioxidants are used in food to protect it from deleterious effects of oxidation and are also employed as dietary supplements to neutralize the adverse effects of oxidative stress. Many of the natural antioxidants of interest are of plant origin and belong to the phenolic and polyphenolic class of compounds as well as carotenoids and antioxidant vitamins, among others. The activity of antioxidants and their mechanism of action is dictated by the structural features of the molecules involved, the system in which they are present as well as processing and storage conditions, among others. While much research has been carried out on natural sources of antioxidants, their widespread use is hindered by regulations, which only permits the use of those that have an RDI (required daily intake) such as vitamins. However, green tea, rosemary and other spices or their extracts thereof, and mixed tocopherols are often used in foods as flavouring agents or under other disguised forms to bypass these unwarranted regulatory issue.

5.2 Common Assays: DPPH, ABTS, FRAP, and SOD

The DPPH, ABTS, FRAP, and SOD assays are cost-effective, accessible methods ideal for labs with limited facilities to assess antioxidant activity.

1. **DPPH Assay**: This rapid, simple assay measures free radical scavenging ability using the DPPH stable radical.

2. **ABTS Assay**: Effective for both hydrophilic and lipophilic compounds, it gauges antioxidant activity by neutralizing ABTS radicals.
3. **FRAP Assay**: Based on reduction potential, this test measures a sample's ability to reduce ferric ions, providing insights into antioxidant capacity.
4. **SOD Assay**: This assesses superoxide dismutase activity, which is essential in antioxidant defence mechanisms.

Each assay requires basic reagents and can be conducted with standard lab tools and is compatible with spectrophotometry, offering valuable insights into antioxidant properties with minimal investment. The standard protocols of these 4 types of *in vitro* antioxidant assays we are discussing in this chapter.

DPPH Assay Protocol

The DPPH (2,2-diphenyl-1-picrylhydrazyl) assay is widely used to assess the free radical scavenging ability of antioxidants in a sample. It is based on the reduction of the DPPH radical, which changes colour upon reacting with an antioxidant.

Principle

DPPH is a stable free radical with a deep violet colour in solution, which absorbs at 517 nm. When an antioxidant donates a hydrogen atom to DPPH, the radical is reduced, resulting in a colour change from violet to yellow. The degree of colour change, quantified by measuring absorbance, correlates with the sample's free radical scavenging ability.

Requirements

- DPPH (2,2-diphenyl-1-picrylhydrazyl) powder
- Methanol (or ethanol)
- Antioxidant sample (e.g., plant extract, standard such as ascorbic acid)
- UV-Visible spectrophotometer
- Micropipettes
- Glass cuvettes
- Test tubes

Methodology

1. **Preparation of DPPH Solution**:
   - Dissolve 4 mg of DPPH• in 100 mL of methanol to prepare a 0.1mM DPPH• solution. Store this solution in the dark until use, as it is sensitive to light.

2. **Sample Preparation**:

   ○ Prepare various concentrations of both test sample and standard antioxidant sample (e.g., 20, 40, 60, 80, 100 μg/mL) in methanol

3. **Working Procedure**:

   ○ Taking 1 ml of test sample and made up to 2.5 ml with ***DMSO solution or Methanol*** then add 0.5 ml DPPH• solution to the reaction mixture. After carefully shaking the reaction mixture it is incubated in dark condition at room temperature for 30 min. After 20 min, the absorbance of the mixture was read at 517 nm.

   ○ For a control, mix 0.5 ml of DPPH• solution with 3.5 mL of *DMSO solution or methanol.*

   ○ Blank solutions comprising of the studied extract solutions (1 ml) and 2 ml of methanol were used as baseline. The negative control comprised 0.5 ml of DPPH• solution and 2.5 ml of methanol, while L-ascorbic acid at the same concentrations as the test samples or extracts would be used as the positive control.

Calculations

The % radical scavenging activity of the test samples or extracts will be calculated using the following equation described by Brand-Williams *et al.*, (1995);

$$\%\,RSA = \frac{Abs\ control - Abs\ sample}{Abs\ control} \times 100$$

Where;

- **Absorbance of Control** is the absorbance of the DPPH solution without any antioxidant.
- **Absorbance of Sample** is the absorbance of the DPPH solution with the antioxidant sample.
- *RSA* is the Radical Scavenging Activity; *Abs control* is the absorbance of DPPH radical + methanol;
- *Abs sample* is the absorbance of DPPH radical + test sample or extract.

Note:

✓ The half-maximal inhibitory concentration (IC_{50}) of the extracts is determined by plotting the percentage inhibition of DPPH free radicals against the concentration of the extracts.

✓ Use software like Microsoft Excel, GraphPad Prism, or similar tools to fit the data to a **dose-response curve** using non-linear regression analysis and calculate IC_{50}.

✓ Prepare a graph by plotting **% scavenging activity** (y-axis) against the **logarithmic concentration of the sample** (x-axis).

✓ The simplest estimate of IC_{50} is to plot x-y and fit the data with a straight line (linear regression). IC_{50} value is then estimated using the fitted line,

$$\text{i.e., } Y = a * X + b,\ IC_{50} = (0.5 - b)/a.$$

✓ Compare the IC_{50} value of test sample with IC_{50} value of standard antioxidant like *Ascorbic acid* or *Rosmarinic acid* or *Quercetin*

Interpretation

Higher percentage values indicate greater antioxidant activity of the sample. A standard, such as ascorbic acid, can be used to create a standard curve for quantifying antioxidant capacity in terms of ascorbic acid equivalents (μg/mL).

ABTS Assay Protocol

The ABTS (2,2'-azino-bis(3-ethylbenzothiazoline-6-sulfonic acid)) assay is a widely used method to measure antioxidant capacity in samples. The assay is based on the ability of antioxidants to quench the blue-green $ABTS^{\bullet+}$ radical cation, leading to a decrease in absorbance.

Principle

The ABTS assay involves the generation of the ABTS radical cation ($ABTS^{\bullet+}$), which has a characteristic absorbance at 734 nm. When an antioxidant donates an electron or hydrogen atom to the $ABTS^{\bullet+}$ radical, it neutralizes it, resulting in a decrease in colour intensity. The reduction in absorbance at 734 nm is proportional to the sample's antioxidant capacity.

Requirements

- ABTS powder
- Potassium persulfate ($K_2S_2O_8$)
- Methanol (or ethanol)
- Antioxidant sample (e.g., plant extract, standard such as Trolox)
- UV-Visible spectrophotometer
- Micropipettes
- Glass cuvettes
- Test tubes

Methodology

1. **Preparation of ABTS•$^+$ Solution**:
   - Dissolve 7 mM of ABTS (e.g., 0.0384 g of ABTS in 10 mL of water) and 2.45 mM potassium persulfate (e.g., 0.0066 g in 10 mL of water) separately.
   - Mix the ABTS solution with the potassium persulfate solution in equal volumes and let the mixture react for 12–16 hours in the dark at room temperature. This creates the ABTS•$^+$ radical solution, which is stable for two days.
2. **Dilution of ABTS•$^+$ Solution**:
   - Before use, dilute the ABTS•$^+$ solution with methanol (or ethanol) to reach an absorbance of approximately 0.7 ± 0.02 at 734 nm.
3. **Sample Preparation**:
   - Prepare different concentrations of the antioxidant sample (e.g., 20, 40, 60, 80, 100 μg/mL) in methanol.
4. **Reaction Mixture**:
   - In separate test tubes, mix 1 mL of the diluted ABTS•$^+$ solution with 10–100 μL of each concentration of the antioxidant sample.
   - For a control, mix 1 mL of the ABTS•$^+$ solution with 1 mL of methanol.
5. **Incubation:**
   - Allow the reaction mixtures to stand for 5–10 minutes at room temperature in the dark.
6. **Measurement**:
   - Measure the absorbance of each sample at 734 nm using a UV-Visible spectrophotometer. Measure the absorbance of the control solution without the antioxidant sample.

Calculations

The percentage inhibition of ABTS radical cation by the sample is calculated using the formula:

$$\text{ABTS Scavenging Activity} = \frac{\text{Abs Control} - \text{Abs Sample}}{\text{Abs Control}} \times 100$$

Where:

- **Absorbance of Control** is the absorbance of the ABTS•$^+$ solution without any antioxidant.
- **Absorbance of Sample** is the absorbance of the ABTS•$^+$ solution with the antioxidant sample.

Interpretation

Higher percentage values indicate stronger antioxidant capacity of the sample. A standard, such as Trolox, can be used to create a standard curve, allowing antioxidant activity to be expressed in terms of Trolox equivalents (TEAC, μM Trolox/mg sample).

NOTE: Trolox is a water-soluble analogue of vitamin E and is widely used as a standard reference antioxidant in assays like ABTS and DPPH. In these assays, the antioxidant capacity of a sample is often expressed in "Trolox Equivalent Antioxidant Capacity" (TEAC), which compares the antioxidant activity of the sample to that of Trolox.

FRAP Assay Protocol

The FRAP (Ferric Reducing Antioxidant Power) assay is a simple and rapid method used to assess the reducing power of antioxidants in a sample. It is based on the ability of antioxidants to reduce ferric ions (Fe^{3+}) to ferrous ions (Fe^{2+}), which results in a colour change measurable by spectrophotometry.

Principle

The FRAP assay measures the antioxidant potential of a sample by evaluating its ability to reduce ferric-tripyridyltriazine (Fe^{3+}-TPTZ) complex to ferrous-tripyridyltriazine (Fe^{2+}-TPTZ), which forms a blue colour. The intensity of this colour, measured at 593 nm, is directly proportional to the reducing power of the antioxidants present in the sample.

Requirements

- Ferric chloride ($FeCl_3 \cdot 6H_2O$)
- TPTZ (2,4,6-tripyridyl-s-triazine)
- Acetate buffer (300 mM, pH 3.6)
- Antioxidant sample (e.g., plant extract, standard such as Trolox or ascorbic acid)
- UV-Visible spectrophotometer
- Micropipettes
- Glass cuvettes
- Test tubes

Methodology

1. **Preparation of FRAP Reagent**:
   - Prepare the following solutions:
     - **300 mM Acetate Buffer** (pH 3.6): Dissolve 3.1 g sodium acetate in 16 mL glacial acetic acid and dilute to 1 L with distilled water.
     - **10 mM TPTZ Solution**: Dissolve 0.031 g TPTZ in 10 mL of 40 mM HCl.
     - **20 mM Ferric Chloride Solution**: Dissolve 0.054 g ferric chloride in 10 mL distilled water.
   - To prepare the FRAP working reagent, mix the acetate buffer, TPTZ solution, and ferric chloride solution in a 10:1:1 ratio (e.g., 10 mL acetate buffer, 1 mL TPTZ solution, 1 mL ferric chloride solution). The reagent should be freshly prepared and kept at 37°C before use.
2. **Sample Preparation**:
   - Prepare various concentrations of the antioxidant sample (e.g., 20, 40, 60, 80, 100 μg/mL) in methanol or water.
3. **Reaction Mixture**:
   - In a test tube, mix 2.85 mL of the FRAP reagent with 150 μL of the sample. For a blank, add 150 μL of methanol or water instead of the sample.
4. **Incubation**:
   - Incubate the mixture at 37°C for 30 minutes.
5. **Measurement**:
   - After incubation, measure the absorbance at 593 nm using a UV-Visible spectrophotometer. Measure the absorbance of the blank as well.

Calculations

The antioxidant power of the sample can be calculated by comparing its absorbance to a standard curve prepared with a known antioxidant (e.g., Trolox or ascorbic acid).

6. **Preparation of Standard Curve**:
   - Prepare a series of Trolox or ascorbic acid standard solutions with known concentrations (e.g., 50, 100, 150, 200, 250 μM).
   - Mix each standard with the FRAP reagent, incubate, and measure absorbance as described above.
   - Plot the absorbance versus the concentration to create a standard curve.
7. **Sample Antioxidant Power Calculation**:
   - Use the standard curve to determine the antioxidant power of the sample, expressed as Trolox or ascorbic acid equivalents (μM of Trolox or ascorbic acid per mg of sample).

Interpretation

Higher absorbance indicates stronger reducing power, meaning greater antioxidant capacity. The results allow comparison of the antioxidant potential of various samples in terms of Trolox or ascorbic acid equivalents.

SOD (Superoxide Dismutase) Assay Protocol

The SOD assay measures the activity of superoxide dismutase, an enzyme that catalyzes the dismutation of superoxide radicals ($O_2{\bullet}^-$) into oxygen and hydrogen peroxide, thus providing a defence against oxidative stress. This assay is commonly based on the inhibition of a reaction between superoxide radicals and a detector molecule.

Principle

The SOD assay relies on the principle that superoxide radicals, generated in the reaction, are detected by a colour-changing dye such as Nitroblue Tetrazolium (NBT) or WST-1. In the presence of SOD, the enzyme competes with the detector molecule for the superoxide radicals, reducing the amount of colour produced. The SOD activity is proportional to the degree of inhibition of colour formation.

Requirements

- NBT (Nitroblue Tetrazolium) or WST-1 (Water-soluble tetrazolium salt) as the dye
- Xanthine and xanthine oxidase (or pyrogallol as an alternative)
- Potassium phosphate buffer (50 mM, pH 7.8)
- Antioxidant sample (e.g., plant extract, or standard enzyme SOD)
- UV-Visible spectrophotometer
- Micropipettes
- Glass cuvettes
- Test tubes

Methodology

8. **Preparation of Reagents**:
    - **50 mM Potassium Phosphate Buffer (pH 7.8)**: Dissolve the required amount of potassium phosphate in distilled water and adjust the pH to 7.8.
    - **NBT Solution (0.3 mM)**: Dissolve NBT in phosphate buffer to achieve a final concentration of 0.3 mM.
    - **Xanthine Solution (0.1 mM)**: Dissolve xanthine in phosphate buffer to reach a concentration of 0.1 mM.

- **Xanthine Oxidase Solution**: Prepare a stock solution in phosphate buffer and dilute it to obtain an activity that generates a stable rate of superoxide production.
- Prepare the reagents freshly before the assay.

9. **Reaction Mixture**:
   - In a test tube, mix the following in this order:
     - 1.5 mL of potassium phosphate buffer (50 mM, pH 7.8)
     - 0.3 mL of NBT solution (0.3 mM)
     - 0.3 mL of xanthine solution (0.1 mM)
     - 0.2 mL of the sample or standard SOD enzyme solution
     - 0.1 mL of xanthine oxidase solution
   - Add the xanthine oxidase last to start the reaction.

10. **Incubation**:
    - Immediately after adding xanthine oxidase, incubate the mixture at room temperature for 10 minutes.

11. **Measurement**:
    - Measure the absorbance at 560 nm using a UV-Visible spectrophotometer. A blank without the sample should be prepared and measured alongside.

Calculations

The SOD activity is calculated based on the inhibition of NBT reduction, which decreases absorbance at 560 nm. The percent inhibition can be calculated using the following formula:

$$\text{SOD Inhibition (\%)} = \frac{\text{Abs Control} - \text{Abs Sample}}{\text{Abs control}} \times 100$$

Where:

- **Absorbance of Control** is the absorbance of the reaction mixture without SOD (or sample).
- **Absorbance of Sample** is the absorbance of the reaction mixture with SOD (or sample).

The SOD activity is typically expressed in terms of units per mg of protein, with one unit of SOD defined as the amount of enzyme required to inhibit 50% of the NBT reduction under assay conditions.

Interpretation

Higher inhibition percentages indicate greater SOD activity, as the enzyme effectively competes with NBT for superoxide radicals, preventing colour formation. The activity can be standardized using a known SOD enzyme to generate a standard curve for accurate quantification of SOD in the sample.

Chapter 6

In Vitro Anti-inflammatory and Antipyretic Assays

6.1 Overview of Inflammation and Fever

Inflammation is the body's natural response to injury, infection, or harmful stimuli. It serves as a defence mechanism to eliminate pathogens, damaged cells, or irritants and to initiate the healing process. This response typically involves increased blood flow, the release of signalling molecules like cytokines, and the recruitment of immune cells to the affected area, leading to symptoms such as redness, swelling, heat, and pain. While essential for healing, acute inflammation is protective, however, prolonged inflammation can lead to chronic diseases such as arthritis, cardiovascular disorders, neurodegenerative diseases and even cancers, due to prolonged immune activation and tissue damage. Anti-inflammatory agents reduce inflammation by inhibiting pathways that produce inflammatory mediators, providing relief from pain and preventing tissue damage.

Fever, or pyrexia, is often a result of inflammation, triggered by substances called pyrogens, which stimulate the hypothalamus to raise the body's temperature set point. This elevated temperature creates an unfavourable environment for pathogens and enhances the immune response. Fever can be beneficial in fighting infections, as it accelerates immune cell activity and inhibits microbial growth. However, excessive or prolonged fever may cause discomfort and, in severe cases, can be harmful, especially in young children or vulnerable populations. Antipyretics, are agents that reduce fever. Antipyretic drugs act on the hypothalamus, adjusting the body's thermostat to lower temperature.

Both inflammation and fever are crucial components of the immune response, but their regulation is essential to prevent tissue damage and maintain overall health.

The relevance of these activities extends to traditional medicine and modern pharmacology. Many natural compounds exhibit anti-inflammatory and antipyretic effects, and their use in traditional remedies underscores their therapeutic potential. Ongoing research seeks safer, more effective anti-inflammatory and antipyretic drugs, aiming to manage symptoms and improve the quality of life for individuals with inflammatory or infectious conditions.

6.2 Cost Effective *In vitro* Anti-inflammatory and Antipyretic Assays

In vitro anti-inflammatory and antipyretic activity assays are essential for evaluating or initial screening of the efficacy of compounds especially in laboratories with limited resources. Cost-effective assays, such as protein denaturation and enzyme inhibition assays for COX, LOX, and other inflammation-related enzymes can provide basic insightful data on natural extracts or synthetic compounds for their therapeutic potential.

For antipyretic activity, though *in vitro* models are less common than *in vivo* assays, the inhibition of prostaglandin synthesis can be tested *in vitro*, as prostaglandins play a role in fever. Using enzyme-linked immunosorbent assays (ELISA) to measure prostaglandin levels is one approach, though it may be challenging in very low-resource labs.

6.2.1 Albumin Denaturation Inhibition Model

The **albumin denaturation inhibition model** is a simple and cost-effective assay widely used to assess anti-inflammatory activity. During inflammation, proteins like albumin can denature, losing their structural integrity. This assay tests a compound's ability to prevent heat-induced denaturation of albumin, a process linked to inflammation. Effective anti-inflammatory compounds stabilize the protein structure, which can be quantified spectrophotometrically. This assay is economical and easy to perform, making it ideal for labs with basic setups.

6.2.2 Enzyme Inhibition Assays

Enzyme inhibition assays target key enzymes involved in the inflammatory pathway, providing specific data on how a compound may reduce inflammation or fever:

1. **Cyclooxygenase (COX) Inhibition Assay**: COX enzymes (COX-1 and COX-2) produce prostaglandins, which contribute to inflammation and fever. Inhibiting COX enzymes, especially COX-2, can lower prostaglandin synthesis and thus reduce inflammation and fever. This assay is commonly used to evaluate the antipyretic and anti-inflammatory potential of compounds.

2. **Lipoxygenase (LOX) Inhibition Assay**: LOX enzymes mediate leukotriene production, another inflammatory pathway. Inhibiting LOX reduces leukotrienes, which play a role in inflammation-related conditions like asthma and arthritis.

3. **Phospholipase Inhibition Assay**: Phospholipase enzymes release arachidonic acid, a precursor to inflammatory mediators. Inhibiting phospholipase activity can interrupt the inflammation cascade at an early stage.

4. **Elastase Inhibition Assay**: Elastase is a proteolytic enzyme involved in tissue inflammation. Inhibiting elastase can help prevent tissue damage in chronic inflammatory diseases.

5. **Xanthine Oxidase (XO) Inhibition Assay**: XO is involved in generating reactive oxygen species, which can exacerbate inflammation. Inhibiting XO activity may help reduce oxidative stress and inflammation.

These assays provide a comprehensive approach for assessing anti-inflammatory and antipyretic effects, empowering small laboratories to conduct impactful, cost-effective research on therapeutic compounds. Each assay requires basic reagents and can be conducted with standard lab tools and is compatible with spectrophotometry, offering valuable insights into anti-inflammatory and antipyretic properties with minimal investment. The standard protocols of 6 types of *in vitro* bio assays we are discussing in this chapter.

Albumin Protein Denaturation Assay Protocol

The albumin protein denaturation assay is a simple and cost-effective *in vitro* method to evaluate anti-inflammatory activity of various compounds or extracts. It is based on the principle that certain agents can inhibit the denaturation of proteins, a process closely associated with inflammation.

Principle

Protein denaturation occurs when proteins lose their secondary and tertiary structures due to external stress, such as heat or chemical agents. This denaturation process mimics some aspects of inflammation in biological systems. Anti-inflammatory compounds can inhibit protein denaturation. In this assay, albumin is subjected to denaturation by heating, and the degree of inhibition of this denaturation by the test sample is measured by observing absorbance changes.

Requirements

- Bovine serum albumin (BSA) solution (1% w/v in distilled water)
- Phosphate-buffered saline (PBS) or distilled water
- Test samples (e.g., plant extracts or anti-inflammatory drugs like diclofenac, aspirin, ibuprofen as a positive control)
- Micropipettes and tips
- Test tubes or 96-well plate
- Water bath
- UV-Visible spectrophotometer
- Cuvettes (if using spectrophotometer)

Methodology

1. **Preparation of Reagents and Solutions**:
   - Prepare a 1% w/v solution of bovine serum albumin (BSA) in PBS or distilled water.
   - Prepare stock solutions of the test samples and the positive control (e.g., diclofenac) in distilled water or an appropriate solvent.
2. **Reaction Mixture Setup**:
   - In each test tube or well of a 96-well plate, add the following:
     - 0.5 mL of 1% BSA solution
     - 0.5 mL of the test sample at various concentrations (or the control solution in the case of the positive control).

For the negative control, use 0.5 mL of distilled water instead of the test sample solution.

3. **Incubation**:
   - Incubate the tubes or wells at 37°C for 20 minutes to equilibrate.
   - After the initial incubation, place the samples in a water bath at 70°C for 10 minutes to induce denaturation of the albumin protein.
4. **Cooling and Measurement**:
   - Allow the samples to cool to room temperature after heating.
   - Measure the absorbance at 660 nm using a UV-Visible spectrophotometer.

Calculations

The Percentage inhibition of protein denaturation is calculated according to Gunathilake, *et al.*, (2018) as follows:

$$\text{Percentage inhibition of denaturation} = \frac{1 - \text{Abs of Sample}}{\text{Abs of control}} \times 100$$

Or Simply

$$\text{Inhibition (\%)} = \frac{\text{Abs Control} - \text{Abs Sample}}{\text{Abs control}} \times 100$$

Where:

- **Absorbance of Control** is the absorbance of the reaction mixture without the test sample.
- **Absorbance of Sample** is the absorbance of the reaction mixture containing the test sample.

Interpretation

Higher inhibition percentages indicate greater anti-inflammatory potential of the test sample, as it suggests the compound's ability to prevent albumin denaturation. By running different concentrations, a dose-dependent response can be assessed. Comparing the sample with a known anti-inflammatory agent like diclofenac helps in determining relative activity.

Note: decrease in absorbance with increase in drug concentration indicates the increase in anti-inflammatory activity.

Note: Compare the percentage inhibition of sample drug with particular concentration of standard drug like ibuprofen, aspirin or diclofenac etc.

Cyclooxygenase (COX) Inhibition Assay Protocol

The Cyclooxygenase (COX) Inhibition Assay is used to evaluate the anti-inflammatory and antipyretic activities of compounds by examining their ability to inhibit the COX enzyme. COX enzymes, particularly

COX-1 and COX-2, catalyze the conversion of arachidonic acid to prostaglandins, which are key mediators of inflammation, pain, and fever. Compounds that inhibit COX activity can reduce inflammation and fever, thus serving as potential anti-inflammatory and antipyretic agents.

Principle

This assay measures the ability of test compounds to inhibit the COX enzymes (COX-1 and COX-2). The inhibition of COX activity is assessed by measuring the decrease in prostaglandin formation from arachidonic acid. The resulting prostaglandins can be quantified using a colorimetric or fluorometric detection system. The degree of COX inhibition reflects the anti-inflammatory and antipyretic potential of the test compounds.

Requirements

- **Enzyme source**: Commercially available COX-1 and COX-2 enzymes or tissue homogenates rich in COX enzymes
- **Substrate**: Arachidonic acid (COX substrate)
- **Reaction buffer**: Tris-HCl (0.1 M, pH 8.0)
- **Test samples**: Plant extracts or compounds with potential COX inhibitory properties
- **Positive control**: Non-steroidal anti-inflammatory drugs (NSAIDs) such as aspirin or ibuprofen
- **Indicator dye** (e.g., N,N,N',N'-tetramethyl-p-phenylenediamine, TMPD)
- **Hydrogen peroxide** (H_2O_2, for TMPD oxidation)
- **Colorimetric or fluorometric COX detection kit**: Alternatively, a coupled assay can be used if prostaglandin formation is measured spectrophotometrically
- **Micropipettes and tips**
- **96-well plate or test tubes**
- **UV-Visible spectrophotometer or microplate reader**

Note: Use microplate reader/ELISA reader in place of spectrophotometer if it is possible to avail it in laboratory as it uses lesser volume of reaction mixture that saves experimental cost.

Methodology

1. **Preparation of Solutions**:
   - Prepare a Tris-HCl reaction buffer (0.1 M, pH 8.0).
   - Dissolve the COX enzymes (COX-1 and COX-2) in the buffer.
   - Prepare arachidonic acid substrate solution according to the manufacturer's instructions or to a concentration optimized for the assay.

- Prepare 100 μM TMPD solution in the assay buffer.
- Prepare different concentrations of the test compounds and positive control (e.g., diclofenac, aspirin or ibuprofen) in the reaction buffer.

2. **Reaction Mixture Setup**:
   - In each well or test tube, add the following in this order:
     - 100 μL of Tris-HCl buffer (pH 8.0)
     - 10 μL of COX enzyme (COX-1 or COX-2)
     - 10 μL of the test sample, control compound, or vehicle (buffer)
   - Incubate the mixture at 37°C for 5 minutes to allow the test compound and enzyme to interact.
   - Start the reaction by adding 10 μL of arachidonic acid substrate to each well or tube.
   - Immediately add 10 μL of TMPD solution and mix gently.
3. **Incubation**:
   - Incubate the reaction mixture at 37°C for 10 minutes.
4. **Measurement**:
   - Measure the absorbance at 590 nm (for TMPD oxidation) using a spectrophotometer or microplate reader or follow the fluorometric detection instructions provided with the kit.

Calculations

Calculate the percentage of COX inhibition by comparing the absorbance of the test sample to the control (without any inhibitor). The percentage inhibition is determined using the following formula:

$$\text{Inhibition (\%)} = \frac{\text{Abs Control} - \text{Abs Sample}}{\text{Abs control}} \times 100$$

Where:

- **Absorbance of Control** is the absorbance of the reaction mixture without the test compound (vehicle only).
- **Absorbance of Sample** is the absorbance of the reaction mixture containing the test compound.

Interpretation

- Higher inhibition percentages indicate stronger COX inhibitory activity of the test sample, suggesting greater anti-inflammatory and antipyretic potential.
- By testing both COX-1 and COX-2 inhibition, one can determine whether the compound is selective (COX-2 specific) or non-selective.

Lipoxygenase (LOX) Inhibition Assay Protocol

The Lipoxygenase (LOX) Inhibition Assay evaluates the anti-inflammatory potential of compounds by examining their ability to inhibit the LOX enzyme. Lipoxygenase enzymes, specifically 5-LOX, catalyze the oxidation of arachidonic acid to leukotrienes, which play a key role in the inflammatory process. Compounds that inhibit LOX activity can reduce inflammation by limiting leukotriene synthesis.

Principle

Lipoxygenase catalyzes the oxygenation of polyunsaturated fatty acids, such as arachidonic acid, to produce hydroperoxides. The inhibition of LOX activity can be determined by measuring the reduction in absorbance or fluorescence due to decreased formation of these oxidized products. The extent of LOX inhibition reflects the anti-inflammatory potential of the test compound.

Requirements

- **Enzyme source**: Soybean lipoxygenase or purified 5-LOX enzyme
- **Substrate**: Linoleic acid or arachidonic acid (LOX substrates)
- **Reaction buffer**: Phosphate buffer (0.1 M, pH 8.0)
- **Test compounds**: Plant extracts or compounds with potential LOX inhibitory properties
- **Positive control**: Known LOX inhibitors (e.g., nordihydroguaiaretic acid - NDGA)
- **Micropipettes and tips**
- **96-well microplate or test tubes**
- **UV-Visible spectrophotometer or microplate reader**

Note: Use microplate reader/ELISA reader in place of spectrophotometer if it is possible to avail it in laboratory as it uses lesser volume of reaction mixture that saves experimental cost.

Methodology

1. **Preparation of Solutions**:
    - Prepare a phosphate buffer (0.1 M, pH 8.0) as the reaction buffer.
    - Dissolve the LOX enzyme in the reaction buffer at an optimized concentration for the assay.
    - Prepare the substrate solution (e.g., linoleic acid or arachidonic acid) at a suitable concentration.
    - Prepare stock solutions of the test samples and the positive control (e.g., NDGA) at various concentrations in distilled water or an appropriate solvent.
2. **Reaction Mixture Setup**:
    - In each well of a 96-well plate (or test tube), add the following in this order:

   - 160 μL of phosphate buffer (pH 8.0)
   - 10 μL of LOX enzyme solution
   - 10 μL of test sample, positive control, or vehicle (buffer only for the control)
 - Incubate the mixture at 25°C for 5 minutes to allow for the interaction of the enzyme with the test compound.

3. **Initiation of Reaction**:
   - Start the reaction by adding 20 μL of the substrate solution (e.g., linoleic acid or arachidonic acid) to each well or tube.
   - Immediately record the initial absorbance at 234 nm using a UV-Visible spectrophotometer or microplate reader.
4. **Incubation and Measurement**:
   - Continue to incubate the reaction mixture at 25°C, monitoring the increase in absorbance at 234 nm for 5–10 minutes. This wavelength corresponds to the formation of conjugated dienes, a product of LOX-catalyzed reaction.
5. **Calculations:** Calculate the percentage inhibition of LOX activity by comparing the absorbance of the test sample to the control. Use the following formula:

$$\text{Inhibition (\%)} = \frac{\text{Abs Control} - \text{Abs Sample}}{\text{Abs control}} \times 100$$

Where:

- **Absorbance of Control** is the change in absorbance of the reaction mixture without the test sample (vehicle only).
- **Absorbance of Sample** is the change in absorbance of the reaction mixture containing the test compound.

Interpretation

Higher inhibition percentages indicate greater LOX inhibitory activity of the test sample, suggesting higher anti-inflammatory potential. The LOX inhibition assay provides insight into the effectiveness of a compound in blocking leukotriene formation, a major pathway in inflammation.

Phospholipase Inhibition Assay Protocol

The Phospholipase Inhibition Assay evaluates the anti-inflammatory potential of compounds by measuring their ability to inhibit phospholipase enzymes, specifically phospholipase A2 (PLA2). PLA2 enzymes are involved in the inflammatory process by hydrolyzing phospholipids to produce arachidonic acid, which is a precursor to pro-inflammatory mediators like prostaglandins and leukotrienes. By inhibiting PLA_2, compounds can reduce inflammation by limiting the production of these mediators.

Principle

Phospholipase A_2 catalyzes the hydrolysis of phospholipids at the sn-2 position, releasing free fatty acids (such as arachidonic acid) and lysophospholipids. In this assay, phospholipid hydrolysis by PLA_2 is measured, and the degree of inhibition by test compounds is evaluated. The inhibition of PLA_2 activity reflects the compound's anti-inflammatory potential.

Requirements

- **Enzyme source**: Purified PLA_2 enzyme (e.g., from snake venom or recombinant PLA_2)
- **Substrate**: Phospholipid substrate (e.g., phosphatidylcholine or phosphatidylethanolamine)
- **Reaction buffer**: Tris-HCl buffer (0.1 M, pH 8.0) with calcium chloride ($CaCl_2$) to activate PLA_2
- **Test compounds**: Plant extracts or compounds with potential PLA_2 inhibitory properties
- **Positive control**: Known PLA_2 inhibitors (e.g., indomethacin or mepacrine)
- **Micropipettes and tips**
- **96-well microplate or test tubes**
- **UV-Visible spectrophotometer or microplate reader**

Methodology

1. **Preparation of Solutions**:
    - Prepare Tris-HCl buffer (0.1 M, pH 8.0) with $CaCl_2$ to ensure optimal PLA_2 activity.
    - Dissolve the PLA_2 enzyme in the reaction buffer at an optimized concentration.
    - Prepare the phospholipid substrate solution at a suitable concentration (follow manufacturer instructions if using commercial kits).
    - Prepare stock solutions of test samples and positive control (e.g., indomethacin) in distilled water or an appropriate solvent.
2. **Reaction Mixture Setup**:
    - In each well of a 96-well plate or test tube, add the following in this order:
        - 150 μL of Tris-HCl buffer with $CaCl_2$
        - 10 μL of PLA_2 enzyme solution
        - 10 μL of the test sample, positive control, or vehicle (buffer only for the control).

- Incubate the mixture at 37°C for 5 minutes to allow the enzyme and test compound to interact.

3. **Initiation of Reaction**:
   - Start the reaction by adding 20 μL of the phospholipid substrate to each well or tube.
   - Mix the contents and immediately record the initial absorbance at 400 nm using a UV-Visible spectrophotometer or microplate reader.
4. **Incubation and Measurement**:
   - Incubate the reaction mixture at 37°C and monitor the increase in absorbance at 400 nm for 5–10 minutes. This wavelength corresponds to the formation of reaction products, indicating phospholipid hydrolysis.
5. **Calculations:** Calculate the percentage inhibition of PLA_2 activity by comparing the absorbance of the test sample to the control. Use the following formula:

   Where:

   - **Absorbance of Control** is the change in absorbance of the reaction mixture without the test sample (vehicle only).
   - **Absorbance of Sample** is the change in absorbance of the reaction mixture containing the test compound.

Interpretation

f) Higher inhibition percentages indicate greater PLA_2 inhibitory activity of the test sample, suggesting stronger anti-inflammatory potential. The phospholipase inhibition assay provides valuable insight into the effectiveness of a compound in blocking arachidonic acid release and, therefore, the downstream production of pro-inflammatory mediators.

Elastase Inhibition Assay Protocol

The Elastase Inhibition Assay evaluates the anti-inflammatory potential of compounds by measuring their ability to inhibit elastase, an enzyme that breaks down elastin and other proteins. Elastase, mainly released by neutrophils during inflammation, plays a key role in inflammatory responses. Its excessive activity can lead to tissue damage in conditions like arthritis and emphysema. Compounds that inhibit elastase can potentially limit tissue destruction and inflammation.

Principle

Elastase catalyzes the hydrolysis of specific peptide bonds in elastin and other proteins. This assay uses a chromogenic or fluorogenic substrate, such as N-Succinyl-Ala-Ala-Ala-p-nitroanilide (SAAN), that releases a coloured or fluorescent product upon cleavage by elastase. The degree of inhibition of elastase by test compounds is measured by monitoring the decrease in absorbance or fluorescence.

Requirements

- **Enzyme source**: Elastase from porcine pancreas or human neutrophils
- **Substrate**: N-Succinyl-Ala-Ala-Ala-p-nitroanilide (SAAN) or a similar elastase substrate
- **Reaction buffer**: Tris-HCl buffer (0.1 M, pH 8.0)
- **Test compounds**: Plant extracts or compounds with potential elastase inhibitory properties
- **Positive control**: Known elastase inhibitors (e.g., oleanolic acid or ursolic acid)
- **Micropipettes and tips**
- **96-well microplate or test tubes**
- **UV-Visible spectrophotometer or microplate reader**

Methodology

1. **Preparation of Solutions**:
   - Prepare a 0.1 M Tris-HCl buffer (pH 8.0) as the reaction buffer.
   - Dissolve the elastase enzyme in the reaction buffer at an optimized concentration suitable for the assay.
   - Prepare a solution of the substrate (e.g., SAAN) at an appropriate concentration according to the enzyme's optimal activity.
   - Prepare stock solutions of test samples and the positive control (e.g., oleanolic acid) in distilled water or an appropriate solvent.
2. **Reaction Mixture Setup**:
   - In each well of a 96-well plate or test tube, add the following in this order:
     - 170 μL of Tris-HCl buffer (pH 8.0)
     - 10 μL of elastase enzyme solution
     - 10 μL of test sample, positive control, or vehicle (buffer only for the control).
   - Incubate the mixture at 25°C for 5 minutes to allow the enzyme to interact with the test compound.
3. **Initiation of Reaction**:
   - Start the reaction by adding 10 μL of the substrate (e.g., SAAN) to each well or tube.
   - Mix the contents and immediately record the initial absorbance at 410 nm using a UV-Visible spectrophotometer or microplate reader.
4. **Incubation and Measurement**:
   - Incubate the reaction mixture at 25°C, monitoring the increase in absorbance at 410 nm over 5–10 minutes. This wavelength corresponds to the release of p-nitroaniline, a product of the enzyme reaction.

5. **Calculations:** Calculate the percentage inhibition of elastase activity by comparing the absorbance of the test sample to the control using the following formula:

$$\text{Inhibition (\%)} = \frac{\text{Abs Control} - \text{Abs Sample}}{\text{Abs control}} \times 100$$

Where:

- **Absorbance of Control** is the absorbance change of the reaction mixture without the test sample.
- **Absorbance of Sample** is the absorbance change of the reaction mixture containing the test compound.

Interpretation

Higher inhibition percentages indicate greater elastase inhibitory activity of the test sample, suggesting stronger anti-inflammatory potential. The elastase inhibition assay thus helps evaluate the ability of a compound to limit proteolytic activity, reducing tissue damage associated with inflammation.

Xanthine Oxidase (XO) Inhibition Assay Protocol

The Xanthine Oxidase (XO) Inhibition Assay evaluates the anti-inflammatory potential of compounds by measuring their ability to inhibit XO enzyme activity. XO catalyzes the oxidation of hypoxanthine to xanthine and xanthine to uric acid, producing reactive oxygen species (ROS) as byproducts. Excessive ROS can contribute to oxidative stress and inflammation. Compounds that inhibit XO can thus help reduce inflammation by limiting ROS production.

Principle

Xanthine oxidase converts xanthine to uric acid, producing hydrogen peroxide (H_2O_2) as a byproduct. This assay typically uses xanthine as a substrate, and the formation of uric acid is monitored by measuring absorbance at 295 nm. A decrease in absorbance indicates inhibition of XO activity, suggesting anti-inflammatory potential of the test compound.

Requirements

- **Enzyme source**: Xanthine oxidase (from bovine milk or a commercial XO preparation)
- **Substrate**: Xanthine
- **Reaction buffer**: Phosphate buffer (50 mM, pH 7.5)
- **Test compounds**: Plant extracts or other compounds with potential XO inhibitory properties
- **Positive control**: Known XO inhibitor (e.g., allopurinol)
- **Micropipettes and tips**
- **96-well microplate or test tubes**
- **UV-Visible spectrophotometer or microplate reader**

Methodology

1. **Preparation of Solutions**:
   - Prepare a 50 mM phosphate buffer (pH 7.5) as the reaction buffer.
   - Dissolve xanthine oxidase in the reaction buffer at an optimized concentration suitable for the assay.
   - Prepare a xanthine solution (substrate) at a concentration of 0.15 mM in the reaction buffer.
   - Prepare stock solutions of test compounds and positive control (e.g., allopurinol) in distilled water or an appropriate solvent.
2. **Reaction Mixture Setup**:
   - In each well of a 96-well plate or test tube, add the following in this order:
     - 140 μL of phosphate buffer (pH 7.5)
     - 30 μL of the xanthine substrate solution
     - 10 μL of the test compound, positive control, or vehicle (buffer only for the control).
   - Incubate the mixture at 25°C for 5 minutes to allow the enzyme to interact with the test compound.
3. **Initiation of Reaction**:
   - Start the reaction by adding 20 μL of the xanthine oxidase enzyme solution to each well or tube.
   - Mix the contents and immediately record the initial absorbance at 295 nm using a UV-Visible spectrophotometer or microplate reader.
4. **Incubation and Measurement**:
   - Incubate the reaction mixture at 25°C for 10–15 minutes.
   - Measure the absorbance at 295 nm at regular intervals or at the end of the incubation period. This wavelength corresponds to the formation of uric acid, indicating xanthine oxidation.
5. **Calculations:** Calculate the percentage inhibition of XO activity by comparing the absorbance of the test sample to the control using the following formula:

$$\text{Inhibition (\%)} = \frac{\text{Abs Control} - \text{Abs Sample}}{\text{Abs control}} \times 100$$

Where:

- **Absorbance of Control** is the absorbance change of the reaction mixture without the test compound.
- **Absorbance of Sample** is the absorbance change of the reaction mixture containing the test compound.

Interpretation

Higher inhibition percentages indicate greater XO inhibitory activity of the test sample, suggesting stronger anti-inflammatory potential. This assay is valuable for assessing a compound's ability to reduce ROS production, indirectly limiting inflammation and oxidative damage.

Chapter 7

In Vitro Antimicrobial Studies

7.1 Models for *In Vitro* Antimicrobial Studies

In vitro antimicrobial activity models are simple, cost-effective, and suitable for laboratories with basic microbiological facilities. These methods provide critical insights into the efficacy of compounds against microbes while eliminating the need for complex infrastructure. Bacteria and fungi can be cultured on affordable media like nutrient agar or Sabouraud Dextrose Agar, prepared in-house if needed. Antibacterial activity is tested through straightforward methods such as disc diffusion, agar well diffusion, or broth dilution, yielding measurable zones of inhibition or MIC values.

Antifungal activity can be assessed via spore germination or mycelial growth inhibition, requiring minimal resources. For antiviral studies, hemagglutination inhibition and plaque assays using embryonated eggs offer viable, low-cost alternatives. Quorum-sensing inhibition (QSI) assays, using organisms like *Chromobacterium violaceum*, provide insights into anti-biofilm properties using simple spectrophotometry.

The significance of these models lies in their accessibility and versatility, allowing any laboratory with basic microbiological setups to perform impactful research. They empower researchers to evaluate antimicrobial potential ethically, paving the way for developing novel therapeutic agents without reliance on advanced infrastructure.

7.2 Selection and Preparation of Microbial Cultures

The selection and preparation of microbial cultures is a fundamental step in antimicrobial studies. Proper handling and maintenance of microbial cultures are crucial to ensure accurate, reproducible results.

7.2.1 Selection of Microbial Strains

For antimicrobial studies, the choice of microbial strains should be based on the research objective. Commonly used bacterial strains include *Escherichia coli*, *Staphylococcus aureus*, *Pseudomonas aeruginosa*, and *Bacillus subtilis*, which serve as representative pathogens for various types of infections. Fungal strains like *Candida albicans* and *Aspergillus niger* are commonly used in antifungal studies. The selection should also consider the strain's clinical relevance and susceptibility patterns. For broader applicability, it is recommended to use standard strains from recognized culture collections such as **MTCC** (Microbial Type Culture Collection and Gene Bank), **NCIM** (National Collection of Industrial Microorganisms), **NCDC** (National Collection of Dairy Cultures), **ATCC** (American Type Culture Collection), and **IARI** (Indian Agricultural Research Institute) Culture Collection.

7.2.2 Culturing Microorganisms

1. **Stock Culture Preparation:**
   - Inoculate the selected microbial strain onto appropriate solid media (e.g., nutrient agar for bacteria, Sabouraud dextrose agar for fungi) and incubate under optimal growth conditions.
   - After colony formation, the culture should be transferred to a sterile tube with glycerol (10-20%) for long-term storage at -80°C.
2. **Routine Subculturing:**
   - Subculture the stock cultures every 2-4 weeks to maintain their viability. Inoculate fresh media with a small amount of the stored culture and incubate under required conditions (e.g., 37°C for most bacteria).
   - Cultures should be used within 24-48 hours after subculturing to avoid the development of mutations that could affect test results.

7.2.3 Preparation of Inoculum

1. **Inoculum Standardization:**
   - To ensure consistent results, the microbial inoculum must be standardized to a specific concentration. This is commonly done using the McFarland standard, which helps in achieving uniform inoculum density.
   - For bacteria, prepare a suspension in saline or phosphate-buffered saline (PBS) and adjust the turbidity to match the desired McFarland standard (e.g., 0.5 McFarland, which is approximately 1 x 10^8 CFU/mL for bacteria).
   - Fungal cultures are often prepared by suspending fungal spores in a sterile solution and counting under a microscope for accurate spore concentration.

7.2.4 Quality Control

To ensure the authenticity and stability of microbial cultures, it is essential to perform periodic checks for purity, sterility, and strain identification. A combination of microscopy and biochemical testing or molecular techniques (e.g., PCR) may be used for verification.

By following these steps, researchers can ensure the preparation of high-quality microbial cultures, leading to reliable and reproducible antimicrobial testing.

7.3 Inexpensive Culture Methods for Bacteria and Fungi

Culturing bacteria and fungi for antimicrobial studies in resource-limited laboratories can be achieved using simple, cost-effective methods that do not compromise the quality of results.

7.3.1 Bacterial Culture Methods

1. **Selection of Media:** Basic and inexpensive media such as Nutrient Agar (NA) or Nutrient Broth (NB) can be used for routine culturing of bacteria. These are widely available and provide essential nutrients for bacterial growth. For selective culturing, simpler formulations like MacConkey Agar (for Gram-negative bacteria) or Manitol Salt Agar (for *Staphylococcus* species) can be easily prepared in the laboratory.
    - **Preparation:** Basic media can be prepared from inexpensive raw materials like peptone, beef extract, and agar powder.
    - **Cost-Effective Alternative:** In-house preparation using ingredients like yeast extract, soy flour, and agar powder reduces the dependency on commercial media.
    - **Common Media for Antibacterial Activity:** For antibacterial testing, Nutrient Agar (NA) and Mueller-Hinton Agar (MHA) are widely used as they provides optimal growth conditions for most pathogenic bacteria and are inexpensive to prepare.
2. **Inoculation and Incubation:** After preparing the media, bacterial samples are inoculated using sterile loops or swabs, then incubated at 37°C for 24-48 hours, depending on the growth rate of the species. Inexpensive incubators or simple temperature-controlled environments (like water baths or air-conditioned rooms) can be used for incubation.

7.3.2 Fungal Culture Methods

1. **Selection of Media:** For fungi, Sabouraud Dextrose Agar (SDA) is a commonly used, low-cost medium that supports the growth of a wide range of fungal species. For dermatophytes, Potato Dextrose Agar (PDA) is an alternative. These media are inexpensive and easy to prepare using simple ingredients like dextrose and agar.
    - **Preparation:** Mix dextrose, agar, and distilled water to create the medium. If required, chloramphenicol can be added to inhibit bacterial contamination.
    - **Common Media for Antifungal Activity:** Potato Dextrose Agar (PDA) and Sabouraud Dextrose Agar (SDA) are typically used for antifungal testing, as it supports the growth of many clinically relevant fungi.
2. **Inoculation and Incubation:** Fungal cultures are typically inoculated by applying a spore suspension or placing fungal fragments on the medium. The cultures are then incubated at 25-30°C, often for 3-5 days, depending on fungal growth rates. This method is inexpensive and requires minimal equipment.
3. **Additional Cost-Saving Techniques:**
    - **Autoclaving:** Basic laboratory autoclaves or pressure cookers can be used to sterilize media and glassware.
    - **Storage:** Fungal and bacterial cultures can be preserved at –20°C or in glycerol stocks for long-term storage, thus reducing the cost of regular purchasing of new cultures.

General Considerations:

Both bacterial and fungal cultures require basic aseptic techniques to maintain sterility. These can be performed with minimal equipment, such as simple sterile loops, petri dishes, and inexpensive incubators or water baths. By using these inexpensive, easy-to-prepare media and techniques, laboratories can efficiently culture a variety of microorganisms without incurring high costs.

7.4 Methods for *In Vitro* Antimicrobial Activity Testing

In vitro antimicrobial activity testing is essential for evaluating the efficacy of antimicrobial agents. Various methods are employed to measure the ability of a substance to inhibit or kill microorganisms. Below are some commonly used techniques for evaluating antibacterial, antifungal, and other antimicrobial activities. These methods are cost-effective and simple, making them suitable for resource-limited laboratories with basic microbiological facilities.

7.4.1 Disk Diffusion Method (Kirby-Bauer Method)

Principle:

The disk diffusion method is one of the most widely used techniques to assess the antimicrobial activity of a substance. In this method, a small paper disk impregnated with the antimicrobial agent is placed on an inoculated agar plate, and the plate is incubated. The antimicrobial agent diffuses radially from the disk, creating a clear zone of inhibition where the microorganism cannot grow.

Procedure:

- Prepare a bacterial inoculum and spread it uniformly on an agar plate (typically **Mueller-Hinton Agar** for bacterial testing).
- Place sterile paper disks impregnated with the antimicrobial agent on the inoculated surface.
- Incubate the plate at 37°C for 18-24 hours.
- Measure the diameter of the zone of inhibition to determine the effectiveness of the antimicrobial agent.

Significance:

This method is inexpensive, easy to perform, and provides qualitative results (e.g., sensitive, intermediate, or resistant). It is widely used for testing antibiotic susceptibility in clinical microbiology.

7.4.2 Agar Well Diffusion Method

Principle:

In the agar well diffusion method, wells are created in the agar plate, which is inoculated with the microorganism. The antimicrobial agent is then added into the well. The agent diffuses radially and creates a zone of inhibition around the well if it has antimicrobial activity.

Procedure:

- Inoculate the agar plate with the test microorganism.
- Use a sterile cork borer or wide portion of 100 μL micropipette tip to create wells in the agar surface.
- Fill the wells with the antimicrobial agent or extract.
- Incubate at the appropriate temperature and observe the zone of inhibition.

Significance:

This method allows for the testing of liquid samples, including plant extracts and essential oils. It is also useful for testing multiple agents simultaneously.

7.4.3 Broth Dilution Method

Principle:

The broth dilution method is used to determine the minimum inhibitory concentration (MIC) of an antimicrobial agent, which is the lowest concentration of the agent that inhibits visible growth of the microorganism.

Procedure:

- Prepare serial dilutions of the antimicrobial agent in a liquid growth medium (such as **Nutrient Broth** or **Sabouraud Dextrose Broth** for fungi).
- Inoculate each dilution with a standardized microbial inoculum.
- Incubate the tubes and observe for turbidity, which indicates microbial growth.
- The MIC is determined as the lowest concentration showing no visible growth.

Significance:

This method provides quantitative data on the antimicrobial potency of an agent, helping to establish appropriate concentrations for use. It is highly reliable for both bacteria and fungi.

7.4.4 Microdilution Method

Principle:

The microdilution method is a more refined version of the broth dilution method, performed in a 96-well microplate format. It is used to determine the MIC in a more high-throughput and less resource-intensive manner.

Procedure:

- Prepare serial dilutions of the antimicrobial agent in a 96-well microplate.
- Inoculate each well with the microorganism and incubate.

- The MIC is determined by observing the well with no visible growth (clear broth).

Significance:

Microdilution allows for testing of multiple antimicrobial agents and microbial strains simultaneously, making it ideal for large-scale screening. It also consumes fewer resources and requires less volume of reagents.

7.4.5 Broth Microdilution for Fungus (Fungus Testing)

Principle:

Similar to bacterial microdilution, the broth microdilution method can be adapted for antifungal testing to determine the MIC against fungi.

Procedure:

- Prepare serial dilutions of antifungal agents in a 96-well plate containing fungal broth.
- Inoculate the wells with fungal spores and incubate.
- Record the lowest concentration that prevents fungal growth.

Significance:

This method is cost-effective for testing antifungal activity, especially with limited resources.

Key Insight

These *in vitro* antimicrobial methods are critical tools for assessing the efficacy of antimicrobial agents. They can be performed with minimal equipment and provide both qualitative and quantitative data on antimicrobial activity. By utilizing these methods, resource-limited laboratories can conduct meaningful antimicrobial testing in a cost-effective and ethically suitable manner.

Endnote

In this chapter, we will explore the detailed protocols for evaluating the antimicrobial properties of substances using various *in vitro* assays. We will focus on methods for **antibacterial activity**, **antifungal activity**, **antiviral activity assays**, and **quorum sensing inhibition assays** (for anti-biofilm activity). Each of these protocols is designed to be cost-effective and ethically sound, making them suitable for laboratories with basic facilities. These assays are essential tools for screening and assessing the antimicrobial potential of natural and synthetic compounds.

Antibacterial Activity Assay Protocol

Well Diffusion Method

In vitro antibacterial activity assays are essential for evaluating the antimicrobial potential of compounds. The well diffusion method is a widely used technique due to its simplicity and cost-effectiveness, especially in resource-limited laboratories. By creating wells in agar plates and introducing different concentrations of the test compound, this method allows for the assessment of antimicrobial effects through zones of inhibition. It provides valuable quantitative data, including the minimum inhibitory concentration (MIC), to determine the compound's potency.

Principle

The well diffusion method is used to determine the antibacterial potential of a compound or phytochemical extract. The compound is introduced into the agar medium through wells, and its antimicrobial activity is assessed by measuring the zone of inhibition formed around each well. The larger the zone, the more effective the compound is in inhibiting bacterial growth. This method also allows for testing multiple concentrations of the sample to determine the minimum inhibitory concentration (MIC) and provide quantitative data.

Requirements

- **Bacterial culture**: A fresh culture of the test bacterium, grown in appropriate broth (e.g., Nutrient Broth), for overnight incubation.
- **Agar medium**: Mueller-Hinton Agar (MHA) for bacterial testing.
- **Antibacterial sample**: The compound or phytochemical extract under investigation.
- **Dilution solvents**: Solvent (e.g., dimethyl sulfoxide (DMSO), or distilled water).
- **100 μL micropipette tip**: Used for creating wells in the agar.
- **Micropipettes**: To transfer 20 μL of each dilution into the wells.
- **Sterile Petri dishes**: For agar medium.
- **Sterile forceps or spreader**: For bacterial inoculation.
- **Incubator**: Set at 37°C for bacterial incubation.
- **Ruler or calliper:** For measuring the zone of inhibition.

Methodology

1. **Preparation of Bacterial Inoculum**:
    - Inoculate the bacterial culture in Nutrient Broth and incubate overnight at 37°C.
    - After incubation, adjust the turbidity of the bacterial suspension to a 0.5 McFarland standard, which corresponds to approximately $1x10^8$ CFU/mL, using sterile saline.

2. **Preparation of Agar Plate**:
   - Pour Mueller-Hinton Agar (MHA) into sterile Petri dishes (about 20-25 mL per plate).
   - Allow the agar to solidify at room temperature.
3. **Inoculation of Agar Plate**:
   - Use a sterile spreader or swab to evenly spread the bacterial inoculum on the surface of the agar plate. Ensure the inoculum is spread uniformly across the entire surface.
4. **Creation of Wells**:
   - After inoculating the agar plate, use a wide portion of a 100 μL micropipette tip to create five wells in the agar. Make sure the wells are evenly spaced and deep enough to hold the solution (approximately 5-6 mm in diameter). Now provide a suitable marking or code to each well on back side of petriplate.
5. **Preparation of Sample Dilutions**:
   - Prepare five serial dilutions of the antibacterial sample in a suitable solvent (e.g., DMSO, or sterile distilled water), starting from a concentration of 100 mg/mL and diluting it stepwise to 6.25 mg/mL (e.g., 100 mg/mL, 50 mg/mL, 25 mg/mL, 12.5 mg/mL, and 6.25 mg/mL). If possible the main stock can be passed though sterile 0.45 or 0.22 μm syringe filters and each dilution should be prepared in a sterile container.
6. **Filling the Wells**:
   - Using a micropipette, transfer 20 μL of each dilution (100 mg/mL, 50 mg/mL, 25 mg/mL, 12.5 mg/mL, and 6.25 mg/mL) into the respective wells. Be sure to avoid spillage into the surrounding agar.
7. **Incubation**:
   - Incubate the inoculated agar plate at 37°C for 18-24 hours.
8. **Measurement of the Zone of Inhibition**:
   - After incubation, observe the plate for the zones of inhibition around each well.
   - Measure the diameter of the clear zone (in millimetres) around each well. The zone of inhibition indicates the extent of antibacterial activity.

Calculations

To quantify the antibacterial activity, use the diameter of the zone of inhibition to calculate the effectiveness of the sample at different concentrations:

1. **Measure the diameter** (mm) of each zone of inhibition around the wells.
2. **Compare the inhibition zones** for each dilution of the sample:
   - The largest zone indicates the highest antimicrobial activity, corresponding to the **highest concentration (100 mg/mL)**.
   - The smallest zone indicates the lowest concentration (6.25 mg/mL).

3. **Plot a Dose-Response Curve** (optional):
   - The diameters of the zones of inhibition can be plotted against the corresponding concentrations to create a dose-response curve. This allows for the determination of the **Minimum Inhibitory Concentration (MIC)**, which is the lowest concentration of the sample that shows no bacterial growth (no zone of inhibition).

Results Interpretation

- **Zone of Inhibition (mm):** The larger the zone of inhibition, the more effective the antibacterial agent is at inhibiting bacterial growth.
- **MIC Determination:** The MIC is determined as the lowest concentration that produces a clear zone of inhibition.

Significance

This well diffusion method is a simple, cost-effective way to screen the antibacterial potential of compounds, particularly for labs with limited resources. The quantitative nature of the results, including the MIC, provides a clear indication of the compound's antimicrobial efficacy.

Antifungal Activity Assay Protocol – 1

Well Diffusion Method

Principle

The well diffusion method is employed to evaluate the antifungal activity of a compound or phytochemical extract. The sample is introduced into agar wells, and its effect on fungal growth is measured by the zone of inhibition formed around the well. The size of the inhibition zone indicates the compound's efficacy in preventing fungal growth. This method provides a straightforward and quantitative approach to assess antifungal potential, allowing for multiple concentrations of the sample to be tested and compared.

Requirements

- **Fungal culture**: A fresh fungal culture, typically of *Candida albicans*, *Aspergillus niger*, or another pathogenic strain.
- **Agar medium**: Sabouraud Dextrose Agar (SDA) for fungal testing.
- **Antifungal sample**: The compound or phytochemical extract being tested.
- **Dilution solvents**: Solvent such as dimethyl sulfoxide (DMSO), or distilled water.
- **100 μL micropipette tip**: Used to create wells in the agar.

- **Micropipettes**: To transfer 20 μL of each dilution into the wells.
- **Sterile Petri dishes**: For agar medium.
- **Sterile forceps or spreader**: For fungal inoculation.
- **Incubator**: Set at 25-30°C for fungal growth.
- **Ruler or calliper**: For measuring the zone of inhibition.

Methodology

1. **Preparation of Fungal Inoculum**:
   - Inoculate the fungal culture (e.g., *Candida albicans*, or *Aspergillus niger*) in Sabouraud Dextrose Agar (SDA) or Potato Dextrose Agar (PDA) and incubate at 25-30°C for 3 to 5 days till the spore formation.
   - After incubation, add 5 to 10 ml of sterile distilled water on the sporing colony and mix the spore in water properly in order to harvest the spores.
   - Now collect this spore suspension in a sterile container or vial for preservation or antimicrobial activity.
2. **Preparation of Agar Plate**:
   - Pour Sabouraud Dextrose Agar (SDA) or Potato Dextrose Agar (PDA) into sterile 90 mm diameter Petri dishes (about 15-20 mL per plate).
   - Allow the agar to solidify at room temperature.
3. **Inoculation of Agar Plate**:
   - Use a sterile spreader or swab to evenly spread the fungal spore inoculum on the surface of the agar plate. Ensure the inoculum is spread uniformly across the entire surface.
4. **Creation of Wells**:
   - After inoculating the agar plate, use a wide portion of a 100 μL micropipette tip to create five wells in the agar. Ensure the wells are spaced evenly and deep enough to hold the solution (approximately 5-6 mm in diameter). Now provide a suitable marking or code to each well on back side of petriplate.
5. **Preparation of Sample Dilutions**:
   - Prepare five serial dilutions of the antifungal sample in a suitable solvent (e.g., DMSO, or sterile distilled water), starting from a concentration of 100 mg/mL and diluting it stepwise to 6.25 mg/mL (e.g., 100 mg/mL, 50 mg/mL, 25 mg/mL, 12.5 mg/mL, and 6.25 mg/mL). If possible the main stock can be passed though sterile 0.45 or 0.22 μm syringe filters and each dilution should be prepared in a sterile container.
6. **Filling the Wells**:
   - Using a micropipette, transfer 20 μL of each dilution (100 mg/mL, 50 mg/mL, 25 mg/mL, 12.5 mg/mL, and 6.25 mg/mL) into the respective wells. Ensure there is no spillage into the surrounding agar.

7. **Incubation**:
    - Incubate the inoculated agar plate at 25-30°C for 48-72 hours (depending on fungal growth rate).
8. **Measurement of the Zone of Inhibition**:
    - After incubation, observe the plate for the zones of inhibition around each well. These clear zones indicate the compound's ability to inhibit fungal growth.
    - Measure the diameter of the clear zone (in millimetres) around each well.

Calculations

To quantify the antifungal activity, use the diameter of the zone of inhibition to calculate the effectiveness of the sample at different concentrations:

1. **Measure the diameter** (in mm) of each zone of inhibition.
2. **Compare the inhibition zones** for each dilution of the sample:
    - The largest zone corresponds to the highest concentration (100 mg/mL).
    - The smallest zone corresponds to the lowest concentration (6.25 mg/mL).
3. **Plot a Dose-Response Curve** (optional):
    - The diameters of the zones of inhibition can be plotted against the corresponding concentrations to create a dose-response curve. This helps determine the **Minimum Inhibitory Concentration (MIC)**, which is the lowest concentration of the sample that prevents visible fungal growth (no zone of inhibition).

Results Interpretation

- **Zone of Inhibition (mm)**: A larger zone indicates greater antifungal activity.
- **MIC Determination**: The MIC is the lowest concentration that produces a clear zone of inhibition.

Significance

This well diffusion method is a simple, cost-effective way to screen the antifungal activity of compounds, particularly for laboratories with limited resources. The quantitative results, including MIC, provide clear information on the compound's efficacy, making it suitable for both natural and synthetic antifungal agents.

Antifungal Activity Assay Protocol – 2

Broth Microdilution Method

The broth microdilution method is a widely recognized and reliable *in vitro* technique for evaluating the antifungal activity of compounds. It is used to determine the minimum inhibitory concentration (MIC) of a substance, which represents the lowest concentration that effectively inhibits fungal growth. This method is particularly useful for screening natural products, phytochemicals, and synthetic agents.

Principle

In this method, serial dilutions of the antifungal agent are prepared in a liquid medium and inoculated with a standardized fungal suspension. The antifungal activity is measured by observing the lowest concentration of the compound that prevents visible fungal growth. This method is quantitative and provides precise results, making it suitable for screening antifungal agents, particularly in resource-limited laboratories.

Requirements

- **Fungal culture**: A fungal strain, such as *Candida albicans*, *Aspergillus niger, or Candida glabrata*, or any other suitable pathogenic fungal strain.
- **Culture medium**: RPMI-1640 medium or Yeast Nitrogen Base (YNB) medium, supplemented with glucose (if required), or Sabouraud Dextrose Broth (SDB).
- **Antifungal compound**: Phytochemical extract, synthetic compound, or natural antifungal substance to be tested.
- **96-well microtiter plates**: For preparing the dilutions and inoculations.
- **Micropipettes and tips**: To transfer the compound and fungal inoculum into the wells.
- **Sterile distilled water or DMSO**: As solvents to dilute the antifungal agent.
- **Fungal inoculum**: Prepared from a fresh culture of the selected fungal strain, adjusted to a specific cell density (usually 0.5 McFarland or equivalent).
- **Sterile 1x phosphate-buffered saline (PBS)**: For adjusting fungal inoculum.
- **Incubator**: To maintain the plate at an appropriate temperature (usually 28-37°C, depending on the fungal strain).
- **Microplate reader**: To measure optical density (OD) at a wavelength of 530-600 nm or visually inspect growth.

Methodology

1. **Preparation of Fungal Inoculum**:
    - Inoculate a fresh fungal strain (e.g., *Candida albicans*) into appropriate broth medium (e.g., Sabouraud Dextrose Broth or RPMI-1640).
    - Incubate the fungal culture at 28-30°C for 24-48 hours.
    - Adjust the fungal suspension to a final concentration of 1×10^3 to 1×10^4 CFU/mL (standardized to 0.5 McFarland or equivalent).

2. **Preparation of the Antifungal Compound**:
   - Dissolve the antifungal compound or phytochemical extract in a suitable solvent (e.g., DMSO or sterile distilled water).
   - Prepare serial dilutions of the antifungal compound in the broth medium. Start with a high concentration (e.g., 100 mg/mL) and dilute it stepwise (e.g., to 50 mg/mL, 25 mg/mL, 12.5 mg/mL, etc.) until you reach the lowest desired concentration.
3. **Preparation of Microdilution Plate**:
   - Dispense 100 μL of the fungal culture medium (broth) into each well of a 96-well microtiter plate.
   - Prepare the dilutions of the antifungal compound (e.g., 100 mg/mL, 50 mg/mL, 25 mg/mL, 12.5 mg/mL, 6.25 mg/mL), and transfer 100 μL of each dilution into the corresponding wells of the microtiter plate.
   - Ensure the wells containing only the fungal culture (no antifungal agent) serve as positive controls, while the wells with only broth medium act as negative controls.
4. **Inoculation**:
   - Add 100 μL of the fungal inoculum (prepared earlier) to each well containing the antifungal agent.
   - The final volume in each well will be 200 μL, containing both the medium and the antifungal compound.
5. **Incubation**:
   - Incubate the microtiter plate at 28-30°C (or the optimal temperature for the fungal strain) for 24-48 hours.
   - During incubation, fungal growth will occur, and the antifungal activity will be reflected by the inhibition of growth in the wells containing the compound.
6. **Reading the Results**:
   - After incubation, measure the optical density (OD) at 530-600 nm using a microplate reader to assess fungal growth. Alternatively, visually inspect the wells for turbidity or absence of growth.
   - The lowest concentration that shows no growth (clear well) is considered the Minimum Inhibitory Concentration (MIC).

Calculations

1. **MIC Determination**:
   - The MIC is defined as the lowest concentration of the compound at which no fungal growth is observed (clear or nearly clear well).
   - Calculate the MIC based on the dilution factor.

2. **Interpretation**:
   - Compare the MIC of the test compound to that of a standard antifungal agent (e.g., fluconazole) for reference.
   - A lower MIC value indicates stronger antifungal activity, while a higher MIC indicates weaker activity.

Results Interpretation

- **MIC Determination**: The minimum concentration of the test compound that inhibits fungal growth is noted as the MIC.
- **Activity**: A lower MIC indicates a more potent antifungal agent. The presence or absence of growth can be confirmed by OD readings or visual observation.

Significance

This broth microdilution method is an effective and widely used technique for assessing the antifungal activity of compounds. It is quantitative, reproducible, and suitable for testing multiple concentrations of compounds, making it ideal for screening natural products, phytochemicals, and synthetic antifungal agents. The method is appropriate for resource-limited laboratories as it requires minimal equipment and can be performed with basic microbiological facilities.

Antiviral Activity Assay Protocol – 1

Hemagglutination Inhibition (HI) Assay

The Hemagglutination Inhibition (HI) Assay is an effective method for screening the antiviral potential of compounds, particularly against viruses that cause hemagglutination. This assay is widely used due to its simplicity, cost-effectiveness, and ability to provide quantitative results. By assessing a compound's ability to inhibit virus-induced agglutination of red blood cells, this method serves as a crucial step in evaluating antiviral efficacy. The following protocol outlines the steps for conducting the HI assay to determine the antiviral activity of a test compound or extract.

Principle

This method evaluates the ability of a compound or phytochemical extract to inhibit the hemagglutination activity of a virus, indicating its potential antiviral properties. The test measures the inhibition of virus-induced hemagglutination by pre-incubating the virus with different concentrations of the compound before adding red blood cells. The absence of hemagglutination in the presence of the compound is considered evidence of antiviral activity.

Requirements

- **Viral stock**: A virus capable of hemagglutination, such as Influenza virus. Live attenuated influenza vaccine (LAIV) strains or vaccine itself can be purchased and safely be used for the purpose minding you have at least BSL-2 lab.
- **Red blood cells (RBCs)**: Human or animal red blood cells (commonly from chickens or rabbits), which are used to assess hemagglutination. One can typically purchase RBS from manufactures (eg. Thermo, Sigma Aldrich, HiMedia, etc.)
- **Phytochemical extract/compound**: The substance to be tested for antiviral activity (e.g., herbal extracts, compounds).
- **Phosphate-buffered saline (PBS)**: To dilute the virus and the extract.
- **96-well microtiter plates**: For performing the assay.
- **Micro-pipettes and tips**: For transferring virus, RBCs, and extracts.
- **Incubator**: To maintain the temperature during incubation (usually 37°C).
- **Centrifuge**: To prepare red blood cell suspensions if necessary.
- **Sterile glassware**: For preparation and dilution of compounds and virus stocks.

Methodology

1. **Preparation of Viral Suspension**:
    - Purchase the live attenuated influenza vaccine (LAIV) strains or vaccine and quantify the virus titer (typically expressed as hemagglutination units, HA units).
    - Prepare a viral suspension with a known HA titer (usually 8 HA units/mL).
2. **Preparation of Red Blood Cell (RBC) Suspension**:
    - Purchase or harvest RBCs from an appropriate animal (e.g., chicken or rabbit).
    - Wash the RBCs three times with PBS (pH 7.2-7.4) to remove any contaminants.
    - Resuspend the RBCs in PBS to a concentration of approximately 0.5-1% (v/v).
3. **Preparation of Compound Dilutions**:
    - Prepare serial dilutions of the compound or phytochemical extract in PBS.
    - Use at least 5 concentrations (e.g., 100 mg/mL, 50 mg/mL, 25 mg/mL, 12.5 mg/mL, 6.25 mg/mL) for testing.
    - Ensure that the solvent used to dissolve the extract does not interfere with the hemagglutination process (preferably use PBS or ethanol).

4. **Incubation of Virus and Compound**:
   - In a 96-well microtiter plate, add 50 μL of each dilution of the compound to separate wells.
   - Add 50 μL of the viral suspension to each well.
   - Mix gently and incubate the plate at 37°C for 30 minutes to allow the virus and the compound to interact.
5. **Hemagglutination Assay**:
   - After incubation, add 50 μL of the red blood cell suspension (0.5-1% RBCs) to each well.
   - Gently shake the plate and incubate for 30-60 minutes at room temperature (or at 37°C, depending on the virus).
   - Observe for hemagglutination. In positive hemagglutination, the RBCs will form a lattice and settle in the center of the well, while in the presence of an antiviral agent, the RBCs will remain dispersed across the well, showing inhibition of agglutination.
6. **Interpretation of Results**:
   - Record the highest dilution of the compound at which no hemagglutination is observed. This concentration is considered the half maximal inhibitory concentration (IC_{50}).
   - The IC_{50} value represents the concentration of the compound that reduces hemagglutination by 50%, which correlates with the antiviral potency of the compound.

Calculations

1. **IC_{50} Determination**:
   - The IC_{50} is determined by plotting the dilution concentrations (x-axis) against the inhibition percentages (y-axis). The IC_{50} is the concentration at which 50% inhibition is observed.
   - A lower IC_{50} value indicates greater antiviral potency.
2. **Activity Assessment**:
   - Compare the results of the antiviral compound with a standard antiviral drug (e.g., oseltamivir for influenza) to determine the relative efficacy of the test compound.
3. **Quantitative Analysis**:
   - Calculate the % inhibition of hemagglutination by the formula:

$$(\%)\,\text{Inhibition} = \frac{\text{Control HA} - \text{Test HA}}{\text{Control HA}} \times 100$$

   - Where **Control HA** is the hemagglutination in the absence of the compound, and **Test HA** is the hemagglutination in the presence of the compound.

Significance

The Hemagglutination Inhibition Assay is an effective method for evaluating the antiviral activity of compounds, especially those targeting enveloped viruses like influenza or other viruses causing hemagglutination. It is a simple, cost-effective technique suitable for use in laboratories with basic virology and microbiological facilities. This assay allows for the identification of potentially antiviral compounds that can be further developed or tested for clinical application.

Antiviral Activity Assay Protocol – 2

Plaque Assay Using Embryonated Eggs

Principle

The plaque assay using embryonated eggs is a method to assess the antiviral potential of a compound or phytochemical extract by evaluating its ability to inhibit viral replication. In this assay, viruses are introduced into the chorioallantoic membrane (CAM) of fertilized chicken eggs. The compound of interest is tested by its ability to prevent the formation of plaques, which are clear zones of infected cells on the membrane. Fewer plaques indicate stronger antiviral activity, as the compound inhibits viral replication.

Requirements

- Embryonated chicken eggs (fertilized eggs, 9-12 days old)
- Virus stock (e.g., live attenuated influenza vaccine (LAIV) strains or vaccine)
- Antiviral compound or phytochemical extract
- Phosphate-buffered saline (PBS)
- Nutrient agar (for plaque formation)
- Incubator (37°C)
- Sterile pipettes and micropipettes
- Microcentrifuge tubes
- Laminar flow hood
- Sterile forceps
- Syringe and needles for inoculation

Methodology

- **Preparation of Eggs:**
  - Select healthy, fertilized chicken eggs and store them at room temperature for 24 hours before use.
  - Disinfect the eggs with 70% ethanol to ensure they are sterile.
  - Use a sterile syringe and needle to create a small hole in the eggshell for inoculation.
- **Virus and Compound Preparation:**
  - Prepare the virus stock solution at a known concentration.
  - Dilute the antiviral compound or phytochemical extract in PBS to achieve the required concentrations (e.g., 100 μg/mL, 50 μg/mL, 25 μg/mL, etc.).
- **Inoculation:**
  - Gently puncture the egg membrane with a sterile needle to inject the virus suspension into the CAM.
  - Inject a known volume (e.g., 100 μL) of virus solution into each egg.
  - For control eggs, inoculate with virus alone, and for test groups, inoculate with virus and the antiviral compound.
  - Seal the hole in the shell with sterile tape and incubate at 37°C for 48-72 hours.
- **Plaque Formation:**
  - After incubation, open the eggs and observe the CAM for plaque formation (clear zones).
  - Gently remove the CAM using sterile forceps and transfer it to a Petri dish.
  - Stain the CAM with crystal violet solution for better visibility of plaques.
- **Counting Plaques:**
  - Count the number of plaques formed in each egg. Each plaque corresponds to an area where viral replication has occurred.

Calculations

Plaque Reduction Percentage: The antiviral activity is quantified by comparing the number of plaques formed in treated eggs with those in control eggs (virus only). The percentage reduction in plaque formation is calculated as follows:

$$(\%)\,\text{Plaque Reduction} = \frac{\text{Plaque in Control} - \text{Plaque in Treated}}{\text{Plaque in Control}} \times 100$$

- **IC_{50} (50% Inhibitory Concentration):** To determine the IC_{50} value, plot the plaque reduction percentage against the concentrations of the compound. The IC_{50} is the concentration at which 50% plaque reduction is observed.

Notes

- Ensure that the embryos are viable and healthy before use.
- The CAM must be handled carefully to avoid contamination.
- The method is applicable for screening a wide range of viruses and antiviral agents.
- The results obtained can be further confirmed using molecular assays (e.g., PCR) to assess viral load.

This assay provides a reliable and reproducible method for evaluating the antiviral potential of compounds or phytochemicals, especially in early-stage drug discovery.

Quorum Sensing Inhibition Assay Protocol

Anti-biofilm Activity

Quorum sensing (QS) is a mechanism of bacterial communication that regulates gene expression in response to cell density or population density, including the production of biofilms. In pathogens, QS controls the production of virulence factors, including biofilm formation. Inhibition of QS can prevent biofilm formation, which is often linked to virulence and antibiotic resistance, and offering a strategy to combat bacterial infections. Quorum Sensing Inhibition Assay (QSIA) evaluates the ability of compounds or phytochemical extracts to interfere with bacterial quorum sensing and inhibit biofilm formation.

Principle

The assay is based on the ability of a test compound to inhibit quorum sensing in bacteria, thereby preventing biofilm formation. This is typically assessed by measuring biofilm biomass or the expression of QS-regulated genes. Inhibition of biofilm formation reflects the anti-quorum sensing and antimicrobial potential of the compound. This assay typically uses *Pseudomonas aeruginosa* or *Chromobacterium violaceum* as model organisms, which produce visible QS-dependent signals (such as violacein pigment or pyocyanin) when grown in the presence of a QS inducer.

Requirements

Biological Material:

1. **Bacterial strains**:
   - *Pseudomonas aeruginosa* (pyocyanin production).
   - *Chromobacterium violaceum* (violacein production).
2. **Optional strains**: QS-reporter strains like bioluminescent *Vibrio fischeri*.

Reagents & Chemicals:

- Luria-Bertani (LB) or nutrient broth.

- Test compound or phytochemical extract (dissolved in water or DMSO).
- Controls:
    - Positive (e.g., known QS inhibitors like furanones).
    - Negative (untreated or solvent only).
- Crystal violet (0.1% w/v) for biofilm staining.
- PBS or sterile distilled water.
- Ethanol (95%) for crystal violet solubilization.

Equipment:

- 96-well microtiter plates (flat-bottom).
- Spectrophotometer or microplate reader (570 nm for biofilm; 520/585 nm for QS signal).
- Incubator (37°C).
- Sterile pipettes and tips.

Methodology

1. **Bacterial Culture Preparation**
    - Inoculate *Pseudomonas aeruginosa* or *Chromobacterium violaceum* in LB broth.
    - Incubate overnight at 37°C with shaking (150 rpm).
    - Standardize culture to $OD_{600} = 0.1$ ($\sim 10^8$ CFU/mL).
2. **Test Compound Preparation**
    - Prepare serial dilutions of the test compound (e.g., 10–1000 μg/mL).
    - Use sterile solvents (e.g., DMSO or PBS).
    - Ensure DMSO concentration is $\leq 1\%$ in the final assay.
3. **Assay Setup**
    - In each well of a sterile 96-well plate, add:
        - 100 μL bacterial suspension ($OD_{600} = 0.1$).
        - 100 μL of test compound (at various concentrations).
        - Positive control: Add a known QS inhibitor.
        - Negative control: Add bacterial culture only.
        - Solvent control: Add the solvent without a test compound.
    - Incubate at 37°C for 24–48 hours.

4. **Biofilm Quantification**
   - Carefully discard the supernatant to remove non-adherent bacteria.
   - Wash wells gently with PBS (3×).
   - Add 200 μL crystal violet (0.1% w/v) to each well.
   - Incubate for 15–20 minutes at room temperature.
   - Rinse wells 3× with PBS to remove excess stain.
   - Solubilize biofilm-bound crystal violet by adding 200 μL ethanol (95%).
   - Measure absorbance at 570 nm using a microplate reader.
5. **QS Signal Quantification**
   - After incubation, check the presence of violacein pigment production (in *Chromobacterium violaceum*) or pyocyanin production (in *Pseudomonas aeruginosa*) as an indicator of QS activity.
   - *Chromobacterium violaceum*: Violacein production can be measured at **585 nm**.
   - *Pseudomonas aeruginosa*: Pyocyanin production can be quantified at **520 nm**.
   - Extract pigment from supernatants for spectrophotometric readings.

Calculations

1. **Biofilm Inhibition Percentage**

$$\%\,\text{Biofilm Inhibition} = \frac{\text{OD Control} - \text{OD Sample}}{\text{OD Control}} \times 100$$

   - **OD Control**: Absorbance of untreated biofilm (negative control).
   - **OD Sample**: Absorbance of biofilm in the presence of the test compound.

2. **QS Signal Inhibition Percentage**

$$\%\,\text{QS Inhibition} = \frac{\text{Pigment Control} - \text{Pigment Sample}}{\text{Pigment Control}} \times 100$$

   - **Pigment Control**: Absorbance of QS signal in untreated sample.
   - **Pigment Sample**: Absorbance of QS signal in treated sample.

3. **3. IC_{50} Calculation**
   - Determine the IC_{50} (concentration at 50% inhibition) by plotting a dose-response curve (concentration vs. inhibition percentage).

Precautions

- Use aseptic techniques to avoid contamination.
- Perform each experiment in triplicate for reproducibility.
- Validate that test compounds do not inhibit bacterial growth directly (ensure effects are QS-specific).

This assay offers a robust framework for identifying potential QS inhibitors, aiding the development of anti-biofilm agents.

Chapter 8

In Vitro Anti-Tubercle Activity

8.1 Overview of Tuberculosis (TB) as a Global Health Challenge

Tuberculosis (TB), caused by *Mycobacterium tuberculosis*, remains a leading infectious disease globally, despite significant advances in medical science and healthcare infrastructure. It is an airborne disease transmitted via respiratory droplets, primarily affecting the lungs but potentially impacting other organs in extrapulmonary TB. According to the World Health Organization (WHO), TB ranks among the top 10 causes of death worldwide, with millions of new cases and fatalities reported annually. The global burden of TB is compounded by the dual challenges of drug resistance and co-infection with HIV.

8.1.1 The Disease Burden

TB poses a significant health challenge, particularly in low- and middle-income countries, where it is both a cause and a consequence of poverty. Factors such as overcrowding, malnutrition, lack of access to healthcare, and poor living conditions exacerbate its spread. In 2022, an estimated 10.6 million people fell ill with TB, and approximately 1.6 million succumbed to the disease, making it one of the most lethal infectious diseases globally. While the disease is treatable and curable with timely intervention, the global efforts to eliminate TB face barriers due to socio-economic disparities and healthcare gaps.

High-burden countries, including India, Indonesia, China, and South Africa, account for a majority of TB cases. Among vulnerable populations, such as children, the elderly, and individuals with weakened immune systems, TB poses an even greater risk. The emergence of drug-resistant TB (DR-TB) has further escalated the crisis, undermining existing treatment regimens and making the disease more challenging to control.

8.1.2 Drug Resistance in TB

Drug-resistant TB has become a critical concern in global health, categorized into multidrug-resistant TB (MDR-TB) and extensively drug-resistant TB (XDR-TB).

- **MDR-TB** refers to strains resistant to at least isoniazid and rifampicin, the two most potent first-line drugs.
- **XDR-TB** exhibits resistance to first-line drugs as well as certain second-line drugs, leaving limited treatment options.

The rise of drug resistance is fueled by incomplete or improper treatments, lack of adherence to lengthy regimens, and poor-quality drugs. MDR-TB accounts for about 3% of new TB cases and up to 18% of previously treated cases, posing severe public health challenges.

8.1.3 Need for Novel Therapeutic Agents

The development of novel anti-TB drugs is imperative to address the growing crisis. Current treatment regimens are long, involving a combination of drugs taken over six to nine months, which increases the risk of non-compliance. Novel therapies need to address several critical issues:

- **Shortened treatment duration**: To improve adherence and reduce the development of resistance.
- **Efficacy against resistant strains**: To combat MDR-TB and XDR-TB effectively.
- **Activity against latent TB**: To target dormant bacteria that evade conventional treatments.

In addition to chemical drugs, natural products, phytochemicals, and repurposed drugs are being actively researched for their anti-tubercular properties. Innovations such as host-directed therapies (HDTs), which enhance the immune response to TB, and nanotechnology-based drug delivery systems are gaining momentum in TB research.

Tuberculosis continues to be a formidable global health challenge, necessitating coordinated efforts to improve diagnostic, preventive, and treatment strategies. Investments in novel therapeutic agents, affordable healthcare infrastructure, and global initiatives like the WHO's *End TB Strategy* are essential to achieve the ambitious goal of eliminating TB as a public health threat by 2035.

8.2 Importance of Screening Anti-Tubercle Agents *In Vitro*

In vitro assays play a critical role in the early-stage development of anti-tubercular drugs by providing a cost-effective, ethical, and scalable alternative to animal models. These laboratory-based assays allow researchers to evaluate the efficacy, potency, and mechanism of action of potential therapeutic agents against *Mycobacterium tuberculosis* or related surrogate strains.

8.2.1 Accelerating Early-Stage Drug Development

In vitro assays enable rapid screening of large compound libraries, identifying promising candidates for further testing. Methods such as the Resazurin Microtiter Assay (REMA), Alamar Blue Assay, and Agar Proportion Method are commonly used to determine the minimum inhibitory concentration (MIC) of compounds, providing insights into their bactericidal or bacteriostatic properties.

These assays also facilitate testing against drug-resistant strains of TB, such as MDR-TB and XDR-TB, allowing researchers to prioritize compounds that overcome resistance mechanisms. Advanced techniques, including high-throughput screening (HTS) and reporter-based assays, enhance efficiency and scalability, significantly reducing the time required for drug discovery pipelines.

8.2.2 Reducing Reliance on Animal Models

In vitro models provide an ethical alternative to animal testing, aligning with the principles of the 3Rs (Replacement, Reduction, and Refinement). By using non-pathogenic or attenuated strains such as *Mycobacterium bovis BCG, M. tuberculosis* H37Ra, or *M. smegmatis*, researchers can simulate mycobacterial infections in a controlled and biosafe manner. These assays help identify active compounds before progressing to *in vivo* studies, thereby minimizing unnecessary use of animals.

Overall, *in vitro* assays are indispensable tools in anti-tubercle drug discovery, offering a robust, ethical, and efficient platform for screening potential therapeutic agents. Their use not only accelerates research timelines but also ensures that only the most promising candidates advance to preclinical and clinical stages.

8.3 Advantages of Using *In Vitro* Methods for Drug Discovery

In vitro methods have revolutionized drug discovery, offering significant advantages in terms of ethics, cost, reproducibility, and scalability. These methods enable researchers to evaluate the potential of therapeutic compounds in a controlled environment, making them indispensable for early-stage drug development.

8.3.1 Ethical Considerations

In vitro assays minimize or eliminate the need for animal testing in the early stages of research. This aligns with the ethical principles of the 3Rs (Replacement, Reduction, and Refinement), reducing harm to animals while maintaining scientific rigor. By using cell-based or microbial models, researchers can address preliminary questions about a compound's efficacy and mechanism of action without resorting to *in vivo* studies.

8.3.2 Cost-Effectiveness

Compared to animal models or clinical trials, *in vitro* methods are significantly more affordable. They require fewer resources, such as specialized facilities, animal care, and labor, making them ideal for resource-limited laboratories. The relatively low cost allows for the rapid screening of large libraries of compounds, accelerating drug discovery timelines.

8.3.3 Reproducibility

In vitro systems provide controlled and standardized conditions, ensuring consistent results across experiments. This reproducibility is crucial for comparing data and validating findings, particularly during preclinical stages of drug development.

8.3.4 Scalability for High-Throughput Screening

Modern *in vitro* methods are highly scalable, enabling the simultaneous testing of hundreds or thousands of compounds. Techniques like microtiter plate assays and automated liquid handling systems enhance the efficiency of high-throughput screening (HTS), expediting the identification of lead candidates.

8.4 Commonly Used Methods of Anti-Tubercle Activity

The identification and evaluation of anti-tubercular compounds rely on a variety of *in vitro* assays, each designed to measure the efficacy of potential drugs against *Mycobacterium tuberculosis* or related non-pathogenic strains. These methods are essential for determining antimicrobial activity, minimum inhibitory concentration (MIC), and potential mechanisms of action.

1. **Resazurin Microtiter Assay (REMA):** REMA is a colorimetric assay widely used for high-throughput screening of anti-tubercular compounds. Resazurin, a redox-sensitive dye, changes colour from blue (oxidized) to pink (reduced) in the presence of viable mycobacterial cells. This non-destructive method is highly sensitive, cost-effective, and suitable for MIC determination.
2. **Alamar Blue Assay:** Similar to REMA, the Alamar Blue Assay employs resazurin as an indicator of metabolic activity. It is particularly valued for its ability to assess drug susceptibility in low-resource settings. This assay is reproducible, scalable, and compatible with both active and dormant mycobacterial cells, making it a versatile choice for TB research.
3. **Agar Proportion Method:** This classical method involves plating *M. tuberculosis* on agar media containing different concentrations of the test compound. The proportion of colonies that grow at each concentration indicates the susceptibility of the strain. While highly accurate, this method is time-consuming and less suitable for high-throughput screening.
4. **Luciferase Reporter Assay (LRA):** The LRA measures bacterial luminescence using genetically engineered *M. tuberculosis* strains expressing luciferase. Luminescence intensity correlates with bacterial viability, offering a rapid and sensitive alternative for testing drug efficacy.
5. **Microplate Dilution Assay:** This method involves culturing mycobacteria in liquid media in 96-well plates with varying drug concentrations. It is an economical and high-throughput approach to determine MIC values.

These assays provide robust, scalable, and cost-effective platforms for evaluating anti-tubercular compounds. The choice of method depends on the laboratory's resources, the stage of drug development, and the specific research objectives.

8.5 *In Vitro* Anti-Microbial Activity for Anti-Tubercle Drug Discovery

In vitro anti-microbial assays are critical for the preclinical evaluation of compounds targeting *Mycobacterium tuberculosis* (M.tb), providing valuable insights into their efficacy and mechanism of action. These assays focus on determining the Minimum Inhibitory Concentration (MIC), bactericidal or bacteriostatic properties, and activity against latent TB, which are pivotal for advancing drug discovery.

1. **Evaluation of MIC:** The MIC represents the lowest concentration of a drug required to inhibit visible bacterial growth. It is a key parameter for assessing the potency of anti-tubercular compounds. Methods such as the Resazurin Microtiter Assay (REMA), Alamar Blue Assay, and Microplate Dilution Method are commonly employed for MIC determination. These assays offer rapid and reliable quantification of a compound's efficacy, allowing for comparisons across a wide range of candidate molecules.
2. **Bactericidal vs. Bacteriostatic Effects:** Understanding whether a compound kills (*bactericidal*) or merely inhibits the growth (*bacteriostatic*) of *M.tb* is essential for therapeutic development.

Time-kill assays and colony-forming unit (CFU) counting methods are often used to distinguish between these effects. Bactericidal drugs are especially important for achieving sterilizing activity and reducing treatment duration.

3. **Activity Against Latent TB:** One of the greatest challenges in TB drug development is addressing latent infections, where *M.tb* resides in a non-replicating, dormant state. Assays using hypoxic culture conditions or nutrient-deprivation models simulate latent TB and help identify compounds capable of targeting dormant bacilli. Techniques such as the Wayne Dormancy Model and modified Alamar Blue Assay are particularly effective in this context.

8.6 Use of Safe Strains in Resource-Limited Labs

In resource-limited laboratories, ensuring biosafety while conducting anti-tubercular research is crucial. Utilizing non-pathogenic or attenuated strains of mycobacteria offers an effective approach to studying drug efficacy without compromising safety. Strains such as *Mycobacterium bovis BCG, M. tuberculosis H37Ra, M. smegmatis, mycolic acid-deficient mutants, and recombinant reporter strains* are commonly used for this purpose due to their reduced virulence and similar biochemical or genetic characteristics to pathogenic *Mycobacterium tuberculosis* (M.tb).

1. ***Mycobacterium bovis* BCG**

   The Bacillus Calmette-Guérin (BCG) strain, derived from *M. bovis,* is an attenuated vaccine strain used globally for TB prevention. It provides a safe alternative for *in vitro* drug screening and immune response studies in TB research. BCG shares many antigens with *M.tb*, making it a reliable model for evaluating host-pathogen interactions, drug susceptibility, and vaccine-related studies.

   - **Applications**:
     - Used as a surrogate for *Mycobacterium tuberculosis* in preliminary drug and phytochemical screening.
     - Useful in high-throughput screening and dormancy models.

2. ***M. tuberculosis* H37Ra**

   H37Ra is an avirulent variant of the virulent *M.tb* H37Rv strain. It retains many genetic and metabolic features of *M.tb* while lacking pathogenicity, making it an excellent substitute for studying anti-tubercular activity. H37Ra is particularly valuable for testing drug mechanisms and host immune responses in environments where biosafety level-3 (BSL-3) facilities are unavailable.

   - **Applications**:
     - Suitable for *in vitro* assays like Resazurin Microtiter Assay (REMA) and Alamar Blue Assay.
     - Used for screening anti-tubercular compounds in resource-limited labs without BSL-3 containment.

3. ***M. smegmatis***

   M. smegmatis is a fast-growing, non-pathogenic mycobacterium commonly used in TB research. It offers advantages such as rapid growth, ease of genetic manipulation, and high biosafety, making it ideal for early drug screening and studying basic mycobacterial biology. Though not a direct surrogate for *M.tb*, its metabolic pathways and cell wall structure share similarities with pathogenic strains, allowing it to serve as a cost-effective model organism.

   - **Applications**:
     - Frequently used as a model organism for initial drug activity assays.
     - Ideal for evaluating mechanisms of action and preliminary high-throughput screening of phytochemicals or synthetic drugs.

4. **Mycolic Acid Deficient Mutants**

   These are genetically engineered *Mycobacterium* strains that lack mycolic acid, a key component of the mycobacterial cell wall, making them avirulent. The absence of essential virulence factors, like mycolic acid, prevents the strains from establishing infections.

   - **Applications:**
     - Used to test inhibitors targeting mycobacterial cell walls or enzymes involved in cell wall synthesis.
     - Used to identify promising drug candidates before progressing to virulent strain testing.

5. **Recombinant Reporter Strains**

   Recombinant strains of *M. bovis* BCG, *M. tuberculosis* H37Ra, or *M. smegmatis* are engineered to express bioluminescent or fluorescent markers. These strains facilitate rapid and non-invasive drug screening. The engineered strains are either attenuated or avirulent, significantly reducing biosafety risks.

   - **Applications**:
     - Enables rapid screening of drug activity using Luciferase Reporter Phage (LRP) assay.
     - High-throughput screening using fluorescence or luminescence markers.
     - Reduces exposure risks while maintaining assay accuracy since strains are avirulent or attenuated.

Benefits of Using Safe Strains

- **Biosafety:** Reduced virulence minimizes risk to researchers and eliminates the need for high-containment facilities.
- **Cost-Effectiveness:** Safe strains require less stringent infrastructure, making them accessible for resource-limited settings.

- **Ethical Compliance:** Safer models reduce the need for animal testing, adhering to ethical research principles.
- **Efficiency:** Rapid-growing strains like *M. smegmatis* accelerate assay turnaround times.

By leveraging these safe strains, researchers in resource-constrained labs can effectively contribute to anti-tubercular drug discovery while maintaining high standards of safety and cost efficiency.

In the context of our chapter on "*In Vitro* Anti-Tubercle Activity Assays", the inclusion of the well diffusion method using *Mycobacterium smegmatis* is both practical and strategic.

The well diffusion method using *Mycobacterium smegmatis* is chosen for its safety, cost-effectiveness, and reliability in preliminary anti-tubercle drug screening. *M. smegmatis* is a non-pathogenic, fast-growing surrogate strain that can be safely handled in Biosafety Level-1 (BSL-1) laboratories, making it ideal for resource-limited settings. The method is simple, time-efficient, and provides measurable inhibition zones to evaluate antimicrobial activity. Despite being avirulent, *M. smegmatis* shares structural and metabolic similarities with *M. tuberculosis*, justifying its use as a model organism. This protocol enables efficient identification of promising compounds for further testing under higher biosafety conditions.

In Vitro Anti-Tubercle Activity Protocol

The *in vitro* evaluation of anti-tubercle activity is essential for preliminary screening of potential drug candidates. Resource-limited laboratories often face challenges in handling pathogenic *Mycobacterium tuberculosis* due to biosafety constraints. To overcome this, *Mycobacterium smegmatis*, a non-pathogenic, fast-growing mycobacterial strain, serves as a cost-effective and safe alternative for preliminary drug screening in BSL-1 laboratories. This protocol describes a simple **well diffusion method** to test the antimicrobial activity of drugs against *M. smegmatis*.

Principle

The well diffusion method evaluates the antimicrobial activity of a test compound by measuring the zone of inhibition around wells containing the compound in an agar medium inoculated with *M. smegmatis*. If the test compound possesses anti-tubercle properties, it will inhibit bacterial growth around the well, resulting in a clear zone that can be measured to determine the compound's efficacy.

Requirements

- Non-pathogenic *Mycobacterium smegmatis* culture (mid-log phase).
- Nutrient agar or Mueller-Hinton Agar (MHA) media.
- Test compounds/plant extracts/drugs (stock solutions).
- Sterile Petri plates.

- Cork borer or sterile micropipette tips.
- Sterile distilled water or DMSO (diluent for test compounds).
- Positive control (e.g., Rifampicin at 10 μg/mL).
- Negative control (solvent such as DMSO or water).
- Micropipettes.
- Incubator set at 37°C.
- Callipers or a ruler (for measuring inhibition zones).

Methodology

1. **Preparation of *M. smegmatis* Inoculum**
    - Prepare a fresh culture of *M. smegmatis* in nutrient broth or tryptic soy broth.
    - Incubate at 37°C with shaking for 24 hours until mid-log phase is reached (OD600 $\approx$ 0.6–0.8).
2. **Preparation of Media**
    - Prepare nutrient agar or Mueller-Hinton Agar (MHA) following the manufacturer's instructions or standard protocol of media preparation.
    - Pour the sterilized media into sterile Petri plates and allow it to solidify.
3. **Inoculation of Agar Plates**
    - Using a sterile cotton swab, evenly spread the *M. smegmatis* inoculum onto the surface of solidified agar plates to create a bacterial lawn.
    - Allow the plates to dry for 5–10 minutes under aseptic conditions.
4. **Well Creation**
    - Use a sterile cork borer or pipette tip to punch wells (6 mm in diameter) into the agar surface. Maintain equal spacing between wells.
    - Remove the agar plugs carefully to form wells.
5. **Loading of Test Compounds**
    - Add 50–100 μL of the test compound solution (at desired concentrations) into the wells.
    - Load the following controls into separate wells:
        - Positive control (e.g., Rifampicin).
        - Negative control (solvent only, e.g., DMSO).
    - Ensure that solutions do not spill outside the wells.

6. **Incubation**

    - Incubate the plates upside down at 37°C for 24–48 hours.

7. **Observation and Measurement**

    - After incubation, observe for zones of inhibition (clear zones around the wells).
    - Measure the diameter of the inhibition zones (in mm) using a ruler or callipers.

Interpretation

- A clear zone of inhibition around the well indicates the antimicrobial activity of the test compound against *M. smegmatis*.
- **Positive Control:** Rifampicin will exhibit a distinct zone of inhibition, serving as a benchmark.
- **Negative Control:** No inhibition zone should appear around the solvent-only well.
- **Test Compounds:** Larger inhibition zones suggest stronger anti-tubercle or anti-mycobacterial activity. In case of no zone of inhibition is the indication that the compound lacks anti-mycobacterial activity.

Chapter 9

In Vitro Models for Antidiabetic Activity

9.1 Overview of *In Vitro* Antidiabetic Activity

Diabetes mellitus is one of the most common metabolic disorders and noninfectious diseases in the world. In diabetic individuals, long-standing hyperglycemia leads to nephropathy, neuropathy, and cardiovascular diseases. World Health Organization reports state that more than 246 million people are affected by noninsulin-dependent diabetes mellitus and this could go up to 438 million by 2030.

Effective management of diabetes involves regulating blood sugar levels through medication, lifestyle changes, and monitoring. Given its prevalence and impact, there is an increasing demand for new, cost-effective, and safe therapeutic agents to manage the condition.

In vitro antidiabetic activity studies, from a cost-effective, ethical, and resource-limited laboratory perspective, focus on accessible, efficient methodologies. Using cell lines, such as yeast models (e.g., *Saccharomyces cerevisiae*), provides a low-cost and ethical alternative for screening potential antidiabetic compounds. Yeast models are ideal for glucose uptake and insulin-like activity assays, as they are easy to culture, require basic laboratory facilities, and offer a high-throughput screening platform. Additionally, yeast cells can be genetically engineered to mimic insulin response, further enhancing their utility in diabetes research. Ethical considerations are addressed by minimizing animal use, relying on *in vitro* models like yeast cells that do not involve live animals.

Cost-effective approaches include enzyme inhibition assays, such as α-glucosidase and α-amylase assays, which require minimal reagents and can be performed using basic equipment. These simplified methods enable researchers to screen compounds for antidiabetic properties while keeping expenses low. Laboratories with limited facilities can utilize these techniques to gather meaningful data on potential antidiabetic agents. Overall, yeast models and basic assays provide an affordable, ethical, and practical approach for *in vitro* antidiabetic research, particularly in resource-constrained environments.

Yeast Glucose Uptake Inhibition Assay

The Yeast Glucose Uptake Inhibition Assay evaluates the antidiabetic potential of compounds by measuring their ability to enhance glucose uptake in yeast cells. Increased glucose uptake can simulate the glucose-lowering effects of insulin, suggesting that a compound might help regulate blood sugar levels. Yeast cells are used because they take up glucose via transporters similar to those in human cells.

Principle

Yeast cells uptake glucose from the medium, reducing glucose concentration. Test compounds are added to yeast cell suspensions to assess whether they enhance glucose uptake, which would result in a lower residual glucose concentration in the medium. By quantifying the remaining glucose, the glucose uptake by yeast in the presence of a test compound can be assessed, indirectly indicating the compound's potential antidiabetic effect. A glucose oxidase-peroxidase **(GOD-POD)** method is commonly used to quantify glucose remaining in the medium by measuring absorbance at 520 nm. However, the **3,5-dinitrosalicylic acid (DNSA) method** can also be used to measure the residual glucose concentration in the medium after yeast cells have had the opportunity to uptake glucose. The DNSA in an alkaline medium under heat, forming a reddish-brown complex. The colour intensity of this complex is proportional to the glucose concentration, which can be measured at 540 nm.

Requirements

- **Yeast Model:** Any *Saccharomyces cerevisiae* strain (MTCC, ATCC or NCIM) or Commercial baker's Yeast may also be used.
- **Glucose Solution:** 1gm/ml or 25 mM solution of glucose stock can be used whose dilutions can be made when required as per the experiment design.
- **Test Samples:** Phytoextract, any drug, compound etc., at 100 mg/ml stock concentration whose dilutions can be made when required as per the experiment design.
- **Standard Drug:** Methazolamide (MTZ) or Metformin (MTF)
- **Centrifuge Machine:** 3000 to 5000 rpm speed is sufficient.
- **Incubator or Water bath:** to maintain temperature of reaction environment at 37°C
- **DNS Reagent:** for glucose estimation in sample (check composition & method to prepare it)

Or

- **Glucose Oxidase-Peroxidase (GOD-POD) kit** for glucose quantification
- **Spectrophotometer:** for taking absorbance in visible range at 540 nm
- **Other Necessary Tools/Equipment:** test tubes, weighing balance, micropipettes, distilled water, marker pen, experiment notebook etc.

Methodology

1. Prepare a 1% suspension of commercial baker's yeast (*S. cerevisiae*) cells in sterile distilled water and incubate overnight at 25°C.
2. Prepare various concentrations of both test sample (phytoextract, drug or compound) and standard drug (MTZ or MTF) from 1 mg/ml to 5 mg/ml

3. Centrifuge this suspension yeast cell suspension 4,000 rpm for 5 minutes) repeatedly until the clear supernatant fluid was obtained.
4. With this clear supernatant again prepare a 10% v/v yeast cell suspension which is the actual need of the experiment.
5. With the clear supernatant, about 10% v/v yeast cell suspension was made ready for the experiment.
6. Prepare various concentrations of both test sample (phytoextract, drug or compound) and standard drug (MTZ or MTF) from 1 mg/ml to 5 mg/ml ***(we can also use any single dilution or concentration of samples).***
7. A control sample is also prepared where ***sterile distilled water*** is used ***in place of*** standard drug or test sample extract**.**
8. Now, to each dilution of samples & standard, add 1 m of 10 mM glucose solution (or any fixed chosen concentration) and allow it to incubate at 37°C for 10 minutes.
9. To start the reaction, add 100 μl of yeast suspension to each reaction, vortex and further incubate the set at 37°C for 60 min.
10. After incubation, centrifuge all the tubes at 3000 rpm and the amount of glucose in the supernatant would be estimated by GOD-POD method or by DNSA method spectrophotometry.

Glucose Estimation by DNSA Method

- After incubating yeast with glucose and test compounds, centrifuge to collect the supernatant.
- This supernatant is subjected to evaluate glucose concentration by DNSA method in both experimental and control sets.
- Pipette 5 mL of each glucose standard and 5 mL of the yeast-incubated supernatant (samples) into separate test tubes.
- Add 500 μL of DNSA reagent to each test tube containing either glucose standards or supernatant samples.
- Place the tubes in a boiling water bath for 10 minutes to allow the colour development.
- The reaction mixture was cooled to room temperature and 1 ml of aliquot was diluted with 2 ml of distilled water whose absorbance was measured at 540 nm using spectrophotometer.

$$\%\,\text{Inhibition in Glucose Uptake} = \frac{\text{Abs}_{\text{Control}} - \text{Abs}_{\text{Sample}}}{\text{Abs}_{\text{Control}}} \times 100$$

Calculations Calculate the percentage increase in glucose uptake by comparing the glucose concentration in the control and test sample using the following formula:

Where:

- **Glucose concentration in Control** is the residual glucose concentration in the absence of test compound.

- **Glucose concentration in Sample** is the residual glucose concentration in the presence of the test compound.

Possible Outcomes

1. If glucose uptake increases = drug/extract/compound is anti-hyperglycaemic
2. If glucose uptake inhibited = drug/extract/compound is **NOT** anti-hyperglycaemic

Experiment Inference Reasoning

Glucose uptake in yeast cells (*S.cerevisiae*) is rapid and occurs down the concentration gradient. Glucose uptake reaches equilibrium and is not accumulative. Phosphorylation accompanies with glucose entry into the cell.

Inference 1: If a sample or drug is capable of increasing glucose uptake effectively, which in turn suggests that it is capable of improving effective glucose utilization at the concentrations used, thereby controlling blood glucose level as also suggested by other reports.

Inference 2: If a sample or drug fails to increase glucose uptake or inhibits the glucose uptake suggests that it is incapable of improving effective glucose utilization from the surrounding and won't be able to be utilized as anti-hyperglycaemic drug. Glucose transporters are stereospecific for certain hexoses and carries glucose, fructose and mannose. This behaviour of decrease in uptake by yeast cell may be attributed to anti-microbial activity of extract at higher concentrations which either kills yeast cell or inhibited its growth and metabolism.

Interpretation

Higher percentages of glucose uptake increase indicate greater antidiabetic potential of the test compound. This assay is a cost-effective, preliminary method to assess the glucose-lowering effects of compounds, indicating potential antidiabetic activity.

α-Amylase Inhibition Assay Protocol

The α-amylase inhibition assay assesses the antidiabetic potential of compounds by measuring their ability to inhibit α-amylase, an enzyme responsible for breaking down complex carbohydrates into glucose. Inhibiting α-amylase slows carbohydrate digestion and reduces postprandial blood glucose levels, indicating potential antidiabetic properties of the compound being tested.

Principle

α-Amylase catalyzes the hydrolysis of starch into maltose and glucose. When a compound inhibits α-amylase activity, less glucose is produced. This inhibition can be quantified by measuring the colour change using a starch-iodine complex (blue colour) or by detecting the reduced release of glucose using specific colorimetric reagents (eg: DNSA or Anthron method). A reduction in the intensity of the colour is indicative of enzyme inhibition.

Requirements

- **α-Amylase enzyme**: Commercially available α-amylase (typically, porcine pancreatic α-amylase at 0.5 mg/mL concentration is commonly used)
- **Starch solution**: 1% (w/v) starch solution in phosphate buffer
- **Test compounds**: Potential antidiabetic compounds or plant extracts
- **Positive control**: Acarbose or another known α-amylase inhibitor
- **Iodine solution**: Used for colour development (0.01 M iodine in 0.05 M potassium iodide)
- **Phosphate buffer**: 0.02 M, pH 6.9 with 6.7 mM NaCl
- **UV-Visible spectrophotometer**: Set to measure absorbance at 540 or 620 nm
- **Water bath or incubator**: Set to 37°C

Methodology

1. **Preparation of Reaction Mixture**:
   - Prepare a 1% starch solution by dissolving starch in phosphate buffer (0.02 M, pH 6.9 with 6.7 mM NaCl).
   - Prepare α-amylase enzyme solution by diluting it in the same phosphate buffer to the required concentration.
2. **Inhibition Reaction**:
   - In a test tube, add 500 μL of the test compound (or control) to 500 μL of the α-amylase enzyme solution.
   - Pre-incubate the mixture at 37°C for 10 minutes to allow the test compound to interact with the enzyme.
3. **Initiation of Reaction**:
   - Add 500 μL of the starch solution to the reaction mixture, and incubate at 37°C for another 10 minutes.
4. **Stopping the Reaction**:
   - After incubation, add 1 mL of the iodine solution to each reaction tube. The iodine reacts with any unhydrolyzed starch, forming a blue-black complex.
5. **Absorbance Measurement**:
   - Measure the absorbance at 540 or 620 nm, depending on the iodine-starch complex.
   - If the colour of the complex formed is too dark, it could be suitably diluted with distilled water and this dilution factor could be adjusted in later calculations.

6. **Control and Blank Preparation**:
   - Prepare a control sample without the test compound (enzyme and starch only).
   - Prepare a blank with the test compound but no enzyme, to account for any intrinsic colour.

Calculations

Calculate the percentage inhibition of α-amylase using the formula:

$$\text{Inhibition (\%)} = \frac{\text{Abs Control} - \text{Abs Sample}}{\text{Abs control}} \times 100$$

Where:

- **Absorbance of Control** is the absorbance without any inhibitor.
- **Absorbance of Sample** is the absorbance with the test compound.

Interpretation

Higher percentages of inhibition indicate greater antidiabetic potential by reducing the rate of starch breakdown. This suggests that the test compound might help control postprandial glucose levels.

α-Glucosidase Inhibition Assay Protocol

The **α-glucosidase inhibition assay** is a widely used method to evaluate the antidiabetic potential of compounds by measuring their ability to inhibit α-glucosidase. α-Glucosidase is an enzyme that hydrolyzes carbohydrates into glucose in the small intestine. Inhibiting this enzyme slows down glucose absorption, which helps manage postprandial blood sugar levels.

Principle

α-Glucosidase catalyzes the breakdown of complex carbohydrates into glucose. When a compound inhibits α-glucosidase activity, it decreases glucose production. The inhibition of α-glucosidase by a test compound can be monitored by measuring the reduced formation of glucose, which can be quantified through a colorimetric reaction using p-nitrophenyl-α-D-glucopyranoside (pNPG) as a substrate. In the presence of α-glucosidase, pNPG is hydrolyzed to release p-nitrophenol, a yellow compound that absorbs at 405 nm. The intensity of the colour is directly proportional to enzyme activity.

Requirements

- **α-Glucosidase enzyme solution**: Typically prepared at 1 U/mL. (commercially available, usually from yeast)
- **pNPG (p-nitrophenyl-α-D-glucopyranoside)**: as a substrate 5 mM solution in phosphate buffer.
- **Test compounds**: The plant extract or isolated compounds under investigation.

- **Positive control**: Acarbose (a known α-glucosidase inhibitor).
- **Phosphate buffer**: 50 mM, pH 6.8.
- **Stop solution**: 0.1 M sodium carbonate.
- **Microplate reader or UV-Visible spectrophotometer:** Set to measure absorbance at 405 nm.
- **96-well plate:** if using a microplate reader
- **Water bath**: For incubation at 37°C.

Note: Use microplate reader/ELISA reader in place of spectrophotometer if it is possible to avail it in laboratory as it uses lesser volume of reaction mixture that saves experimental cost.

Methodology

1. **Preparation of Reaction Mixture**:
    - In a test tube, mix 50 μL of the test compound (dissolved in phosphate buffer) with 50 μL of the α-glucosidase enzyme solution.
    - For the control, use 50 μL of buffer instead of the test compound.
    - Pre-incubate the mixture at 37°C for 10 minutes.
2. **Substrate Addition:**
    - Add 50 μL of pNPG solution (5 mM) to each tube to initiate the reaction.
    - Incubate the tubes at 37°C for an additional 15 minutes.
3. **Stopping the Reaction**:
    - After incubation, add 100 μL of sodium carbonate (0.1 M) to each tube to stop the reaction.
    - This step stabilizes the colour and allows absorbance measurement.
4. **Absorbance Measurement**:
    - Measure the absorbance of each sample at 405 nm using a spectrophotometer or a microplate reader.

Calculations

Calculate the percentage inhibition of α-glucosidase activity using the formula:

$$\text{Inhibition (\%)} = \frac{\text{Abs Control} - \text{Abs Sample}}{\text{Abs control}} \times 100$$

Where:

- **Control Absorbance** is the absorbance of the reaction without the test compound.
- **Sample Absorbance** is the absorbance of the reaction with the test compound.

IC_{50} Calculation: The IC_{50} value (concentration at which 50% inhibition occurs) can be determined by plotting the inhibition percentages against the log concentrations of the test samples and performing a nonlinear regression analysis (e.g., using software like GraphPad Prism or Microsoft Excel).

Interpretation

A higher percentage of α-glucosidase inhibition suggests stronger antidiabetic potential of the test compound, as it implies that the compound may reduce glucose absorption by inhibiting α-glucosidase activity. This assay is commonly used for initial screening of natural products or pharmaceutical agents for antidiabetic activity.

Chapter 10

In Vitro Hepatoprotective Assays

10.1 Overview of Hepatoprotective Activity

The liver is a vital organ that performs numerous functions such as detoxification, protein synthesis, and the production of biochemicals necessary for digestion. Hepatic diseases, including hepatitis, cirrhosis, fatty liver disease, and drug-induced liver injury (DILI), are among the most common health problems worldwide. These conditions can lead to liver failure, which is a significant cause of morbidity and mortality globally.

10.1.1 Hepatic Problems and Global Prevalence

Liver diseases affect millions of people worldwide. Hepatitis, particularly Hepatitis B and C, is a major global health problem, with an estimated 300 million people living with chronic viral hepatitis. Non-alcoholic fatty liver disease (NAFLD) is another rising concern, primarily linked to obesity and metabolic syndrome, affecting over 25% of the global population. Furthermore, alcohol consumption and excessive use of certain pharmaceuticals are primary contributors to liver damage, leading to conditions like alcoholic liver disease (ALD) and drug-induced liver injury (DILI), which remains a leading cause of acute liver failure.

As the liver plays a critical role in detoxifying harmful substances from the body, its dysfunction can lead to a wide range of systemic problems. Therefore, the search for effective hepatoprotective agents has become a major area of research in both pharmaceuticals and alternative medicine.

10.1.2 Development of New Drugs

The treatment of hepatic diseases has traditionally been challenging, with many therapies either insufficient in efficacy or associated with severe side effects. For example, antiviral treatments for Hepatitis C have greatly improved, but cost and accessibility remain issues in low- and middle-income countries. Similarly, while drugs for alcohol-induced liver disease exist, there is still no universally effective drug for managing NAFLD and cirrhosis.

In recent years, the search for hepatoprotective drugs has shifted towards natural products and phytochemicals, many of which exhibit antioxidant, anti-inflammatory, and anti-fibrotic properties. Phytochemicals derived from plants like *Silybum marianum* (milk thistle), *Andrographis paniculata* (andrographis), and *Curcuma longa* (turmeric) have shown promising hepatoprotective effects in both *in vitro* and *in vivo* studies. Furthermore, synthetic drugs targeting specific molecular pathways involved in liver inflammation and fibrosis, such as peroxisome proliferator-activated receptor (PPAR) agonists, are under investigation for their potential to manage chronic liver diseases.

10.2 Cost-effective Experimental Methods Without Ethical Issues

Developing new hepatoprotective drugs requires extensive research and testing, which often involves expensive animal models and clinical trials that raise ethical concerns. However, advancements in alternative testing methods have allowed researchers to assess hepatoprotective activity more effectively while minimizing the ethical implications of animal use.

Cost-effective *in vitro* assays, such as those utilizing liver cell lines like HepG2 or primary hepatocytes, provide a viable alternative to animal testing. These cell culture models enable researchers to screen for hepatoprotective activity, assess cytotoxicity, and study mechanisms of liver injury and regeneration. Additionally, high-throughput screening platforms allow for the rapid testing of multiple compounds, reducing both time and financial costs.

Biochemical assays, such as measuring the levels of liver enzymes (e.g., ALT, AST) in cell cultures or serum, provide an easy and efficient method to evaluate the hepatoprotective effects of different compounds. Moreover, novel approaches like 3D liver models and organ-on-chip technology are emerging as promising alternatives to traditional models, offering more physiologically relevant data while still being cost-effective.

Overall, the hepatoprotective activity of various compounds, especially plant-derived products, holds great promise in addressing the global challenge of liver diseases. With the development of cost-effective and ethically sound experimental methods, future research can continue to uncover novel hepatoprotective agents that will help combat hepatic diseases without compromising on ethical standards or financial feasibility.

10.2.1 Yeast-Based Models and Enzyme Assays for Hepatoprotective Studies

Saccharomyces cerevisiae Model

Saccharomyces cerevisiae, commonly known as baker's yeast, has emerged as an alternative model for liver protection studies due to its genetic similarity to mammalian cells, simplicity, cost-effectiveness, genetic tractability, and ease of manipulation. This yeast model is particularly useful for screening hepatoprotective compounds in early-phase drug discovery. This yeast model provides a robust platform for studying cellular responses to oxidative stress and toxic insults, which mimic liver damage pathways in higher organisms. The simple growth conditions of *S. cerevisiae* and its ability to metabolize toxic substances make it a valuable tool for assessing the protective effects of natural and synthetic compounds against liver damage. The yeast can be genetically engineered to express human liver enzymes or proteins involved in liver metabolism, allow the study of hepatoprotective mechanisms, including antioxidant activity, enzyme regulation, and cell viability. This model eliminates the ethical concerns associated with animal studies and serves as an initial screening tool for liver-protective compounds.

Enzyme Inhibition Assays for Liver Protection Assessment

Enzyme inhibition assays are essential for evaluating hepatoprotective potential by studying the modulation of key liver enzymes involved in oxidative stress and detoxification pathways. Enzyme inhibition assays, such as those measuring the activity of liver-specific enzymes (e.g., ALT, AST, and CYP_{450} enzymes), are frequently used to assess liver protection in these models. Hepatoprotective compounds are tested for their ability to inhibit the activity of enzymes that are involved in the liver's detoxification pathways. Additionally, antioxidant assays, including DPPH, FRAP, and ABTS, are commonly employed to measure the ability of compounds to neutralize reactive oxygen species (ROS), which contribute to liver cell damage. Together, these assays help identify potential liver-protective agents in a cost-effective and ethical manner. The following assays are commonly used:

1. **Alanine Aminotransferase (ALT) Inhibition Assay:** Measures the ability of compounds to reduce ALT activity, a marker of liver cell damage and leakage into the bloodstream.
2. **Aspartate Aminotransferase (AST) Inhibition Assay:** Evaluates AST activity modulation, which reflects liver function and protection against cellular damage.
3. **Glutathione S-Transferase (GST) Inhibition Assay:** Assesses the role of compounds in enhancing detoxification by supporting glutathione conjugation pathways.
4. **Superoxide Dismutase (SOD) Inhibition Assay:** Tests antioxidant capacity by measuring the inhibition of oxidative stress induced by superoxide radicals.
5. **Catalase (CAT) Inhibition Assay:** Determines the compound's ability to modulate hydrogen peroxide detoxification, preventing oxidative damage.
6. **Lactate Dehydrogenase (LDH) Release Assay:** Quantifies cell membrane integrity by measuring LDH release, indicating protection against cytotoxicity.

Together, these assays provide a comprehensive understanding of liver protection mechanisms and facilitate the discovery of effective hepatoprotective agents.

Each assay requires basic reagents and can be conducted with standard lab tools and is compatible with spectrophotometry, offering valuable insights into hepatoprotective properties with minimal investment. The standard protocols of these 7 types of *in vitro* hepatoprotective assays we are discussing in this chapter.

In Vitro Hepatoprotective Activity Protocol on Yeast Model

Principle

The *Saccharomyces cerevisiae* model is used to assess hepatoprotective activity by evaluating the yeast's ability to survive under oxidative stress or toxic insults in the presence of test compounds. Yeast cells mimic liver cellular pathways, including detoxification and oxidative stress responses, enabling the assessment of protective effects of compounds. Oxidative stress is induced using agents like hydrogen peroxide (H_2O_2) or ethanol, and cell viability is used as a marker for hepatoprotection. Here a rapid and cost-effective approach to screening hepatoprotective agents using *S. cerevisiae* as a model system is presented.

Materials and Equipment

Materials:

- ***Saccharomyces cerevisiae*** strain (wild type or genetically modified)
- Yeast extract peptone dextrose (YPD) medium
- H_2O_2 or ethanol (oxidative stress inducers)
- Test compounds (e.g., phytochemicals or synthetic drugs)
- 96-well microplate
- Phosphate-buffered saline (PBS)
- 2,3,5-Triphenyl Tetrazolium Chloride (TTC) or MTT for viability assay
- Dimethyl sulfoxide (DMSO)

Equipment:

- Autoclave
- Incubator shaker (30°C)
- Microcentrifuge
- Microplate reader (for absorbance measurements)

Methodology

1. **Preparation of Yeast Culture**
   - Inoculate ***S. cerevisiae*** in YPD medium.
   - Incubate at 30°C with shaking (200 rpm) until the culture reaches an OD_{600} of 0.8–1.0 (logarithmic phase).
2. **Induction of Oxidative Stress**
   - Harvest yeast cells by centrifugation at 3000 rpm for 5 minutes.
   - Wash cells with PBS and resuspend them in PBS.
   - Induce oxidative stress by adding H_2O_2 (1–2 mM final concentration) or ethanol (5–10%) to the suspension in a 96-well plate and incubate for 1 hour.
3. **Treatment Groups and Test Compounds** Divide the wells into the following groups:**Negative Control (NC):** Yeast cells under oxidative stress without any treatment.
   - **Positive Control (PC):** Yeast cells under oxidative stress treated with a known hepatoprotective compound (e.g., silymarin).

- **Test Groups (TG):** Yeast cells under oxidative stress treated with test compounds at different concentrations (e.g., 10, 50, and 100 μg/mL).
- **Blank (BL):** Yeast cells without stress or treatment.

Add 100 μL of the appropriate solution (PBS, test compound, or positive control) to each well.

4. **Incubation**
   - Incubate the microplate at 30°C for 24 hours in a shaker incubator.
5. **Cell Viability Assay**
   - Add 20 μL of TTC or MTT solution (0.5 mg/mL) to each well.
   - Incubate for 2 hours at 30°C to allow the formation of formazan crystals.
   - Dissolve the crystals using 100 μL of DMSO per well.
   - Measure the absorbance at 490 nm (TTC) or 570 nm (MTT) using a microplate reader.

Data Analysis

Percentage Cell Viability

$$\%\,\text{Viability} = \frac{\text{Abs of Treated Cells}}{\text{Abs of Untreated Cells}} \times 100$$

Percentage Protection

$$\%\,\text{Protection} = \frac{\text{Abs Treated Cell} - \text{Abs Negative Control}}{\text{Abs of Positive control} - \text{Abs Negative Control}} \times 100$$

Interpretation of Results

- Increased cell viability and reduced ROS levels in the test compound + toxicant group compared to the toxicant control indicate hepatoprotective activity.
- Enhanced activity of antioxidant enzymes (SOD, catalase) supports the mechanism of action.

Alanine Aminotransferase (ALT) Inhibition Assay Protocol

The ALT inhibition assay evaluates the hepatoprotective potential of compounds by measuring their ability to inhibit the activity of ALT, an enzyme associated with liver function. Elevated ALT levels indicate liver damage, and inhibition of ALT activity suggests protective effects against liver injury.

Principle

Alanine Aminotransferase (ALT) catalyzes the conversion of alanine and α-ketoglutarate to pyruvate and glutamate. The inhibition of ALT activity reduces pyruvate formation, which can be measured by its reaction with 2,4-dinitrophenylhydrazine (DNPH) to produce a chromophore absorbable at 520 nm. A reduction in absorbance reflects the compound's hepatoprotective potential.

Requirements

Materials

- **ALT enzyme**: Commercially available ALT or extracted from liver tissue.
- **Alanine**: Substrate for the enzyme reaction.
- **α-Ketoglutarate**: Cofactor for the ALT reaction.
- **Test compounds**: Potential hepatoprotective compounds or plant extracts.
- **Positive control**: Known ALT inhibitor (e.g., silymarin).
- **2,4-Dinitrophenylhydrazine (DNPH)**: For pyruvate detection.
- **Sodium hydroxide (NaOH)**: For colour development.
- **Phosphate buffer**: 100 mM, pH 7.4.
- **Distilled water**: For reagent preparation.

Equipment

- UV-Visible spectrophotometer (set at 520 nm).
- Microplate reader (optional).
- Water bath or incubator set at 37°C.
- Pipettes and tips.

Methodology

1. **Preparation of Reaction Mixture**
    1. Prepare a 100 mM phosphate buffer (pH 7.4).
    2. Dissolve ALT enzyme in the buffer to the required concentration.
    3. Prepare alanine (100 mM) and α-ketoglutarate (5 mM) solutions in the same buffer.
2. **Inhibition Reaction**
    1. In a reaction tube or microplate well, add:
        - 100 μL ALT enzyme solution.
        - 100 μL of the test compound at various concentrations (e.g., 10–100 μg/mL).
    2. Pre-incubate the mixture at 37°C for 10 minutes to allow interaction between the enzyme and the test compound.

3. **Initiation of Reaction**

    1. Add 100 μL alanine and 100 μL α-ketoglutarate to the reaction mixture to start the reaction.
    2. Incubate at 37°C for 20 minutes.

4. **Stopping the Reaction**

    1. Stop the reaction by adding 100 μL DNPH reagent to each tube.
    2. Allow the mixture to sit at room temperature for 10 minutes for colour development.

5. **Colour Development**

    1. Add 1 mL of 0.4 N NaOH to each reaction tube to stabilize the chromophore.

6. **Absorbance Measurement**

    1. Measure the absorbance at 520 nm using a spectrophotometer.

7. **Control and Blank Preparation**

    - **Control**: Reaction mixture without the test compound (enzyme and substrate only).
    - **Blank**: Reaction mixture with the test compound but no enzyme, to account for background absorbance.

Calculations

Calculate the percentage inhibition of ALT activity using the formula:

$$\text{Inhibition}\,\% = \frac{\text{Abs Control} - \text{Abs Sample}}{\text{Abs control}} \times 100$$

Interpretation

- **Higher percentage inhibition**: Indicates greater hepatoprotective potential by reducing ALT activity.
- **Positive control comparison**: Test compounds with inhibition close to or better than the positive control are promising hepatoprotective agents.

Aspartate Aminotransferase (AST) Inhibition Assay Protocol

The AST inhibition assay evaluates the hepatoprotective potential of compounds by assessing their ability to inhibit AST activity. Aspartate Aminotransferase (AST) is an enzyme involved in amino acid metabolism, and its elevated levels indicate liver damage. Inhibiting AST activity reflects the hepatoprotective action of the tested compound.

Principle

AST catalyzes the transamination of aspartate and α-ketoglutarate to form oxaloacetate and glutamate. Oxaloacetate reacts with 2,4-dinitrophenylhydrazine (DNPH) to form a hydrazone complex that can be detected spectrophotometrically at 520 nm. A decrease in absorbance in the presence of a compound indicates inhibition of AST activity, reflecting hepatoprotective potential.

Requirements

Materials

- **AST enzyme**: Commercially available or extracted from liver tissue.
- **Aspartate**: Substrate for the enzyme reaction.
- **α-Ketoglutarate**: Cofactor for the reaction.
- **Test compounds**: Potential hepatoprotective agents or plant extracts.
- **Positive control**: Known AST inhibitor (e.g., silymarin).
- **2,4-Dinitrophenylhydrazine (DNPH)**: For detection of oxaloacetate.
- **Sodium hydroxide (NaOH)**: For colour development.
- **Phosphate buffer**: 100 mM, pH 7.4.
- **Distilled water**: For reagent preparation.

Equipment

- UV-Visible spectrophotometer set at 520 nm.
- Microplate reader (optional).
- Water bath or incubator at 37°C.
- Pipettes and tips.

Methodology

1. **Preparation of Reaction Mixture**
    1. Prepare a 100 mM phosphate buffer (pH 7.4).
    2. Dissolve AST enzyme in the buffer to the required concentration.
    3. Prepare aspartate (100 mM) and α-ketoglutarate (5 mM) solutions in the buffer.
2. **Inhibition Reaction**
    1. In a reaction tube or microplate well, add:
        - 100 μL AST enzyme solution.

- 100 µL of the test compound at various concentrations (e.g., 10–100 µg/mL).

2. Pre-incubate the mixture at 37°C for 10 minutes to allow interaction between the enzyme and the test compound.

3. Initiation of Reaction

1. Add 100 µL aspartate and 100 µL α-ketoglutarate to the reaction mixture to start the reaction.
2. Incubate at 37°C for 20 minutes.

4. Stopping the Reaction

1. Add 100 µL DNPH reagent to each tube to stop the reaction.
2. Let the mixture stand at room temperature for 10 minutes to allow hydrazone complex formation.

5. Colour Development

1. Add 1 mL of 0.4 N NaOH to each tube to stabilize the colour.

6. Absorbance Measurement

1. Measure the absorbance at 520 nm using a spectrophotometer.

7. Control and Blank Preparation

- **Control**: Reaction mixture without the test compound (enzyme and substrate only).
- **Blank**: Reaction mixture with the test compound but no enzyme, to account for background absorbance.

Calculations

Calculate the percentage inhibition of AST activity using the formula:

$$\text{Inhibition}\ (\%) = \frac{\text{Abs Control} - \text{Abs Sample}}{\text{Abs control}} \times 100$$

Interpretation

- **Higher percentage inhibition**: Indicates stronger hepatoprotective activity of the test compound.
- **Positive control comparison**: Results close to or better than the positive control indicates significant hepatoprotective potential.

Glutathione S-Transferase (GST) Inhibition Assay Protocol

The **Glutathione S-Transferase (GST) inhibition assay** evaluates hepatoprotective potential by measuring a compound's ability to inhibit GST activity. GST is an enzyme that detoxifies xenobiotics by conjugating them with glutathione (GSH). Elevated or unregulated GST activity can indicate liver stress. Inhibiting GST under controlled conditions may reflect hepatoprotective effects of the compound.

Principle

GST catalyzes the conjugation of glutathione (GSH) with electrophilic compounds such as **1-chloro-2,4-dinitrobenzene (CDNB)** to form a GSH-CDNB conjugate. This reaction results in an increase in absorbance at 340 nm, which is directly proportional to enzyme activity. The presence of an inhibitor reduces this absorbance, indicating the inhibitory potential of the compound.

Requirements

Materials

- **GST enzyme**: Commercially available (e.g., from rat liver or recombinant GST).
- **Glutathione (GSH)**: Substrate for GST.
- **1-Chloro-2,4-dinitrobenzene (CDNB)**: Model electrophilic substrate.
- **Test compounds**: Plant extracts or synthetic compounds with potential hepatoprotective activity.
- **Positive control**: Known GST inhibitor (e.g., ethacrynic acid).
- **Phosphate buffer**: 100 mM, pH 6.5.
- **Dimethyl sulfoxide (DMSO)**: For dissolving hydrophobic compounds.
- **Distilled water**: For reagent preparation.

Equipment

- Microplate reader or spectrophotometer set at 340 nm.
- Pipettes and tips.
- Incubator or water bath (set at 37°C).

Methodology

1. **Preparation of Reagents**
    1. Prepare a 100 mM phosphate buffer (pH 6.5).
    2. Dissolve GST enzyme in the buffer to the required concentration.
    3. Prepare GSH (10 mM) and CDNB (10 mM) solutions in phosphate buffer.
2. **Preparation of Reaction Mixture**

    In a 96-well plate or test tube, prepare the reaction mixture as follows:

    - 50 μL GST enzyme solution.
    - 50 μL of test compound at varying concentrations (e.g., 10–100 μg/mL).
    - 50 μL GSH solution (10 mM).

3. **Pre-Incubation**
    1. Pre-incubate the reaction mixture at 37°C for 10 minutes to allow the test compound to interact with the enzyme.
4. **Initiation of Reaction**
    1. Add 50 μL CDNB solution to the reaction mixture to start the enzymatic reaction.
    2. Incubate at 37°C for 5 minutes.
5. **Absorbance Measurement**
    1. Measure the absorbance at 340 nm at 1-minute intervals for 5 minutes using a spectrophotometer or microplate reader.
6. **Control and Blank Preparation**
    - **Control**: Reaction mixture without the test compound (enzyme, GSH, and CDNB only).
    - **Blank**: Reaction mixture with the test compound but no enzyme, to account for background absorbance.

Calculations

GST Activity (Control)

$$\text{GST Activity (nmol / min)} = \frac{\Delta A_{340}}{\varepsilon \times \text{path length}} \times \text{Reaction volume (in mL)}$$

Where:

- ΔA_{340} = Change in absorbance at 340 nm per minute.
- ε = Extinction coefficient of CDNB-GSH conjugate (9.6 $mM^{-1}cm^{-1}$).
- **Path length** = 1 cm for a cuvette; adjust for microplate wells.

Percentage Inhibition

$$\text{Inhibition \%} = \frac{\text{GST activity Control} - \text{GST activity Sample}}{\text{GST activity Control}} \times 100$$

Interpretation

- **Higher inhibition percentages**: Suggest significant hepatoprotective potential.
- Compare with the **positive control** for benchmarking the efficacy of the test compound.

Superoxide Dismutase (SOD) Inhibition Assay

This assay evaluates the ability of test compounds to inhibit the activity of the superoxide dismutase (SOD) enzyme. SOD plays a critical role in the defence against oxidative stress by converting superoxide radicals into oxygen and hydrogen peroxide. Oxidative stress is a key factor in liver damage, and compounds that can modulate SOD activity may exhibit hepatoprotective properties. This cost-effective method involves monitoring the reduction of nitroblue tetrazolium (NBT) to formazan, which provides a measurable indication of enzyme inhibition.

Principle

Superoxide dismutase catalyzes the dismutation of superoxide radicals (O_2^-) into oxygen and hydrogen peroxide. The inhibition of this enzyme can be assessed by measuring the formation of formazan from the reduction of nitroblue tetrazolium (NBT) by superoxide radicals. A decrease in formazan production, as measured by absorbance at 560 nm, indicates the inhibitory potential of the test compounds on SOD activity.

Requirements

Materials

- SOD enzyme (commercially available).
- Nitroblue tetrazolium (NBT) (1 mM solution).
- Phenazine methosulfate (PMS) (0.12 mM solution).
- Nicotinamide adenine dinucleotide (NADH) (1 mM solution).
- Phosphate buffer (50 mM, pH 7.8).
- Test compounds (dissolved in water or DMSO).
- Positive control: e.g., Ascorbic acid or known antioxidant.
- Distilled water for reagent preparation.

Equipment

- UV-Visible spectrophotometer (set to **560 nm**).
- Pipettes and microplates/test tubes.
- Incubator or water bath (37°C).

Methodology

1. **Preparation of Reaction Mixture**
   - **Phosphate buffer**: Prepare 50 mM phosphate buffer (pH 7.8).
   - Mix the following reagents freshly before use:

        - 200 μL NBT (1 mM solution).
        - 100 μL NADH (1 mM solution).
        - 100 μL PMS (0.12 mM solution).
        - 500 μL phosphate buffer.
    - Final volume for each reaction should be 1 mL.

2. **Reaction Setup**
    - **Control**: Add 50 μL of SOD enzyme (no test compound).
    - **Test sample**: Add 50 μL of test compound solution and 50 μL of SOD enzyme.
    - **Blank**: Replace SOD enzyme with phosphate buffer (background correction).
3. **Initiation of Reaction**
    - Add the above reagents into separate test tubes or microplate wells.
    - Incubate the mixtures at 37°C for 5 minutes.
4. **Stopping the Reaction**
    - Measure absorbance immediately at 560 nm using a spectrophotometer.
5. **Observations**
    - The control will have maximum absorbance due to formazan formation.
    - tndicates inhibition of SOD activity.

Calculations

Percentage Inhibition of SOD Activity

$$\text{Inhibition}\,(\%) = \frac{\text{Abs Control} - \text{Abs Sample}}{\text{Abs control}} \times 100$$

Interpretation

- **Higher inhibition percentages** suggest stronger SOD inhibition, indicating potential hepatoprotective activity through antioxidant mechanisms.
- This assay provides insights into the compound's ability to modulate oxidative stress, a critical factor in liver protection.

Catalase (CAT) Inhibition Assay Protocol

This assay evaluates the hepatoprotective potential of compounds by examining their ability to inhibit the activity of catalase (CAT), an enzyme responsible for detoxifying hydrogen peroxide (H_2O_2) into water and oxygen. Since oxidative stress is a major factor in liver damage, compounds that modulate catalase activity may exhibit hepatoprotective effects. The protocol utilizes a colorimetric approach to measure enzyme activity, providing a cost-effective and straightforward method for analysis.

Principle

Catalase catalyzes the decomposition of hydrogen peroxide into water and oxygen. The assay quantifies catalase activity by measuring the residual H_2O_2 after the reaction, using a chromogenic reagent like potassium permanganate ($KMnO_4$) or ammonium molybdate. A reduction in the rate of H_2O_2 breakdown indicates inhibition of catalase activity by the test compound.

Requirements

Materials

- Catalase enzyme (commercially available).
- Hydrogen peroxide (H_2O_2, 30% stock, diluted to 10 mM).
- Potassium permanganate ($KMnO_4$, 6 mM solution) or ammonium molybdate (1% w/v).
- Phosphate buffer (50 mM, pH 7.0).
- Test compounds (dissolved in water or DMSO).
- Positive control: e.g., Ascorbic acid or other known antioxidants.
- Distilled water for reagent preparation.

Equipment

- UV-Visible spectrophotometer (set to 240 nm or 540 nm, depending on the detection reagent).
- Pipettes and microplates/test tubes.
- Incubator or water bath (37°C).

Methodology

1. **Preparation of Reaction Mixture**
   - **Phosphate buffer**: Prepare 50 mM phosphate buffer (pH 7.0).
   - Mix the following in test tubes or microplate wells:
     - 500 μL H_2O_2 solution (10 mM).

  - 200 μL phosphate buffer.
  - 50 μL catalase enzyme solution.
  - 50 μL test compound or control solution.

2. **Pre-Incubation**
   - Incubate the test tubes containing the catalase enzyme and test compound at 37°C for 10 minutes to allow interaction.
3. **Initiation of Reaction**
   - Add 500 μL of H_2O_2 solution to initiate the reaction.
   - Incubate the reaction mixture at 37°C for 5 minutes.
4. **Stopping the Reaction**
   - For potassium permanganate: Add 500 μL of $KMnO_4$ solution to stop the reaction.
   - For ammonium molybdate: Add 1 mL of ammonium molybdate solution.
5. **Absorbance Measurement**
   - Measure the absorbance at 240 nm for direct H_2O_2 quantification or 540 nm for colorimetric detection using $KMnO_4$ or ammonium molybdate.
6. **Control and Blank Preparation**
   - **Control**: Reaction without the test compound.
   - **Blank**: Reaction mixture without the catalase enzyme.

Calculations

Percentage Inhibition of Catalase Activity

$$\text{Inhibition (\%)} = \frac{\text{Abs Control} - \text{Abs Sample}}{\text{Abs control}} \times 100$$

Interpretation

- **Lower H_2O_2 degradation** and higher inhibition percentages suggest a stronger inhibitory effect on catalase activity by the test compound.
- The hepatoprotective potential can be inferred if the compound demonstrates significant antioxidant properties by modulating catalase activity.

Lactate Dehydrogenase (LDH) Release Assay

This assay evaluates the hepatoprotective potential of compounds by measuring the release of lactate dehydrogenase (LDH) enzyme from damaged liver cells (or cell lines) into the surrounding medium. The amount of LDH released is indicative of cellular damage, as LDH is normally found in the cytoplasm of cells. Compounds that reduce LDH leakage can help in determining hepatoprotective effects against liver injury, which is often caused by oxidative stress or toxins. This assay is commonly used to screen for hepatoprotective compounds due to its simplicity and reliability.

Principle

Lactate dehydrogenase (LDH) catalyzes the conversion of lactate to pyruvate, producing NADH in the process. In the event of liver cell damage, LDH is released into the extracellular environment, which can be quantitatively measured. The assay involves measuring the optical density of the released LDH in the medium after exposure to hepatotoxic agents and treatment with test compounds. The reduction in LDH release upon treatment suggests hepatoprotection.

Requirements

Materials

- **Cell culture**: Hepatocyte cell line (e.g., HepG2, primary hepatocytes).
- **Culture medium**: RPMI-1640 or DMEM, supplemented with 10% fetal bovine serum (FBS).
- **Toxic agent**: E.g., hydrogen peroxide (H_2O_2), acetaminophen, or other hepatotoxins.
- **Test compounds**: Potential hepatoprotective compounds (plant extracts, phytochemicals, synthetic drugs).
- **LDH assay kit**: Commercial LDH cytotoxicity assay kit (e.g., Lactate Dehydrogenase Cytotoxicity Assay Kit, available from various suppliers).
- **Phosphate-buffered saline (PBS)**.
- **96-well microplate**.
- **Incubator**: Set at 37°C, 5% CO_2.
- **Microplate reader**: For measuring absorbance at 490 nm (or other wavelengths specified by the kit).

Equipment

- **Incubator**: 37°C with 5% CO_2 for cell culture maintenance.
- **Centrifuge**: For cell harvesting.
- **Microplate reader**: To measure LDH release.
- **Pipettes** and **sterile tips**.

Methodology

1. **Cell Culture and Pre-Treatment**
   - Seed the hepatocyte cell line (e.g., HepG2) in a 96-well microplate at a density of approximately 1×10^5 cells/well and allow cells to adhere and grow for 24 hours.
   - After the cells are fully attached, treat them with the test compound (at varying concentrations, e.g., 10, 50, 100 μg/mL) and incubate for 1–2 hours.
2. **Induction of Hepatotoxicity**
   - Expose the cells to a toxic agent (e.g., H_2O_2, acetaminophen) to induce cell damage. The concentration and exposure time will depend on the hepatotoxicity inducer (typically 200 μM H_2O_2 for 1 hour).
   - Include a **negative control** (untreated cells) and a **positive control** (cells treated with hepatotoxin without test compound).
3. **Incubation and LDH Release**
   - After incubation with the toxic agent, incubate the cells for an additional 24–48 hours at 37°C, allowing for the release of LDH from damaged cells into the culture medium.
4. **Assay Preparation**
   - Collect the culture medium and transfer 50 μL of the medium to a fresh 96-well microplate for LDH measurement.
5. **LDH Measurement**
   - Add 50 μL of the LDH substrate solution (from the assay kit) to each well of the microplate containing the culture supernatant.
   - Incubate the microplate at room temperature for 30–60 minutes to allow colour development.
   - Measure the absorbance at 490 nm using a microplate reader.
6. **Calculation of LDH Activity**
   - Determine the LDH activity in the test samples by comparing the absorbance values to the standard curve provided by the LDH assay kit.
   - **Calculate the percent LDH release** by the following formula:

Calculations

Percentage LDH Release

$$\%\text{LDH Released} = \frac{\text{Abs Sample}}{\text{Abs of Positive Control}} \times 100$$

Where:

- **Absorbance of Sample** is the optical density of the test compound-treated group.
- **Absorbance of Positive Control** is the optical density of the hepatotoxin-treated group.

Percentage Hepatoprotection

$$\text{Protection (\%)} = \left(1 - \frac{\text{Absorbance of Treated Sample}}{\text{Absorbance of Positive Control}}\right) \times 100$$

Interpretation

- A higher percentage of **LDH release** indicates greater cytotoxicity or cell damage.
- **Lower LDH release** in the test compound-treated groups suggests hepatoprotective effects, as the compound helps to preserve cell integrity.
- The results can be used to assess the ability of test compounds to prevent liver damage or to identify potential hepatoprotective drugs or phytochemicals.

Chapter 11

Kidney Protective Activity Assays

11.1 Overview of Nephroprotective Activity

Nephroprotective activity refers to the protective effect of certain substances, particularly plant-based compounds, against kidney damage caused by various factors like oxidative stress, toxins, or inflammation. With the rise of chronic kidney disease (CKD) worldwide, there is growing interest in identifying natural nephroprotective agents. For laboratories with limited facilities, conducting nephroprotective studies using cost-effective and ethically suitable *in vitro* pharmacological models can be a feasible approach.

11.1.1 *In Vitro* Pharmacological Models for Nephroprotective Activity

In vitro studies offer an ethical and cost-effective alternative to animal models, particularly when working with limited resources. Common *in vitro* assays to assess nephroprotective activity involve the use of renal cell lines, such as **human renal proximal tubular cells (HK-2)** or **Vero cells**, and the induction of nephrotoxicity using chemicals like **cisplatin**, **gentamicin**, or **ethylene glycol**. These models are simple, reproducible, and require minimal equipment, making them suitable for labs with budget constraints.

A key component of these studies is the evaluation of **cell viability**. Techniques such as the **MTT assay** or **trypan blue exclusion** test allow for the determination of cell damage caused by nephrotoxic agents and the protective effects of potential nephroprotective compounds. These assays are inexpensive and can be performed with basic laboratory equipment like a microplate reader or a spectrophotometer.

11.1.2 Biochemical Markers and Oxidative Stress Evaluation

Oxidative stress is a major contributor to nephrotoxicity, and assessing **reactive oxygen species (ROS)** generation is essential for evaluating nephroprotective effects. Cost-effective methods, such as **DPPH assay** or **ABTS assay**, can be used to measure the antioxidant potential of plant extracts or compounds. These assays, which require basic laboratory setups, can provide important data on the ability of the compounds to scavenge free radicals and reduce oxidative stress, which is a crucial mechanism in protecting kidney cells from damage.

Additionally, evaluating **lactate dehydrogenase (LDH)** and **creatinine levels** in culture media can offer insights into cellular damage and nephrotoxicity. Elevated LDH and creatinine levels are indicative of kidney injury, and their reduction in the presence of a nephroprotective agent suggests its efficacy.

11.1.3 Inflammation and Cytokine Assessment

Nephroprotective compounds may also exert their effects through anti-inflammatory pathways. *In vitro* models can assess the expression of inflammatory cytokines such as **TNF-α**, **IL-6**, and **IL-1**β through enzyme-linked immunosorbent assay (ELISA), which is a straightforward and affordable technique suitable for labs with limited facilities. These cytokines are often upregulated in response to nephrotoxic injury, and their inhibition is a sign of effective nephroprotection.

11.2 Ethical Considerations and Sustainability

Using *in vitro* models ensures ethical suitability, as these studies do not involve the use of animals. Furthermore, the use of plant-based compounds for nephroprotective activity aligns with the growing interest in natural and sustainable therapies. Plants offer a rich source of bioactive compounds, and their use in nephroprotective studies is a step towards finding low-cost and ethical alternatives to synthetic drugs.

Overall, conducting nephroprotective studies *in vitro* using cost-effective and ethically suitable methods is not only feasible but also essential for laboratories with limited resources. By utilizing simple and reproducible assays, such as cell viability tests, antioxidant assays, and inflammation markers, researchers can gain valuable insights into the nephroprotective potential of natural compounds while maintaining ethical integrity. These studies provide an accessible entry point for labs working within constraints and can contribute to the discovery of novel, safe, and affordable nephroprotective agents.

11.3 Urease Inhibition Assay for Labs with Limited Facilities

Urease inhibitors, in particular, have gained attention for their potential in preventing kidney-related issues associated with bacterial infections, such as those caused by *Helicobacter pylori* and *Proteus vulgaris*, which produce urease, an enzyme that converts urea into ammonia. Ammonia can accumulate and impair kidney function, making urease inhibition an attractive therapeutic target. For labs with limited resources, conducting *in vitro* pharmacological assays like the Urease Inhibition Assay can provide valuable insights into nephroprotective activity without the need for complex or expensive equipment.

Urease Inhibition Assay: A Cost-effective Approach

The urease inhibition assay is a straightforward and cost-effective *in vitro* method to assess the nephroprotective potential of plant extracts, compounds, or synthetic drugs. This assay is particularly suitable for labs with basic facilities, as it primarily involves monitoring the enzymatic activity of urease in the presence of test samples. Here's a brief overview of how the assay can be conducted:

1. **Sample Preparation**: Test samples (e.g., plant extracts, purified compounds) are dissolved in an appropriate solvent, such as water or dimethyl sulfoxide (DMSO). For effective results, the test samples should be concentrated or extracted from materials with known nephroprotective properties.

2. **Enzyme Source**: Urease is typically sourced from *Jack beans* (*Canavalia ensiformis*) or bacterial strains like *Helicobacter pylori* and *Proteus vulgaris*. The enzyme can be purchased commercially or isolated from these sources.

3. **Assay Procedure**: The assay involves incubating the enzyme with the test sample in a reaction mixture containing urea as the substrate. The hydrolysis of urea produces ammonia, which can be quantified using colorimetric or spectrophotometric methods. The test sample's ability to inhibit urease activity is determined by comparing the ammonia release in the presence of the sample to that of a control group (without the sample).

4. **Measurement**: Ammonia production can be measured using an ammonia-specific reagent like Nessler's reagent, which reacts with ammonia to form a yellow-coloured complex. The intensity of the colour, measured using a UV-Vis spectrophotometer, correlates with the ammonia concentration and indicates urease activity.

Benefits for Limited-Facility Labs

For labs with limited facilities, this assay is advantageous in several ways:

- **Cost-effective**: The reagents required for this assay (urea, ammonia assay kits, or Nessler's reagent) are inexpensive and readily available.
- **Simple Equipment**: Only basic equipment like a spectrophotometer, micropipettes, and a water bath is needed. These are standard items found in most research labs.
- **Ethically Suitable**: The assay does not require the use of animals, making it ethically suitable for labs adhering to ethical guidelines. It can be an alternative to animal-based nephroprotective studies.
- **Adaptability**: This assay can be easily adapted to study a variety of samples, including herbal extracts, purified bioactive compounds, or synthetic inhibitors.

The Urease Inhibition Assay is a valuable tool for assessing nephroprotective activity in a cost-effective and ethically sound manner. Its simple setup, minimal equipment requirements, and reproducibility make it ideal for labs with limited facilities. By employing this assay, researchers can screen a wide range of compounds and natural products for their potential to protect kidney function, offering a promising avenue for drug discovery and development in nephrology. Thus, the standard protocols of this of *in vitro* nephroprotective activity assay we are discussing in this chapter.

Urease Inhibition Assay Protocol

The urease inhibition assay is used to determine the nephroprotective potential of compounds by evaluating their ability to inhibit urease activity. Urease is an enzyme found in many organisms, including the bacterium *Helicobacter pylori*, and is involved in the hydrolysis of urea into ammonia and carbon dioxide. The excess production of ammonia can lead to kidney toxicity and related complications. Inhibition of urease can therefore be beneficial in preventing nephrotoxicity, which can be used to evaluate the nephroprotective potential of a compound.

Principle

Urease catalyzes the hydrolysis of urea to produce ammonia and carbon dioxide. The ammonia released can be quantified using colorimetric methods. When a test compound inhibits urease activity, less ammonia is produced, which is indicative of urease inhibition. The inhibition can be measured by comparing the amount of ammonia produced in the presence and absence of the test compound. The assay is performed by incubating urease with the test compound and measuring the reduction in ammonia production.

Requirements

Materials

- **Urease enzyme**: Commercially available urease (e.g., from *Canavalia ensiformis* or *Jack bean*)
- **Substrate**: Urea solution (typically 0.1 M in phosphate buffer)
- **Test compounds**: Potential nephroprotective compounds (e.g., plant extracts, synthetic drugs)
- **Positive control**: A known urease inhibitor (e.g., acetohydroxamic acid, thiourea)
- **Buffer solution**: Phosphate buffer (0.1 M, pH 7.0)
- **Colorimetric reagent**: Nessler's reagent (or other ammonia-detecting reagents)
- **Microplate reader**: For absorbance measurement at 450 nm (or the appropriate wavelength for the specific reagent used)
- **Pipettes** and **sterile tips**
- **96-well microplate**
- **Centrifuge** (if needed for enzyme purification or preparation)

Equipment

- **Incubator**: For maintaining reaction temperature (usually 37°C)
- **Microplate reader**: For absorbance measurement at the appropriate wavelength
- **Pipettes** and **sterile tips**

Methodology

1. **Preparation of Reagents**
    - Prepare **urease enzyme solution** by dissolving the enzyme in phosphate buffer (0.1 M, pH 7.0) to the required concentration, typically around 0.1–1 mg/mL.
    - Prepare **urea solution** at a concentration of 0.1 M in phosphate buffer (pH 7.0).
    - Prepare **Nessler's reagent** (or the ammonia-detecting reagent) according to the supplier's instructions.

2. **Pre-incubation of Test Compounds**
   - Seed 96-well microplates with 50 μL of the test compound at various concentrations (e.g., 10, 50, 100 μg/mL).
   - Add 50 μL of urease enzyme solution to each well.
   - Incubate the plate at 37°C for 10–15 minutes to allow the test compound to interact with the enzyme.
3. **Initiation of Reaction**
   - After pre-incubation, add 50 μL of urea solution (0.1 M) to each well to start the reaction.
   - Incubate the plate at 37°C for 30 minutes to allow the hydrolysis of urea.
4. **Stopping the Reaction**
   - After incubation, add 100 μL of Nessler's reagent to each well.
   - Incubate for 10–15 minutes to allow the colour to develop. The ammonia released from urea hydrolysis will react with Nessler's reagent to produce a yellowish-brown colour.
5. **Absorbance Measurement**
   - Measure the absorbance at 450 nm using a microplate reader.
   - Ensure to measure the blank (phosphate buffer) and controls (positive and negative controls) at the same time.
6. **Control and Blank Preparation**
   - **Negative control**: Perform the assay without the test compound to measure basal urease activity.
   - **Positive control**: Include a known urease inhibitor (e.g., acetohydroxamic acid or thiourea) to confirm that the urease activity can be effectively inhibited.

Calculations

1. **Calculation of Urease Inhibition**

   The urease inhibition percentage is calculated based on the reduction in ammonia production:

$$\%\,\text{Urease Inhibition} = \frac{\text{Abs Control} - \text{Abs Sample}}{\text{Abs control}} \times 100$$

   Where:

   - **Absorbance of Control** is the absorbance from the positive control (urease with no inhibitor).
   - **Absorbance of Sample** is the absorbance from the test compound-treated group.

2. **Nephroprotective Potential**

   The test compound's nephroprotective potential is proportional to the percent urease inhibition. Higher inhibition suggests better nephroprotective activity by preventing urease-mediated kidney damage.

Interpretation

- **Higher urease inhibition** indicates stronger inhibition of urease activity and suggests that the test compound has nephroprotective properties by reducing urease-mediated damage.
- **No inhibition or minimal inhibition** suggests that the compound does not have significant nephroprotective effects in this assay.

Chapter 12

Anti-Aging and Skin-Protective Activity Assays

12.1 Overview of Anti-aging and Skin protection Assay

Anti-aging and skin protection are key areas of focus in dermatological research, as they are essential for maintaining skin health and preventing premature aging. The global demand for natural and effective skin care products has spurred interest in exploring plant-based compounds, which can provide anti-aging and skin-protective benefits. For laboratories with limited facilities, conducting *in vitro* pharmacological assays to assess these effects in a cost-effective and ethically suitable manner is a practical approach.

12.1.1 *In Vitro* Models for Anti-Aging and Skin Protection

In vitro studies are a reliable alternative to animal testing, especially when working within budget constraints. The use of skin cell lines such as **human dermal fibroblasts (HDF)**, **keratinocytes (HaCaT)**, and **melanocytes** provides a reproducible platform for evaluating skin protection and anti-aging effects. These cell lines are often used to mimic the physiological functions of skin cells, such as collagen synthesis, wound healing, and melanin production, which are crucial in aging and skin protection.

A key assay for evaluating anti-aging potential is the **collagen synthesis assay**. Collagen is a vital protein that maintains the skin's structural integrity, and its reduction is a hallmark of aging. Assays that measure the **pro-collagen secretion** from fibroblasts, such as enzyme-linked immunosorbent assays (ELISA), can provide valuable information about the ability of a compound to stimulate collagen production. These assays are affordable and require only basic laboratory equipment.

12.1.2 Oxidative Stress and Antioxidant Activity

Oxidative stress plays a significant role in skin aging, leading to wrinkles, fine lines, and pigmentation changes. *In vitro* assays to measure the **antioxidant activity** of plant extracts or compounds can be easily adapted to labs with limited facilities. The **DPPH** (2,2-diphenyl-1-picrylhydrazyl) and **ABTS** (2,2'-azino-bis(3-ethylbenzothiazoline-6-sulfonic acid)) assays are commonly used to assess free radical scavenging abilities. These assays are simple, cost-effective, and do not require complex instrumentation, making them ideal for small laboratories.

Additionally, assessing **reactive oxygen species (ROS)** production in skin cells exposed to oxidative stress-inducing agents is a valuable tool for evaluating anti-aging potential. The use of fluorescent probes like **DHE (dihydroethidium)** can help quantify ROS generation, and the reduction in ROS levels after treatment with a compound suggests its antioxidant capacity.

12.1.3 Skin Hydration and Protection Assays

Skin hydration is another critical factor in skin health and aging. Dehydration of the skin leads to the formation of wrinkles and a dull appearance. Simple assays that measure **transepidermal water loss (TEWL)** or **skin barrier integrity** can be conducted using available resources. *In vitro* models using **HaCaT cells** or **HDF cells** can be treated with plant extracts to determine their effect on water retention and barrier function.

Moreover, **UV-induced skin damage** is a significant cause of aging. *In vitro* assays can be performed to evaluate the protective effects of compounds against UV-induced DNA damage. The use of the **Comet Assay** or **micronucleus test** helps assess the DNA protective effects of extracts by detecting DNA strand breaks or mutations caused by UV exposure.

12.1.4 Skin Anti-infective Assays

Skin infections caused by bacterial and fungal pathogens, such as *Staphylococcus epidermidis*, *Staphylococcus aureus*, *Corynebacterium granulosum*, *Propionibacterium acnes*, *Candida albicans*, *Trichophyton rubrum* and *Microsporum canis* are prevalent worldwide. These infections often lead to significant discomfort and cosmetic concerns. *In vitro* antimicrobial assays are crucial for the development of new drug leads targeting these infections. Techniques such as disk diffusion, broth microdilution, and agar well diffusion are commonly employed to evaluate the antimicrobial efficacy of natural or synthetic compounds against pathogens.

For acne, assays targeting *Propionibacterium acnes* focus on inhibitory effects on biofilm formation, a key factor in acne pathogenesis. Similarly, antifungal assays against dermatophytes like *T. rubrum* assess the minimum inhibitory concentration (MIC) of potential antifungal agents. These methods provide rapid and cost-effective means for screening plant extracts, nanoparticles, or synthetic molecules. Identifying potent skin anti-infective agents through such assays aids in developing topical formulations for managing acne, ringworm, and other skin infections.

12.1.5 Ethical and Cost-Effective Considerations

In vitro pharmacological assays provide an ethically suitable alternative to animal studies, ensuring that skin protection and anti-aging research is conducted without the use of animals. Furthermore, the use of plant-based compounds for skin protection aligns with the growing consumer preference for natural and sustainable products. Many of these assays are inexpensive and require minimal laboratory infrastructure, making them ideal for research in labs with limited resources.

12.2 Cost Effective Skin Protective and Anti-Aging Assays

Skin protection and anti-aging studies focus on combating oxidative stress, maintaining skin structure, and preventing damage caused by UV exposure. Several *in vitro* assays are employed to evaluate these protective and anti-aging effects of natural compounds.

1. **Antioxidant Activity Assays (DPPH, ABTS, and FRAP Assay)**: These assays are designed to measure the ability of compounds to neutralize free radicals, which contribute to skin aging. The **DPPH** and **ABTS** assays assess radical scavenging ability, while the **FRAP** assay evaluates the reducing power of compounds, indicating their potential to protect skin cells from oxidative damage.
2. **Collagenase Inhibition Assay**: Collagenase breaks down collagen in the skin, leading to wrinkles and sagging. This assay tests the ability of a compound to inhibit collagenase, promoting collagen stability and skin firmness, thus helping prevent skin aging.
3. **Elastase Inhibition Assay**: Elastase degrades elastin, which is essential for skin elasticity. The elastase inhibition assay measures a compound's potential to protect skin elasticity by preventing elastin breakdown.
4. **Hyaluronidase Inhibition Assay**: Hyaluronidase degrades hyaluronic acid, which is crucial for skin hydration. Inhibiting this enzyme helps preserve moisture and maintain skin plumpness.
5. **Tyrosinase Inhibition Assay**: Tyrosinase is involved in melanin synthesis. Inhibiting this enzyme can reduce hyperpigmentation, leading to an even skin tone.
6. **UV Protection Assay (SPF Estimation)**: This assay estimates a compound's sun protection factor (SPF), assessing its ability to protect the skin from harmful UV radiation and prevent photoaging.
7. **Longevity Assay on Drosophila Model**: This model is used to evaluate the effects of compounds on lifespan and healthspan. It offers a cost-effective and ethical method to assess anti-aging potential *in vivo*.
8. **Anti-Acne Activity on *C. anes* Model:** The *Cutibacterium acnes* (formerly *Propionibacterium acnes*) model, combined with *in vitro* antimicrobial activity assays, evaluates compounds for their ability to inhibit bacterial growth, disrupt biofilm formation, and reduce inflammation in acne treatment.

Evaluating anti-aging and skin protection properties through cost-effective and ethically suitable *in vitro* assays offers a practical solution for laboratories with limited resources. Simple assays, such as collagen synthesis, antioxidant activity, and UV protection tests, provide valuable insights into the effectiveness of natural compounds in combating skin aging and offering protection. These assays are affordable, ethically sound, and compatible with basic lab tools and spectrophotometry, ensuring minimal investment. Since antioxidant and elastase assays have been discussed in earlier chapters, so to be to be straightforward, standard protocols of the 5 types of *in vitro* anti-aging and skin protection assays we are discussing in this chapter enabling researchers to develop safe, cost-effective skincare solutions.

Collagenase Inhibition Assay Protocol

This simplified and cost-effective method for assessing collagenase inhibition potential focuses on spectrophotometric analysis. The protocol uses a synthetic peptide substrate (such as N-(3-(2-furyl)-acryloyl)-L-alanylalanylhydrazide) that undergoes a colour change upon cleavage by collagenase. This change in absorbance can be measured using a UV-Vis spectrophotometer, making it accessible and affordable for many laboratories.

Principle

Collagenase catalyzes the breakdown of a synthetic peptide substrate. When the substrate is cleaved by collagenase, it results in the release of products that cause a change in absorbance at a specific wavelength (e.g., 340 nm). The degree of absorbance decrease correlates with collagenase activity, and the inhibition of this activity by test compounds can be quantified by comparing the absorbance in the presence and absence of the inhibitor.

Requirements

Materials

- **Collagenase enzyme**: Commercially available collagenase (e.g., from *Clostridium histolyticum*)
- **Synthetic peptide substrate** (e.g., N-(3-(2-furyl)-acryloyl)-L-alanylalanylhydrazide)
- **Test compounds**: Plant extracts or synthetic compounds to be tested
- **Positive control**: Known collagenase inhibitor (e.g., EDTA or doxycycline)
- **Phosphate buffer**: 0.1 M, pH 7.4
- **UV-Vis spectrophotometer**: Set to measure absorbance at 340 nm
- **96-well microplate** or cuvettes
- **Pipettes and sterile tips**
- **Incubator**: Set to 37°C

Methodology

1. **Preparation of Reagents**
    - Prepare collagenase enzyme solution in phosphate buffer (0.1 M, pH 7.4) to a concentration of 0.5–1.0 mg/mL.
    - Prepare the synthetic peptide substrate in phosphate buffer at a concentration of 1 mg/mL or as specified by the manufacturer.
2. **Pre-incubation of Test Compounds**
    - In a 96-well microplate (or cuvette), add 50 μL of the test compound or positive control at varying concentrations (e.g., 10, 50, 100 μg/mL).
    - Add 50 μL of the collagenase enzyme solution to each well or cuvette.
    - Pre-incubate at 37°C for 10–15 minutes to allow the compound to interact with the enzyme.

3. **Initiation of Reaction**
   - Add 50 μL of the synthetic peptide substrate to each well or cuvette.
   - Incubate the reaction mixture at 37°C for 30 minutes to allow collagenase to cleave the substrate.
4. **Stopping the Reaction**
   - After incubation, the reaction can be stopped by adding a stopping solution, such as TCA (trichloroacetic acid), if needed. However, for some setups, stopping may not be necessary as the colour change is detectable even with ongoing enzyme activity.
5. **Spectrophotometric Measurement**
   - Measure the absorbance at 340 nm using a UV-Vis spectrophotometer. The decrease in absorbance at this wavelength correlates with the collagenase activity, as the substrate is cleaved by the enzyme.
6. **Control and Blank Preparation**
   - **Control (without inhibitor)**: Prepare a sample without the test compound to measure baseline enzyme activity.
   - **Blank**: Prepare a blank containing only the substrate and buffer to account for any background absorbance.

Calculations

1. **Calculation of Collagenase Inhibition**

   The percentage inhibition of collagenase activity is calculated by comparing the absorbance of the sample to the control:

$$\%\,\text{Collagenase Inhibition} = \frac{\text{Abs Control} - \text{Abs Sample}}{\text{Abs control}} \times 100$$

   Where:

   - **Absorbance of Control** is the absorbance without the test compound (i.e., only enzyme and substrate).
   - **Absorbance of Sample** is the absorbance with the test compound present.

Interpretation

- **Higher inhibition** corresponds to better anti-aging or skin protection potential, as the test compound prevents collagen breakdown by inhibiting collagenase activity.
- **Lower inhibition** suggests the compound does not significantly affect collagenase activity.

This simplified protocol is cost-effective, as it uses readily available materials and relies on basic spectrophotometric analysis for determining enzyme activity. It also requires minimal reagents and can be adapted for high-throughput screening in a 96-well plate format.

Hyaluronidase Inhibition Assay Protocol

This assay measures the ability of a compound to inhibit hyaluronidase, an enzyme that degrades hyaluronic acid, a key component of the extracellular matrix in the skin. Inhibition of hyaluronidase activity suggests potential anti-aging and skin protection properties by preventing the breakdown of hyaluronic acid, which helps maintain skin hydration and elasticity.

Principle

Hyaluronidase catalyzes the hydrolysis of hyaluronic acid, breaking it down into smaller fragments. The ability of a compound to inhibit this enzyme can be assessed by measuring the decrease in the degradation of hyaluronic acid. The assay uses a colorimetric or spectrophotometric method to quantify the breakdown of hyaluronic acid by the enzyme and the inhibitory effect of test compounds.

Requirements

Materials

- **Hyaluronidase enzyme**: Commercially available hyaluronidase (e.g., from *Bacillus subtilis* or *Bovine Testes*)
- **Hyaluronic acid solution**: 1 mg/mL hyaluronic acid in phosphate buffer
- **Test compounds**: Plant extracts or synthetic compounds to be tested
- **Positive control**: Known hyaluronidase inhibitor (e.g., quercetin, sodium chloride)
- **Sodium tetraborate (borax)**: Used for colour development
- **Sodium chloride**: To prepare the inhibitor solution
- **Phosphate buffer**: 0.1 M, pH 7.4
- **UV-Vis spectrophotometer**: Set to measure absorbance at 600 nm
- **96-well microplate** or cuvettes
- **Pipettes and sterile tips**
- **Incubator**: Set to 37°C

Methodology

1. **Preparation of Reagents**
    - Prepare **hyaluronidase enzyme solution** by diluting it in phosphate buffer to a concentration of 0.1–0.2 mg/mL.
    - Prepare hyaluronic acid solution by dissolving 1 mg/mL of hyaluronic acid in phosphate buffer.
    - Prepare the test compound solutions at various concentrations (e.g., 10, 50, 100 μg/mL).

- Prepare a positive control solution of a known inhibitor at an appropriate concentration (e.g., 1 mM sodium chloride).

2. **Pre-incubation of Test Compounds**
   - In a 96-well microplate (or cuvette), add 50 μL of the test compound to each well (or cuvette) at varying concentrations.
   - Add 50 μL of the hyaluronidase enzyme solution to each well.
   - Pre-incubate the mixture at 37°C for 10–15 minutes to allow the enzyme and test compound to interact.
3. **Initiation of Reaction**
   - Add 100 μL of hyaluronic acid solution to each well, and incubate at 37°C for 30 minutes. The hyaluronic acid will be degraded by hyaluronidase during this time.
4. **Stopping the Reaction**
   - After incubation, add 100 μL of borate solution (e.g., 0.2% borax in water) to each well. This reacts with the degradation products to form a colour that can be measured spectrophotometrically.
5. **Spectrophotometric Measurement**
   - Measure the absorbance at 600 nm using a UV-Vis spectrophotometer. The absorbance corresponds to the amount of hyaluronic acid degradation, with higher absorbance indicating more degradation.
6. **Control and Blank Preparation**
   - **Control (without inhibitor)**: Prepare a sample without the test compound to measure baseline hyaluronidase activity.
   - **Blank**: Prepare a blank without hyaluronic acid to account for any background absorbance.

Calculations

1. **Calculation of Hyaluronidase Inhibition**

   The percentage inhibition of hyaluronidase activity is calculated by comparing the absorbance of the sample with the control:

$$\%\,\text{Hyaluronidase Inhibition} = \frac{\text{Abs Control} - \text{Abs Sample}}{\text{Abs control}} \times 100$$

   Where:

   - **Absorbance of Control** is the absorbance without the test compound (only enzyme and substrate).
   - **Absorbance of Sample** is the absorbance with the test compound present.

Interpretation

- **Higher inhibition** of hyaluronidase indicates better potential for anti-aging and skin protection, as the test compound prevents the breakdown of hyaluronic acid.
- **Lower inhibition** suggests the compound has less effect on hyaluronidase activity, and therefore less potential for skin protection.

This protocol offers a simple, cost-effective method for assessing the hyaluronidase inhibitory potential of compounds using spectrophotometric analysis. By measuring the degradation of hyaluronic acid, it provides insight into the potential of test compounds for skin protection and anti-aging applications.

Tyrosinase Inhibition Assay Protocol

The tyrosinase inhibition assay is commonly used to evaluate the ability of a compound to inhibit tyrosinase activity, a key enzyme in melanin synthesis. Inhibiting tyrosinase can help reduce hyperpigmentation, dark spots, and promote even skin tone, making it valuable for anti-aging and skin protection applications. The inhibition is quantified by measuring the decrease in dopaquinone formation using spectrophotometry.

Principle

Tyrosinase catalyzes the oxidation of L-tyrosine to dopaquinone, which leads to the formation of melanin. The assay evaluates the ability of compounds to inhibit this enzyme, reducing melanin production. The assay measures the reduction in dopaquinone formation by monitoring absorbance at 475 nm, where dopaquinone absorbs light. A decrease in absorbance indicates inhibition of tyrosinase activity by the test compound.

Requirements

Materials:

- **Tyrosinase enzyme**: Mushroom tyrosinase (500-1000 units/mL)
- **L-tyrosine**: 1 mM solution in phosphate buffer (0.1 M, pH 6.8)
- **Test compounds**: Phytochemical extracts or synthetic compounds
- **Positive control**: Known tyrosinase inhibitor (e.g., kojic acid, arbutin)
- **Phosphate buffer**: 0.1 M, pH 6.8
- **Dimethyl sulfoxide (DMSO)**: For dissolving test compounds
- **96-well microplate** or cuvettes
- **UV-Vis spectrophotometer**: For absorbance measurements at 475 nm
- **Incubator**: Set to 25°C or room temperature
- **Pipettes** and **sterile tips**

Reagents:

- **L-tyrosine** (substrate)
- **Phosphate buffer** (0.1 M, pH 6.8)
- **Tyrosinase enzyme solution** (500-1000 units/mL)
- **Test compounds** (phytochemicals or synthetic compounds)

Methodology

1. **Preparation of Reagents:**
    - **Tyrosinase solution**: Dilute tyrosinase enzyme in phosphate buffer to achieve a concentration of 500-1000 units/mL.
    - **L-tyrosine solution**: Prepare a 1 mM solution in phosphate buffer (0.1 M, pH 6.8).
    - **Test compound solutions**: Dissolve test compounds in DMSO to obtain working concentrations (e.g., 10, 50, 100 μg/mL).
2. **Pre-incubation of Test Compounds:**
    - In a 96-well microplate (or cuvettes), add 50 μL of each test compound solution (at varying concentrations) to the wells.
    - Add 50 μL of the tyrosinase enzyme solution to each well.
    - Incubate the reaction mixture at 25°C for 10-15 minutes to allow the compound to interact with the enzyme.
3. **Initiation of Reaction:**
    - After the incubation, add 100 μL of L-tyrosine solution to each well to initiate the reaction. Tyrosinase will catalyze the conversion of L-tyrosine to dopaquinone, which will lead to a colour change.
    - Incubate at 25°C for 20-30 minutes to allow the reaction to proceed.
4. **Spectrophotometric Measurement:**
    - After the incubation, measure the absorbance of each well at 475 nm using a UV-Vis spectrophotometer. Dopaquinone absorbs light at this wavelength, and the intensity of the colour indicates the level of tyrosinase activity.
    - If using a 96-well microplate, transfer the plate to the microplate reader and record the absorbance for each well.
5. **Control and Blank Preparation:**
    - **Control (without inhibitor)**: Prepare a sample without the test compound to measure baseline tyrosinase activity (only enzyme and substrate).

- **Blank**: Prepare a blank with the substrate (L-tyrosine) but without the enzyme and test compound to account for any background absorbance.

Calculations

Percentage Inhibition Calculation: The percentage inhibition of tyrosinase activity is calculated as follows:

$$\% \text{Inhibition} = \frac{\text{Abs Control} - \text{Abs Sample}}{\text{Abs control}} \times 100$$

Where:

- **Absorbance of Control** is the absorbance of the control sample (without the test compound).
- **Absorbance of Sample** is the absorbance of the sample with the test compound.

Interpretation

- **Higher inhibition** suggests that the test compound is effective in reducing tyrosinase activity and may have skin lightening or anti-aging effects by preventing melanin synthesis.
- **Lower inhibition** suggests minimal or no effect on tyrosinase activity.

This assay provides a simple, cost-effective method to evaluate the tyrosinase inhibitory activity of compounds using a spectrophotometric approach. By measuring the reduction in dopaquinone formation, it helps to determine the anti-aging and skin protection potential of various phytochemicals or synthetic compounds.

UV Protection Assay (SPF Estimation) Protocol

This assay estimates the Sun Protection Factor (SPF) of compounds or phytochemical extracts *in vitro*, which indicates their potential for skin protection against harmful UV radiation, evaluates the ability of a compound or phytochemical extract to absorb or reflect ultraviolet (UV) radiation. The assay uses spectrophotometry to measure UV absorption at specific wavelengths.

Principle

The SPF is a measure of a substance's ability to absorb or block UV radiation. Compounds or extracts are dissolved in a suitable solvent and applied to a transparent substrate. SPF is a measure of the photoprotective efficacy of a substance against UV-induced skin damage, particularly from UVB (290–320 nm). The assay involves measuring the UV absorbance of the test sample in the UVB range and calculating its SPF using a mathematical formula based on absorbance data.

Requirements

Materials:

- **Test samples**: Phytochemical extracts or formulations
- **Solvent**: Ethanol, methanol, or water (depending on the solubility of the sample)
- **Reference standard**: Commercial sunscreen with known SPF value
- **Quartz cuvettes**: For precise UV absorbance readings in spectrophotometric analysis
- **Phosphate buffer**: pH 7.4 (optional, for preparing aqueous solutions)
- **Distilled water**

Equipment:

- **UV-Vis spectrophotometer**: Capable of measuring absorbance in the UV range (290–320 nm)
- **Pipettes** and **tips**
- **Sonicator** (optional): For proper mixing of test samples

Methodology

1. **Preparation of Solutions:**
   - Dissolve the test sample in a suitable solvent to prepare a solution with a known concentration (e.g., 0.5 mg/mL or as appropriate for the sample).
   - For comparative analysis, prepare a solution of the reference standard (commercial sunscreen).
2. **Baseline Adjustment:**
   - Calibrate the spectrophotometer with the solvent as the blank.
   - Measure and adjust the baseline to zero absorbance.
3. **Measurement of Absorbance:**
   - Fill a quartz cuvette with the test sample solution and place it in the spectrophotometer.
   - Record the absorbance at wavelengths ranging from 290 nm to 320 nm at 5 nm intervals (290, 295, 300, 305, 310, 315, 320 nm).
   - Repeat the process for the reference standard and blank.
4. **Replicates:**
   - Perform the analysis in triplicates to ensure accuracy and reproducibility.

Calculations

1. **Determine SPF Value:** Use the following formula for SPF estimation:

$$\boldsymbol{SPF} = \sum_{290}^{320} EE(\lambda) \times I(\lambda) \times Abs(\lambda)$$

Where:

- **EE(λ)** = Erythemal Effectiveness at wavelength λ (provided in standard tables, e.g., FDA or ISO standards).
- **I(λ)** = Solar Intensity at wavelength λ (provided in standard tables).
- **Abs(λ)** = Absorbance of the sample at wavelength λ.
- The values of **EE(λ)** and **I(λ)** are constants provided in published standards (e.g., ISO 24443).

Example EE(λ) and I(λ) values:

Wavelength (nm)	EE(λ)	I(λ)
290	0.015	0.05
295	0.081	0.08
300	0.287	0.20
305	0.327	0.50
310	0.186	0.70
315	0.083	0.90
320	0.018	0.95

- Multiply the absorbance at each wavelength by the respective EE(λ) and I(λ) values.
- Sum the results across all wavelengths and multiply by a constant factor (if specified by the protocol).
- **Control:** For comparative purposes, measure the SPF of a standard sunscreen product under the same conditions.

Calculation Example:

If the absorbance values of a sample at the specified wavelengths are as follows:

Wavelength (λ)	Absorbance (Abs(λ))	EE (λ) × I(λ)	Product (Abs(λ) × EE(λ) × I(λ))
290 nm	0.6	0.015	0.009
295 nm	0.5	0.081	0.0405
300 nm	0.4	0.287	0.1148
305 nm	0.3	0.327	0.0981
310 nm	0.2	0.186	0.0372
315 nm	0.1	0.083	0.0083
320 nm	0.05	0.018	0.0009

*Sometimes, only the value of EE(λ) can be used in calculation considering value of I(λ) as 1.

Summing the products gives:

$$SPF = 0.009 + 0.0405 + 0.1148 + 0.0981 + 0.0372 + 0.0083 + 0.0009 = 0.3088$$

This value is multiplied by any standard correction factor provided by the protocol (if applicable).

Interpretation

- Higher SPF values indicate greater UV protection and potential for anti-aging and skin protection applications.
- Compare the SPF value of the test sample to the reference standard for relative efficacy.

This UV Protection Assay provides a simple, cost-effective, and reliable method for estimating the SPF of compounds or phytochemical extracts. By calculating SPF, researchers can assess the anti-aging and skin protection potential of natural products or formulations, aiding in the development of safer, plant-based sunscreens and skincare products.

Protocol for Longevity Assay on Drosophila Model

This assay evaluates the anti-aging potential of compounds or phytochemical extracts by assessing their effects on the lifespan of *Drosophila melanogaster*. The model provides insights into oxidative stress resistance, metabolic pathways, and overall longevity influenced by the test compound.

Principle

The longevity assay using *Drosophila melanogaster* (fruit fly) is a widely used model to evaluate the anti-aging potential of compounds or phytochemical extracts, due to its short lifespan of fruit flies, ease of genetic manipulation, and similarity to mammalian aging pathways. The assay involves administering the test compound via diet and monitoring survival rates over time in comparison to control group. Enhanced longevity or delayed aging signs suggest anti-aging potential. Changes in lifespan indicate the compound's ability to modulate aging processes, potentially through antioxidant, anti-inflammatory, or stress-resistance pathways.

Requirements

1. **Biological Materials**:
    - *Drosophila melanogaster* (wild-type strain or age-sensitive mutant strain)
    - Fly food media (cornmeal-agar or other suitable media)
    - Test compound or phytochemical extract
    - Control substances:

1. Negative control: Fly food without the test compound.
2. Positive control: A known anti-aging compound (e.g., resveratrol).

2. **Reagents**:
   - Agar
   - Sugar
   - Yeast
   - Cornmeal
   - Nipagin (methylparaben, as a preservative)
   - Propionic acid (as an antifungal agent)
   - Solvent (e.g., ethanol or DMSO, depending on the solubility of the test compound)
3. **Equipment**:
   - Incubator (maintained at 25°C, 12-hour light/dark cycle and 60% relative humidity)
   - Fly vials or bottles
   - CO_2 anesthetizer or chill table for handling flies.
   - Micropipettes
   - Analytical balance
   - Fine-tipped forceps
   - Stereomicroscope (optional)

Methodology

1. **Preparation of Fly Media**:
   - Prepare a standard cornmeal-agar fly food by mixing:
     - 1% agar
     - 5% sugar
     - 2% yeast
     - 8% cornmeal
     - 0.1% nipagin
     - 0.1% propionic acid
   - Dissolve the test compound or extract in a suitable solvent (e.g., ethanol) and mix it with the fly media at desired concentrations. Ensure the solvent does not exceed 0.5% to avoid toxic effects.

2. **Fly Rearing and Grouping**:
   - Rear flies under standard conditions (25°C, 12-hour light/dark cycle).
   - Collect newly emerged flies (1–2-day-old) to ensure uniform age.
   - Anesthetize flies using CO_2 or by chilling on ice and separate them by sex using a stereomicroscope. Use only male or female flies to avoid confounding effects due to mating.
   - Divide flies into groups (20–30 flies per group) with at least three replicates:
     - **Negative control:** Standard food without the test compound.
     - **Positive control:** Food containing a known anti-aging compound.
     - **Test groups:** Food with different concentrations of the test compound.
3. **Setting Up the Assay**:
   - Place vials in an incubator at 25°C and 60% humidity.
   - Transfer flies to fresh food every 2–3 days to prevent microbial contamination, depletion of food and ensure fresh exposure to the test compound.
   - Record the number of dead flies daily.
4. **Monitoring Lifespan and End of Assay**:
   - Record the number of surviving flies daily or at regular intervals until all flies in each group have died.
   - Note the date of each fly's death to calculate lifespan parameters.

Calculations

1. **Survival Curve Analysis:** Use the Kaplan-Meier survival analysis to plot the percentage of surviving flies over time for each group.

   Survival Percentage (%) = Number of surviving flies / Initial number of flies × 100
2. **Mean Lifespan**: Calculate the mean lifespan for each group using the formula:

   Mean Lifespan= $\sum$ (Days Survived by Each Fly)/Total Number of Flies

   Maximum Lifespan: Identify the longest lifespan observed in each group.
3. **Statistical Analysis**:
   - Compare survival curves between groups using the log-rank test.
   - Compare the mean and maximum lifespans between control and treated groups using statistical methods such as ANOVA or a Kaplan-Meier survival analysis.
   - Perform pairwise comparisons (e.g., Tukey's test or log-rank test) to identify significant differences.

% Increase =

4. **Percent Increase in Lifespan**: For treated groups, calculate the percentage increase in mean lifespan compared to the control:

$$\% \text{ Increase} = \frac{\text{Mean Lifespan of Treated G} - \text{Mean Lifespan of Control}}{\text{Mean Lifespan of Control}} \times 100$$

Interpretation

- An increase in mean lifespan or maximum lifespan or survival percentage indicates that the test compound has potential anti-aging effects.
- Additional assays (e.g., oxidative stress resistance, mitochondrial activity) can be performed to elucidate the mechanism.
- **Improved resistance to oxidative stress:** Indicates enhanced protective effects on metabolic and cellular pathways.
- **Dose-dependent effects:** Highlight optimal concentrations for therapeutic use.

The longevity assay using *Drosophila melanogaster* is a cost-effective, ethically acceptable, and reliable method for evaluating the anti-aging potential of compounds or phytochemical extracts. It provides valuable insights into the impact of test substances on aging pathways, paving the way for potential applications in skin protection and age-related research.

In Vitro Anti-Acne Activity Assay Protocol

In vitro antimicrobial activity assays are crucial for assessing the potential of compounds against acne-causing bacteria like *Cutibacterium acnes*. The well diffusion method is a widely employed technique due to its simplicity and effectiveness in determining the antimicrobial activity of test compounds through measurable inhibition zones.

Principle

The well diffusion method evaluates the antibacterial efficacy of a compound by introducing it into wells created on an agar medium inoculated with *C. acnes*. The compound diffuses into the agar, inhibiting bacterial growth, which is observed as a clear zone around the well. This method also helps in estimating the Minimum Inhibitory Concentration (MIC) by testing multiple concentrations of the compound.

Requirements

- ***Cutibacterium acnes* (ATCC-11827 or similar strain):** Fresh anaerobic culture grown in Reinforced Clostridial Medium (RCM).
- **Agar medium:** Reinforced Clostridial Agar (RCA).
- **Antibacterial sample:** Compound or phytochemical extract under investigation.

- **Positive control:** A known anti-acne drug (e.g., clindamycin).
- **Dilution solvents:** DMSO or distilled water.
- **100 μL micropipette tip:** For creating wells in the agar.
- **Micropipettes:** To transfer 20 μL of each dilution into the wells.
- **Sterile Petri dishes:** For agar medium.
- **Anaerobic chamber or jars:** For *C. acnes* incubation.
- **Incubator:** Set to 37°C.
- **Ruler or calliper:** For measuring zones of inhibition.

Methodology

1. **Preparation of Bacterial Inoculum**
    - Grow *C. acnes* in RCM broth under anaerobic conditions for 48–72 hours at 37°C.
    - Adjust the bacterial suspension turbidity to match a 0.5 McFarland standard ($\sim 1 \times 10_6$ CFU/mL).
2. **Preparation of Agar Plates**
    - Pour molten RCA (~20–25 mL per plate) into sterile Petri dishes and allow to solidify.
3. **Inoculation of Agar Plate**
    - Evenly spread 100 μL of the bacterial suspension over the agar surface using a sterile spreader.
4. **Creation of Wells**
    - Use a 100 μL micropipette tip to create 5 wells (~5–6 mm diameter) in the agar at evenly spaced intervals.
5. **Filling the Wells**
    - Prepare serial dilutions of the antibacterial sample (e.g., 100 μg/mL to 6.25 μg/mL).
    - Transfer 20 μL of each dilution into separate wells following all aseptic techniques.
6. **Positive Control**
    - Perform a separate experiment with known anti-acne drug (e.g., clindamycin) at similar concentration
7. **Incubation**
    - Place the plates in an anaerobic jar or chamber and incubate at 37°C for 48–72 hours.
8. **Observation**
    - Examine the plates for clear zones of inhibition around the wells, indicating antibacterial activity.

Results Interpretation

- Larger inhibition zones correspond to higher antibacterial efficacy.
- The smallest concentration showing a clear zone indicates the MIC.
- Compare MIC values of test samples against controls.

Significance

This MIC-based method is a simple efficient and cost-effective way to screen and evaluate anti-acne potential of test compounds, supporting the development of new treatments targeting *C. acnes*.

Chapter 13

Astringent Activity Using Simple *In Vitro* Models

13.1 Overview of Astringent Activity And *In Vitro* Studies

13.1.1 Astringent

An **astringent** is a substance that causes the contraction or shrinkage of tissues, typically reducing secretions and tightening the skin. This action is often accompanied by a dry, puckering sensation in the mouth, which is why many tannin-containing foods and beverages, like red wine, tea, or unripe fruits, are described as astringent.

Astringents are commonly used in cosmetics and healthcare products to reduce oiliness, close pores, and promote skin tightening. **Medically, astringents can help stop bleeding and treat skin irritations**.

13.1.2 Astringent Property

The **astringent property** refers to the ability of a substance to precipitate proteins and cause tissue contraction. This effect can be seen both in topical applications (like skin tightening) and in the mucous membranes of the body (such as the mouth, stomach, or intestines). This activity is primarily associated with phenolic compounds, tannins, and other plant-derived phytochemicals. Astringents are widely used in medicinal formulations for their ability to reduce inflammation, control bleeding, and treat conditions like diarrhoea, wounds, and skin irritations. The mechanism behind this property typically involves:

1. **Protein Precipitation:** Astringent compounds, often tannins or polyphenols, interact with proteins, forming complexes that lead to precipitation. This process reduces secretions and causes tissues to contract.
2. **Tissue Constriction:** When applied to skin or mucous membranes, astringents cause the cells and tissues to constrict, leading to a reduction in moisture, pore size, or inflammation. This property is why astringents are used in products for acne treatment, skin toners, and aftershaves.
3. **Drying Effect:** Astringents help dry out excess oils or fluids from the skin, which is beneficial for controlling oily skin or wounds.

Common Examples of Astringents

- **Tannins** found in tea, wine, and some fruits (like unripe bananas).
- **Witch hazel** is a popular astringent used in skincare products.
- **Alum** and **zinc oxide** are used in wound care for their astringent and antiseptic properties.

13.2 Cost-Effective *In Vitro* Studies

Investigating astringent activity through *in vitro* methods is an economical and ethically favourable approach, particularly for laboratories with limited facilities. Laboratories with basic infrastructure can employ simple and reproducible methods to evaluate astringent activity, including:

1. **Protein Precipitation Assay:** This method measures the ability of test compounds to precipitate proteins, such as bovine serum albumin (BSA). It involves incubating the test sample with a protein solution and quantifying precipitation through spectrophotometry.
2. **Tannin Content Estimation:** Total tannin content, a marker of astringent activity, can be measured using the Folin-Ciocalteu assay to quantifies tannic acid, a primary astringent compound measured at 765 nm. Results are expressed as tannic acid equivalents. This cost-effective method is widely available in basic phytochemical labs.
3. **Polyphenol Content Assay:** The total polyphenol content is determined using the Folin-Ciocalteu reagent. Plant extracts are mixed with the reagent and sodium carbonate, and the absorbance at 765 nm indicates polyphenol concentration, expressed as gallic acid equivalents.
4. **Collagen Contraction Assay:** Collagen-based models are used to assess tissue contraction. This is a low-cost method that evaluates the contraction of collagen gels treated with test compounds. Collagen matrices are prepared and exposed to the sample, and contraction is measured by gel size reduction after incubation.
5. ***In Vitro* Wound Healing Models:** Scratch assays using fibroblast or keratinocyte cell lines are a useful and ethically acceptable way to study tissue regeneration and contraction effects.

13.2.1 Ethical Suitability

In vitro assays avoid the use of animals, aligning with ethical standards while maintaining scientific relevance. These assays focus on simplicity and replicability, making them ideal for small-scale labs or academic setups.

13.2.2 Considerations for Limited Facilities

To maximize output, labs can use readily available reagents and low-cost instruments such as UV-visible spectrophotometers. Collaborative sharing of resources and outsourcing advanced analytical needs can further support research. Each assay requires basic reagents and can be conducted with standard lab tools and is compatible with spectrophotometry, offering valuable insights into astringent properties with minimal investment. Since estimation of total polyphenols and total tannic acid have been discussed in earlier chapters, so to be to be straightforward, standard protocols of the 2 types of *in vitro* astringent activity assays we are discussing in this chapter.

Protein Precipitation and Tightening Effects Assay Protocol

This cost-effective and accessible method evaluates the astringent activity of compounds or phytochemical extracts. The assay measures protein precipitation and simulates tissue-tightening effects, essential features of astringents.

Principle

Astringent compounds interact with proteins, causing them to precipitate and form insoluble complexes. The extent of protein precipitation can be measured spectrophotometrically by monitoring the decrease in protein concentration in the supernatant. A greater reduction in absorbance indicates higher astringent potential.

Protocol – I Spectrophotometry at 660 nm

Astringency is associated with the ability to precipitate proteins. Here's a basic method for assessing astringent activity that measures the absorbance at 660 nm. Otherwise, only protein precipitation can also be monitored as qualitative examination.

Requirements

Materials:

- Bovine serum albumin (BSA) or egg albumin (as a protein source)
- Plant extract or compound (to be tested for astringency)
- 1% Ferric chloride ($FeCl_3$) solution
- Phosphate buffer (pH 6.8)
- Test tubes
- Spectrophotometer (optional)

Methodology

1. **Preparation of Protein Solution:**
    - Dissolve Bovine Serum Albumin (BSA) or egg albumin in phosphate buffer (pH 6.8) to make a 1% (w/v) protein solution.
2. **Preparation of Extract Solution:**
    - Prepare the plant extract or test compound solution at different concentrations in distilled water.
3. **Incubation:**
    - Mix 2 mL of protein solution with 2 mL of the plant extract or test compound in a test tube.

- Incubate the mixture at 37°C for 10–30 minutes, depending on the sensitivity of the protein to precipitation.

4. **Precipitation Detection:**
   - After incubation, add 1 mL of 1% Ferric chloride ($FeCl_3$) solution to each mixture. The formation of a precipitate indicates protein precipitation, which correlates with astringent activity.

5. **Quantification (optional):**
   - If you want to quantify the astringency, centrifuge the mixtures at 3,000 rpm for 10 minutes.
   - Measure the absorbance of the supernatant using a spectrophotometer at 660 nm. A decrease in absorbance suggests a higher level of protein precipitation and thus higher astringency.

Control:

- Use a control containing only protein solution and buffer without any extract to compare the results.

Interpretation

- A greater degree of protein precipitation indicates a stronger astringent property of the test compound or extract.

Protocol – II Spectrophotometry at 280 nm

Astringency is associated with the ability to precipitate proteins. Here's a basic method for assessing astringent activity that measures the absorbance at 280 nm.

Requirements

Materials

- Protein source: Bovine Serum Albumin (BSA) or Egg Albumin.
- Buffer: Phosphate-Buffered Saline (PBS, pH 7.4).
- Test compounds: Plant extracts or synthetic compounds.
- Solvent for extract preparation: Water, ethanol, or acetone.
- UV-Vis spectrophotometer (280 nm).
- Centrifuge.
- Microcentrifuge tubes.
- Pipettes and tips.

Methodology

1. **Preparation of Reagents**
   - Prepare a 1% BSA solution in PBS (1 g of BSA in 100 mL PBS).
   - Prepare test compound or extract solutions in suitable solvents at varying concentrations (e.g., 50, 100, 200 μg/mL).
2. **Protein Precipitation Assay**
   - In a microcentrifuge tube, mix 1 mL of BSA solution with 1 mL of test compound solution.
   - Incubate the mixture at room temperature for 30 minutes.
   - Centrifuge at 10,000 rpm for 10 minutes to pellet the precipitated proteins.
   - Collect the supernatant and measure absorbance at 280 nm using a UV-Vis spectrophotometer.
3. **Controls**
   - **Negative control:** Use PBS without the test compound to measure baseline protein absorbance.
   - **Positive control:** Use a known astringent compound (e.g., tannic acid).

Calculations

The percentage protein precipitation is calculated by comparing the absorbance of the sample with the standard:

$$\text{Protein Precipitation (\%)} = \frac{\text{Abs Control} - \text{Abs Sample}}{\text{Abs control}} \times 100$$

Where:

- **Absorbance of Control:** Absorbance of the negative control (protein without test compound).
- **Absorbance of Sample:** Absorbance of the test sample.

Interpretation

Higher protein precipitation percentages indicate stronger astringent activity. Dose-dependent inhibition provides additional insights into the efficacy of the test compound.

Collagen Contraction Assay Protocol

This protocol evaluates the ability of compounds or phytochemical extracts to enhance collagen contraction, simulating the tightening effect characteristic of astringent activity. The assay involves forming collagen gels and measuring the reduction in gel size upon treatment with test compounds. The protocol here discussed is cost-effective and ideal for *in vitro* studies in resource-limited laboratories.

Principle

Collagen gels mimic the extracellular matrix. Astringent compounds interact with collagen fibrils, promoting gel contraction, which reflects tissue tightening effects. The reduction in gel area or volume after treatment indicates the astringent potential of the test compound or extract.

Requirements

1. **Reagents and Chemicals:**
   - Type I Collagen (e.g., rat-tail collagen)
   - Phosphate-buffered saline (PBS, pH 7.4)
   - NaOH (0.1 M, for neutralizing collagen solution)
   - Test compound or phytochemical extract
   - Distilled water
   - Ethanol (if needed for dissolving the extract)
2. **Equipment:**
   - 24-well or 96-well culture plates
   - Pipettes and micropipettes
   - Incubator maintained at 37°C
   - Ruler or image analysis software (e.g., ImageJ) for measuring gel diameter
   - Analytical balance

Methodology

1. **Preparation of Collagen Gel:**
   - Mix Type I collagen, PBS, and NaOH to adjust the pH to 7.4.
   - Dispense 500 μL of the mixture into each well of a 24-well plate.
   - Allow the gel to polymerize at 37°C for 30–60 minutes.
2. **Treatment with Test Compound:**
   - After polymerization, overlay the gel with 200 μL of test compound solution (prepared in PBS or culture medium).
   - Use different concentrations (e.g., 50, 100, 200 μg/mL).
   - Include controls:

- **Negative control:** PBS or solvent without test compound.
- **Positive control:** Known astringent (e.g., tannic acid).

3. **Incubation:**
   - Incubate the plate at 37°C for 24 hours.
4. **Measurement of Contraction:**
   - After incubation, measure the diameter of the gel in each well manually using a ruler or digitally by capturing images and using imaging software.
   - Record the gel area or diameter.
5. **Calculation of Contraction:**

   The percentage of contraction is calculated using the following formula:

$$(\%)\text{Contraction} = \frac{\text{Initial Gel Area} - \text{Final Gel Area}}{\text{Initial Gel Area}} \times 100$$

   For measurements based on diameter:

$$(\%)\text{Contraction} = \frac{\text{Initial Gel Diameter} - \text{Final Gel}}{\text{Diameter}} \times 100$$

Notes

- Ensure the collagen solution is handled on ice to prevent premature polymerization.
- Maintain consistent gel volumes and initial diameters for accuracy.
- For cell-free assays, ensure the test compound does not directly destabilize collagen to avoid false-positive results.
- Results can be plotted as concentration vs. percentage contraction to determine the IC_{50} (concentration for 50% contraction).

Interpretation

- A higher percentage of contraction indicates stronger astringent activity.
- Dose-dependent activity suggests the compound's efficacy in promoting tissue tightening effects. IC_{50} values provide a comparative measure of the potency of different test compounds or extracts.

Chapter 14

In Vitro Cardioprotective Studies

14.1 Overview of cardioprotective studies using *in vitro* models

Cardiovascular diseases (CVDs) are responsible for a significant number of global deaths, prompting the need for effective and safe therapies. *In vitro* studies offer a cost-effective and ethically suitable approach for screening potential cardioprotective agents. Laboratories with limited resources can conduct several simple assays to evaluate the cardioprotective potential of natural compounds or phytochemical extracts. These assays can assess mechanisms such as lipid peroxidation, antioxidant activity, and clot dissolution, all of which are critical to heart health.

1. **Lipid Peroxidation Assays:**

   Lipid peroxidation is a key mechanism of cellular damage in cardiovascular diseases, leading to the formation of reactive oxygen species (ROS) that can damage cell membranes and tissues. Measuring lipid peroxidation *in vitro* provides insight into the ability of a compound to prevent oxidative stress, which is implicated in heart disease.

   The **Malondialdehyde (MDA) assay** is a commonly used method to measure lipid peroxidation. MDA, a byproduct of lipid peroxidation, reacts with thiobarbituric acid (TBA) to form a pink-coloured complex, which can be quantified using a spectrophotometer. This assay is simple, cost-effective, and requires minimal laboratory equipment. A reduction in MDA levels indicates the potential cardioprotective effect of a compound by inhibiting lipid peroxidation.

2. **Antioxidant Activity Assays:**

   Antioxidants play a critical role in protecting cardiovascular cells from oxidative damage by neutralizing free radicals. Several cost-effective antioxidant activity assays are available, which can be performed using standard laboratory equipment.

   - **DPPH (2,2-Diphenyl-1-picrylhydrazyl) Radical Scavenging Assay**: This assay is one of the simplest and widely used methods to assess the antioxidant potential of compounds. DPPH is a stable free radical that changes colour from purple to yellow when it reacts with an antioxidant. The reduction in absorbance is measured spectrophotometrically, with higher scavenging activity corresponding to stronger antioxidant potential.

   - **ABTS (2,2'-Azino-bis(3-ethylbenzothiazoline-6-sulfonic acid)) Assay**: ABTS radical scavenging is another widely used assay. ABTS reacts with potassium persulfate to generate the ABTS radical cation, which exhibits a green colour. Antioxidants neutralize this radical, leading to a decrease in absorbance. This assay is simple and adaptable for high-throughput screening, making it suitable for laboratories with limited resources.

These assays are inexpensive and easy to perform, requiring only basic reagents and equipment such as a spectrophotometer.

3. **Simple Clot Dissolution Assays:**

   Blood clot formation and thrombosis are major contributors to heart attacks and strokes. *In vitro* clot dissolution assays are important for evaluating the antithrombotic potential of compounds. One of the simplest models involves the use of **fibrinogen and thrombin** to induce clot formation in a test tube.

   - **Fibrin Clot Lysis Assay**: Fibrinogen is mixed with thrombin to form a clot *in vitro*. The clot is then exposed to different concentrations of the test compound, and the degree of clot dissolution is monitored. The clot can be quantified by measuring the absorbance or weight of the remaining clot after a defined period. Compounds that enhance clot dissolution may possess antithrombotic activity, which is beneficial in preventing cardiovascular events.

This assay requires minimal equipment and can be performed using commercially available reagents, making it ideal for laboratories with limited facilities.

Overall, *in vitro* cardioprotective studies using lipid peroxidation assays, antioxidant activity assays (such as DPPH and ABTS), and clot dissolution models provide an effective, low-cost, and ethically sound approach to evaluate the potential of natural compounds or synthetic agents in protecting heart health. These assays are simple, easy to perform, and require minimal equipment, making them ideal for labs with limited resources. By focusing on these basic but informative models, researchers can gain valuable insights into the cardioprotective properties of compounds, contributing to the development of safe, affordable treatments for cardiovascular diseases.

Simple Clot Dissolution Assay Protocol (Weight-Based)

This assay evaluates the thrombolytic or clot-dissolving potential of compounds or phytochemical extracts, which may be indicative of cardioprotective properties. It involves the formation of a fibrin clot and the measurement of clot dissolution upon exposure to the test compound. It provides a quantitative assessment of the cardioprotective potential of the test compounds.

Principle

The fibrinolytic activity is assessed by monitoring the dissolution of a clot formed by fibrinogen in the presence of thrombin. When exposed to a fibrinolytic agent, the clot breaks down, and the extent of dissolution correlates with the thrombolytic or clot-dissolving activity of the compound. When treated with a fibrinolytic agent, these clots dissolve, resulting in a decrease in clot weight. The extent of clot dissolution is calculated by comparing the initial and final weights of the clot, with greater weight loss indicating higher fibrinolytic activity. This is a simple assay to screen for the cardioprotective effects of test substances.

Requirements

Materials

- Fibrinogen (human or bovine fibrinogen).
- Thrombin (human or bovine thrombin).
- Test compounds: Phytochemical extracts or synthetic compounds dissolved in appropriate solvents (e.g., DMSO, ethanol).
- Positive control: Known fibrinolytic agent (e.g., streptokinase, urokinase).
- Negative control: PBS or solvent without test compound.
- Pre-weighed containers (e.g., microcentrifuge tubes, filter paper).
- Weighing balance (sensitive to 0.001 g).
- Water bath or incubator at 37°C.
- Pipettes and sterile tips.

Methodology

1. **Preparation of Reagents**
   - Prepare 1% fibrinogen solution in PBS or saline.
   - Prepare thrombin solution in PBS or saline at a concentration of 0.1–1.0 U/mL.
   - Prepare the test compound solutions in appropriate concentrations (e.g., 10, 50, 100 μg/mL).
2. **Clot Formation**
   - Add 200 μL of fibrinogen solution to a microcentrifuge tube or pre-weighed container.
   - Add 10 μL of thrombin solution to initiate clot formation.
   - Incubate at 37°C for 30–60 minutes to allow the clot to form completely.
   - Carefully aspirate and discard the supernatant without disturbing the clot.
   - Weigh the container with the clot and record the weight (initial clot weight).
3. **Treatment with Test Compounds**
   - Add 200 μL of the test compound solution to the container with the clot.
   - Include a positive control (fibrinolytic agent) and a negative control (PBS or solvent without test compound).
   - Incubate at 37°C for 1–2 hours to allow clot dissolution.

4. Separation and Drying of Clot

- Carefully remove the remaining clot and place it in a pre-weighed drying container (e.g., filter paper or aluminium foil).
- Dry the clot in an oven or desiccator at 37°C until constant weight is achieved (typically 12–24 hours).
- Weigh the dried clot and record the weight (final clot weight).

Calculations

$$\text{Clot Dissolution (\%)} = \frac{\text{Initial Clot Weight} - \text{Final Clot Weight}}{\text{Initial Clot Weight}} \times 100$$

Interpretation

- **Higher percentage clot dissolution** indicates greater fibrinolytic activity and better cardioprotective potential of the test compound.
- **Lower percentage clot dissolution** suggests limited or no fibrinolytic activity.

This weight-based clot dissolution assay is simple, cost-effective, and provides a reliable measure of the fibrinolytic activity of compounds, making it suitable for *in vitro* cardioprotective studies in laboratories with limited resources.

Chapter 15

In Vitro Neuroprotective Activity Assays on a Budget

15.1 Overview of Neuroprotection and Neurodegeneration

Neurodegeneration refers to the progressive loss of structure or function of neurons, often leading to conditions such as Alzheimer's disease, Parkinson's disease, and amyotrophic lateral sclerosis (ALS). These disorders impose a significant global health burden, with rising prevalence due to aging populations. Neurodegeneration involves mechanisms such as oxidative stress, protein misfolding, mitochondrial dysfunction, and neuroinflammation, highlighting the complexity of these conditions.

Neuroprotection aims to preserve neuronal function and prevent further degeneration. This approach focuses on targeting pathways involved in oxidative stress, inflammation, and apoptosis. For instance, antioxidants, anti-inflammatory agents, and mitochondrial stabilizers are being explored as potential neuroprotective therapies. Despite substantial research, developing effective drugs remains challenging due to the complexity of the blood-brain barrier (BBB), which limits drug delivery to the central nervous system.

Drug development in this field faces several hurdles, including high costs, limited translational success from preclinical models to clinical trials, and incomplete understanding of disease mechanisms. Current therapies for neurodegenerative disorders, such as acetylcholinesterase inhibitors for Alzheimer's or dopamine precursors for Parkinson's, primarily offer symptomatic relief rather than halting or reversing disease progression.

Recent advances, such as gene therapy, stem cell approaches, and precision medicine, hold promise for neuroprotection. Additionally, natural compounds with antioxidant and anti-inflammatory properties are gaining attention as cost-effective and safer alternatives. Overcoming these challenges requires an integrated approach, combining innovative technologies with a deeper understanding of neurodegenerative pathways to develop effective, disease-modifying treatments.

15.1.1 Applications in Cognitive Disorders

Cognitive disorders, such as Alzheimer's disease, dementia, and age-associated cognitive decline, are characterized by impairments in memory, attention, and problem-solving abilities. Enzyme inhibition models, including Acetylcholinesterase (AChE), Monoamine Oxidase (MAO), and GABA Transaminase (GABA-T) assays, play a crucial role in the development of therapeutics for these conditions.

- **AChE Inhibitors**: These are widely used in managing Alzheimer's disease. By preventing the breakdown of acetylcholine, AChE inhibitors enhance cholinergic transmission, improving memory and cognitive function.

- **MAO Inhibitors**: Targeting MAO enzymes restores the balance of monoamine neurotransmitters, which is beneficial in treating cognitive decline associated with depression and Parkinson's disease.
- **GABA-T Inhibitors**: By increasing GABA levels, these inhibitors help manage anxiety and epilepsy-related cognitive impairments.

These *in vitro* models provide a cost-effective and ethically suitable approach for identifying potential neuroprotective agents, aiding in the discovery of novel therapies to improve cognitive health.

15.2 Low-cost enzyme inhibition models relevant to neuroprotection

Neurodegenerative diseases, such as Alzheimer's, Parkinson's, and epilepsy, involve complex pathophysiological mechanisms, including enzyme dysregulation. Cost-effective *in vitro* assays provide valuable insights into the neuroprotective potential of compounds by targeting these enzymatic pathways. Laboratories with limited resources can leverage enzyme inhibition models as ethically suitable and low-cost tools for such studies.

1. **Acetylcholinesterase (AChE) Inhibition Assay**

   AChE plays a critical role in degrading acetylcholine, a neurotransmitter essential for learning and memory. Excessive AChE activity is linked to cholinergic dysfunction observed in Alzheimer's disease. The AChE inhibition assay is a widely used *in vitro* model to screen neuroprotective agents.

   - **Principle**: The assay involves using acetylthiocholine as a substrate, which is hydrolyzed by AChE to produce thiocholine. The reaction is detected by a colorimetric method using Ellman's reagent (DTNB), forming a yellow chromophore.
   - **Utility**: A reduction in AChE activity indicates the neuroprotective potential of the test compound.

2. **Monoamine Oxidase (MAO) Inhibition Assay**

   MAO enzymes regulate the breakdown of neurotransmitters like dopamine, serotonin, and norepinephrine. Dysregulated MAO activity contributes to neurodegenerative diseases, including Parkinson's and depression.

   - **Principle**: The assay measures the ability of compounds to inhibit MAO-A or MAO-B activity using substrates like kynuramine. The enzymatic reaction produces hydrogen peroxide or other detectable products.
   - **Utility**: MAO inhibitors can restore neurotransmitter balance, offering therapeutic potential.

3. **GABA Transaminase (GABA-T) Inhibition Assay**

   GABA-T is involved in degrading GABA, an inhibitory neurotransmitter. Dysregulated GABA metabolism is implicated in epilepsy and anxiety disorders.

   - **Principle**: The assay evaluates GABA-T activity using substrates like GABA and measuring reaction byproducts (e.g., succinic semialdehyde) using spectrophotometric or fluorometric methods.

- **Utility**: GABA-T inhibitors enhance GABAergic activity, providing neuroprotective effects.

By targeting key enzymatic pathways, such assays contribute to understanding neurodegenerative mechanisms and identifying therapeutic leads. Each assay requires basic reagents and can be conducted with standard lab tools and is compatible with spectrophotometry, offering valuable insights into neuroprotection and neurodegeneration properties with minimal investment. The standard protocols of these 3 types of enzyme inhibition based *in vitro* assays we are discussing in this chapter.

Acetylcholinesterase (AChE) Inhibition Assay Protocol

This assay evaluates the ability of compounds or phytochemical extracts to inhibit acetylcholinesterase (AChE), an enzyme responsible for breaking down acetylcholine. Inhibition of AChE is linked to neuroprotection and has therapeutic implications for neurodegenerative diseases such as Alzheimer's disease.

Principle

Acetylcholinesterase catalyzes the hydrolysis of acetylcholine into choline and acetate. In this assay, a chromogenic substrate (e.g., acetylthiocholine iodide) reacts with AChE to produce thiocholine, which reacts with 5,5'-dithiobis-(2-nitrobenzoic acid) (DTNB) to form a yellow-coloured product. The intensity of the yellow colour is measured spectrophotometrically, and a decrease in absorbance in the presence of test compounds indicates AChE inhibition.

Requirements

Materials

- Acetylcholinesterase enzyme: Commercially available (e.g., from *Electrophorus electricus* or human recombinant AChE).
- Chromogenic substrate: Acetylthiocholine iodide (ATCI).
- DTNB (Ellman's reagent): 5,5'-dithiobis-(2-nitrobenzoic acid).
- Test compounds: Phytochemical extracts or synthetic compounds dissolved in appropriate solvents (e.g., DMSO, ethanol).
- Positive control: Donepezil, galantamine, or tacrine.
- Phosphate buffer: 0.1 M, pH 8.0.
- 96-well microplate or cuvettes.
- UV-Vis spectrophotometer (405–412 nm) or microplate reader.
- Pipettes and sterile tips.

Methodology

1. Preparation of Reagents

- Prepare AChE enzyme solution in phosphate buffer (0.1 M, pH 8.0).
- Prepare ATCI substrate solution in phosphate buffer (1–2 mM).
- Prepare DTNB solution in phosphate buffer (1 mM).
- Prepare test compound solutions at varying concentrations (e.g., 10, 50, 100 μg/mL).
- Prepare a positive control solution (e.g., galantamine or donepezil).

2. Assay Setup

1. In a 96-well microplate or cuvettes, add the following components:
   - 100 μL of AChE enzyme solution.
   - 50 μL of test compound or positive control.
   - 50 μL of DTNB solution.
2. Pre-incubate the mixture at room temperature for 10–15 minutes to allow interaction between the enzyme and the test compound.

3. Initiation of Reaction

- Add 50 μL of ATCI solution to initiate the reaction.

4. Measurement

- Incubate the mixture at 37°C for 20–30 minutes.
- Measure the absorbance at 405–412 nm using a UV-Vis spectrophotometer.

5. Control and Blank Preparation

- Negative control: Replace the test compound with buffer to measure baseline enzyme activity.
- Blank: Include all components except the enzyme to account for non-enzymatic activity.

Calculations

$$(\%)\,\text{Inhibition of AChE Activity} = \frac{\text{Abs Control} - \text{Abs Sample}}{\text{Abs Control}} \times 100$$

Where:

- Abs Control : Absorbance of the negative control (enzyme without test compound).
- Abs Sample : Absorbance of the test sample with the compound.

Interpretation

- **Higher percentage inhibition** indicates stronger AChE inhibitory activity, suggesting potential neuroprotective effects.
- **Lower percentage inhibition** indicates weaker or no AChE inhibitory activity.

This assay provides a cost-effective, reproducible, and efficient way to screen compounds for neuroprotective potential, making it suitable for *in vitro* studies on phytochemicals or synthetic compounds targeting neurodegenerative conditions.

Monoamine Oxidase (MAO) Inhibition Assay Protocol

This assay measures the ability of a compound or phytochemical extract to inhibit monoamine oxidase (MAO) activity, a key enzyme involved in the breakdown of neurotransmitters such as dopamine, serotonin, and norepinephrine. Assessing MAO inhibition is crucial for exploring neuroprotection and understanding the neurodegenerative potential of test compounds.

Principle

Monoamine oxidase catalyzes the oxidative deamination of monoamine substrates, producing hydrogen peroxide and aldehydes. A chromogenic or fluorogenic substrate (e.g., kynuramine) is used, forming a detectable product measurable via spectrophotometry (UV-Vis) or fluorometry. The presence of an inhibitor reduces product formation, indicating the compound's inhibitory potential.

Requirements

Materials & Equipment

- **MAO enzyme**: Commercially available MAO-A or MAO-B (e.g., from human recombinant sources).
- **Substrate**: Kynuramine or other suitable monoamine substrate.
- **Positive control**: Known MAO inhibitor (e.g., clorgyline for MAO-A, selegiline for MAO-B).
- **Reaction buffer**: 0.1 M phosphate buffer (pH 7.4).
- **Test compounds**: Phytochemical extracts or synthetic compounds dissolved in appropriate solvents (e.g., DMSO).
- **Peroxidase enzyme**: For coupling reactions when using kynuramine.
- **Chromogen**: Amplex Red or 4-aminoantipyrine with phenol, to detect hydrogen peroxide.
- **Microplate:** 96-well plate for high-throughput analysis.
- **Microplate reader:** For absorbance (at ~490 nm) or fluorescence (excitation/emission ~530/590 nm).

- Pipettes and sterile tips.
- Incubator set at 37°C.

Methodology

1. **Preparation of Reagents**
   - **MAO enzyme solution**: Prepare enzyme stock in phosphate buffer (final concentration ~0.5–1.0 U/mL).
   - **Substrate solution**: Prepare kynuramine (0.5–1.0 mM) or alternative substrate in phosphate buffer.
   - **Chromogen solution**: Dissolve Amplex Red or other chromogen in buffer following manufacturer instructions.
   - **Test compounds**: Prepare stock solutions in DMSO and dilute to working concentrations (e.g., 10, 50, 100 μg/mL).
2. **Reaction Setup**
   1. **In each well of a 96-well plate**, add:
      - 50 μL of phosphate buffer (pH 7.4).
      - 20 μL of MAO enzyme solution.
      - 10 μL of test compound or positive control.
      - 10 μL of chromogen solution.
   2. **Pre-incubate at 37°C** for 10 minutes.
   3. Initiate the reaction by adding 10 μL of the substrate solution.
   4. Incubate at 37°C for 30 minutes.
3. **Measurement**
   - Measure absorbance at 490 nm (or fluorescence at excitation/emission ~530/590 nm) using a microplate reader.
   - Record readings for the test compound, positive control, negative control (no inhibitor), and blank (no enzyme).

Calculations

$$(\%)\,\text{Inhibition of MAO Activity} = \frac{\text{Abs Control} - \text{Abs Sample}}{\text{Abs Control}} \times 100$$

Where:

- **Control**: Reaction without inhibitor (baseline activity).
- **Sample**: Reaction with test compound.

Interpretation

- **High inhibition**: Suggests neuroprotective potential by reducing neurotransmitter degradation, beneficial for conditions like Parkinson's or Alzheimer's.
- **Low inhibition**: Indicates limited interaction with MAO enzymes.

Notes

- Ensure solvent concentrations (e.g., DMSO) are uniform and below 1% to avoid interference.
- Use separate assays for MAO-A and MAO-B to identify isoform-specific inhibition.
- This protocol is adaptable for high-throughput analysis and resource-limited laboratories.

GABA Transaminase (GABA-T) Inhibition Assay Protocol

This assay evaluates the ability of a compound or phytochemical extract to inhibit GABA transaminase (GABA-T), the enzyme responsible for degrading gamma-aminobutyric acid (GABA). By inhibiting GABA-T, compounds can potentially enhance GABA levels in the brain, offering neuroprotection and therapeutic potential for neurological disorders like epilepsy and anxiety.

Principle

GABA-T catalyzes the conversion of GABA into succinic semialdehyde (SSA). This reaction requires an acceptor molecule such as α-ketoglutarate. SSA can be detected by coupling with a colorimetric or fluorometric assay that measures downstream products. The presence of a GABA-T inhibitor reduces the formation of SSA, which is quantified spectrophotometrically or fluorometrically.

Requirements

Materials and Equipment

- **GABA-T enzyme**: Commercially available or purified enzyme (e.g., from bovine brain).
- **Substrate**: GABA (gamma-aminobutyric acid).
- **Acceptor**: α-Ketoglutarate (optional cofactor: pyridoxal-5-phosphate).
- **Test compounds**: Phytochemical extracts or synthetic compounds.
- **Positive control**: Known GABA-T inhibitor (e.g., vigabatrin).

- **Reaction buffer**: 50 mM phosphate buffer (pH 8.0).
- **Detection reagent**: NADH for coupled reaction or a derivatizing reagent like 2,4-dinitrophenylhydrazine (DNPH).
- **Microplate**: 96-well plate for high-throughput analysis.
- **Microplate reader**: For absorbance (at 340 nm for NADH or 450–500 nm for DNPH).
- Pipettes and sterile tips.
- Incubator set at 37°C.

Methodology

1. **Preparation of Reagents**
   - **GABA-T enzyme solution**: Prepare stock solution in phosphate buffer (final concentration ~0.1–0.5 U/mL).
   - **Substrate solution**: Dissolve GABA in phosphate buffer (final concentration ~10 mM).
   - **Acceptor solution**: Dissolve α-ketoglutarate in phosphate buffer (final concentration ~5 mM).
   - **Detection reagent**: Prepare NADH (0.2 mM) or DNPH (following manufacturer's instructions).
   - **Test compounds**: Prepare stock solutions in DMSO and dilute to working concentrations (e.g., 10, 50, 100 μg/mL).
2. **Reaction Setup**
   1. In a 96-well plate, add:
      - 50 μL of phosphate buffer (pH 8.0).
      - 20 μL of GABA-T enzyme solution.
      - 10 μL of test compound or positive control.
   2. **Pre-incubate at 37°C** for 10 minutes.
   3. Initiate the reaction by adding:
      - 10 μL of GABA substrate solution.
      - 10 μL of α-ketoglutarate solution.
   4. Incubate the reaction mixture at 37°C for 30 minutes.
3. **Detection**
   1. For NADH-based detection:
      - Add 10 μL of NADH solution to each well.
      - Measure absorbance at 340 nm.

2. For DNPH-based detection:
    - Add DNPH reagent to derivatize SSA.
    - Incubate for 10 minutes at room temperature.
    - Measure absorbance at 450–500 nm.
3. Record readings for the test compound, positive control, negative control (no inhibitor), and blank (no enzyme).

Calculations

$$(\%)\,\text{Inhibition of GABA - T Activity} = \frac{\text{Abs Control} - \text{Abs Sample}}{\text{Abs Control}} \times 100$$

Where:

- **Control**: Reaction without inhibitor (baseline activity).
- **Sample**: Reaction with test compound.

Interpretation

- **High inhibition**: Suggests neuroprotective potential by enhancing GABA levels, which can alleviate conditions like epilepsy or anxiety.
- **Low inhibition**: Indicates limited interaction with GABA-T.

Notes

- Use appropriate blanks to account for background absorbance.
- Ensure uniform solvent concentrations across samples to avoid interference.
- This protocol can be adapted for high-throughput analysis with minimal modifications.

Chapter 16

Anthelmintic and Anti-parasitic Activity Assays

16.1 Overview of Anthelmintic and Anti-parasitic Activity

Anthelmintic and anti-parasitic activity encompasses the ability of compounds or extracts to inhibit or kill parasitic worms (helminths) and protozoans. Helminth infections, such as those caused by *Ascaris*, *Strongyloides*, or *Schistosoma*, and protozoal diseases like malaria (caused by *Plasmodium*), leishmaniasis (*Leishmania spp.*), and giardiasis (*Giardia lamblia*), pose significant global health challenges, particularly in tropical and subtropical regions.

Screening for anthelmintic activity involves *in vitro* models using helminths (e.g., *Pheretima posthuma* or *Haemonchus contortus*), where parameters like motility, paralysis, or death are monitored. For anti-protozoal activity, cell-based assays using host cells infected with protozoa or free-living protozoan cultures help evaluate the inhibition of parasite growth or cytotoxicity.

Protozoan studies often utilize species like *Plasmodium falciparum* or *Trypanosoma cruzi*, focusing on metabolic inhibition or interference with parasite-specific enzymes. Natural compounds, particularly phytochemicals like alkaloids, flavonoids, and terpenoids, have shown promising activity against both helminths and protozoans, offering safer, cost-effective alternatives to synthetic drugs. These assays are affordable and ethically suitable, enabling the identification of potential treatments in resource-limited labs.

16.1.1 Affordable *Pheretima posthuma* Models for Helminth Inhibition Testing

The use of *Pheretima posthuma* (earthworm) models offers a cost-effective and simple approach for evaluating anthelmintic activity. Earthworms share physiological similarities with parasitic helminths, particularly in their muscle and neuromuscular system, making them a reliable substitute for initial testing. In this model, test compounds are applied to *Pheretima posthuma in vitro*, and parameters like paralysis and death are monitored over time. These models are widely used to screen plant extracts, synthetic drugs, and bioactive compounds. The ease of availability, minimal ethical concerns, and straightforward protocols make this model ideal for resource-limited laboratories to assess potential anthelmintic agents.

Anthelmintic Activity Assay Protocol

This protocol evaluates the anthelmintic potential of compounds or phytochemical extracts using earthworms (*Pheretima posthuma* or *Eisenia fetida*), which share physiological similarities with intestinal parasites.

Principle

The test compound or phytochemical extract is assessed for its ability to induce paralysis or death in earthworms. The paralysis is typically associated with the interference of neuromuscular function, while the death is attributed to metabolic disruption or loss of vital physiological functions. Both effects are observed over time. The time to paralysis and death is recorded to assess the potency of the compound.

Requirements

Materials

1. **Earthworms**: *Pheretima posthuma* or *Eisenia fetida*, 5–8 cm in length, 0.2–0.5 cm in width.
2. **Test compounds**: Extracts or synthetic compounds dissolved in suitable solvents (e.g., PBS, water, or DMSO).
3. **Positive control**: Standard anthelmintic drug (e.g., albendazole or piperazine citrate or levamisole).
4. **Negative control**: Solvent without the test compound (e.g., PBS).
5. **Buffers/solutions**: Phosphate-buffered saline (PBS) or physiological saline.
6. **Petri dishes or beakers**: For incubating worms in test solutions.
7. **Forceps**: For handling earthworms.

Equipment

- Timer: For recording the time to paralysis or death.
- Incubator (optional): For maintaining a constant temperature (25–37°C).
- Light microscope (optional) for detailed observations.

Methodology

1. **Preparation of Test Solutions**
    1. Dissolve the test compound in PBS, saline, or appropriate solvent.
    2. Prepare test solutions at varying concentrations (e.g., 10, 50, 100, 200 μg/mL).
    3. Prepare positive and negative control solutions.
2. **Earthworm Collection and Selection**
    1. Collect live and healthy earthworms of uniform size (5–8 cm).
    2. Wash the worms thoroughly with water to remove soil and debris.
    3. Keep the worms in physiological saline until testing.

3. Experimental Setup

1. Divide the worms into groups of 6–8 per test solution, including controls.
2. Place each group in a Petri dish or beaker containing 10–20 mL of the test solution.
3. Maintain one group in the positive control solution and another in the negative control solution.

4. Incubation and Observation

1. Observe the worms for signs of paralysis or death.
   - **Paralysis**: Complete immobility, even when gently stimulated with a needle.
   - **Death**: No movement and a faded or discoloured body.
2. Record the time to paralysis and time to death for each group.
3. Confirm death by transferring the worms to warm water (50°C) for 10 minutes.

Calculations

Percentage Paralysis

$$(\%)\text{Paralysis} = \frac{\text{Number of affected worms}}{\text{Total number of worms tested}} \times 100$$

Percentage Mortality

$$(\%)\text{Mortality} = \frac{\text{Number of dead worms}}{\text{Total number of worms tested}} \times 100$$

Time-based Effectiveness

Calculate the mean time to paralysis and death for each test concentration and compare with controls.

Effective Dose (ED_{50})

Determine the concentration of the test compound that causes 50% mortality or paralysis. The ED_{50} value represents the concentration of the test compound required to cause 50% mortality or paralysis in the worms. This can be calculated using dose-response curves if data points for various concentrations are available.

Interpretation

- **High Anthelmintic Potential**: Lower concentrations and shorter times to paralysis or death.
- **Low Anthelmintic Potential**: Higher concentrations or no significant effect.

Notes

- Ensure the test concentrations are non-toxic to the worms, and do not exceed the necessary range to avoid nonspecific toxicity.

- Maintain consistency in worm size and age to minimize variability in the results.
- Use a sufficient number of worms per test to ensure reliable and statistically significant results.
- Replicates (e.g., n = 3 or more per concentration) are recommended for robust data.
- Perform experiments in triplicate for statistical accuracy.

This simple, cost-effective assay offers a reliable method to screen anthelmintic compounds using easily available earthworms as model organisms.

Chapter 17

Inexpensive Cytotoxicity and Anticancer Activity Assays

In vitro cytotoxicity and anticancer activity assays provide crucial insights into the therapeutic potential of natural and synthetic compounds. For labs with limited facilities, cost-effective methodologies are essential to balance scientific rigor with budget constraints without violating ethical considerations. Simple yet reliable assays, such as MTT, trypan blue exclusion, and sulforhodamine B (SRB) assays, can effectively measure cell viability and proliferation. These methods utilize readily available resources, reducing dependency on high-end equipment. Additionally, cell line models like HeLa or MCF-7, maintained using low-cost culture media, enable systematic screening of compounds. This chapter explores practical approaches to execute cytotoxicity studies in resource-limited settings without compromising accuracy.

17.1 Overview of Cytotoxicity and Anticancer Activity

Cytotoxicity and anticancer activity assays are indispensable tools for evaluating the potential therapeutic effects of compounds. These assays, performed *in vitro* using diverse biological models, allow researchers to assess the efficacy and safety of novel compounds while minimizing costs and ethical complexities. This section provides an overview of cost-effective models, including onion root tips model, microbial systems, chick embryo models, and cancer cell lines, alongside a brief discussion of the limitations of animal and human models.

17.1.1 Antimitotic Activity Using the Onion Root Tip Model

The onion root tip model is a simple, cost-effective, and reliable method for studying antimitotic activity, serving as an alternative to expensive and ethically complex animal or human cell-based systems. The rapidly dividing meristematic cells in the onion (*Allium cepa*) root tips make this model particularly suitable for assessing the effects of potential anticancer agents on the mitotic process.

In this model, onion bulbs are grown in water to develop root tips, which are then exposed to the test compounds. After treatment, the root tips are fixed, stained with dyes like acetocarmine or Feulgen stain, and examined microscopically to analyse mitotic index, chromosomal abnormalities, and mitotic arrest. Compounds causing disruptions such as microtubule destabilization, chromosomal fragmentation, or spindle assembly defects are identified as having potential antimitotic or anticancer activity.

The onion root tip model is relevant to eukaryotic cell systems as the fundamental process of mitosis is highly conserved across plants, animals, and humans. This model has been instrumental in the preliminary screening of plant extracts and synthetic compounds, such as microtubule inhibitors and DNA-damaging agents.

This method is cost-effective, avoids ethical concerns, and offers rapid results, making it an excellent preliminary tool for anticancer drug discovery, especially in resource-limited settings.

17.1.2 Microbial Models: Bacterial, Yeast, and Fungal Systems

Microbial models, including bacteria, yeast, and fungi, are excellent tools for preliminary cytotoxicity screening. These systems are inexpensive, require minimal culture maintenance, and provide rapid results.

- **Bacterial models**: Certain bacterial species, such as *Escherichia coli* and *Bacillus subtilis*, are used to evaluate general cytotoxic effects, often through growth inhibition assays. These methods help determine compound toxicity, though their relevance to eukaryotic systems is limited.
- **Yeast models**: Yeast species like *Saccharomyces cerevisiae* serve as simple eukaryotic models for cytotoxicity studies. Their genetic similarity to higher eukaryotes makes them valuable for understanding the cellular impact of potential anticancer agents. Cytotoxicity in yeast can be assessed using growth curve analysis or viability assays like the methylene blue test.
- **Fungal models**: Filamentous fungi such as *Aspergillus* and *Penicillium* can also be employed to screen compounds for cytotoxic or antifungal activity. They are particularly useful for studies involving natural products. For example, *Aspergillus nidulans*, known for forming bald colonies due to mutations in its regulatory pathways, is a model organism in cytotoxicity studies. Such strains facilitate the assessment of protein kinase inhibitors and natural product-based therapies, providing insights into cellular signaling and compound efficacy. These fungal systems offer robust and versatile platforms for cost-effective cytotoxicity and anticancer screening, particularly for early-stage drug discovery.

17.1.3 Chick Embryo Chorioallantoic Membrane (CAM) Assay

The CAM assay is an *ex vivo* model that offers a cost-effective alternative to mammalian systems for studying anticancer activity and angiogenesis. The chick embryo's chorioallantoic membrane, a vascularized structure, provides an excellent platform for testing the effects of compounds on tumour growth, invasion, and vascularization. Advantages include ease of use, low cost, and reduced ethical considerations compared to animal models. Tumour cells can be implanted on the CAM, and the effects of test compounds are observed through changes in angiogenesis or tumour size. This assay bridges the gap between *in vitro* and *in vivo* studies, making it a valuable intermediate model.

17.1.4 Cancer Cell Line Models

Cancer cell lines represent the gold standard for *in vitro* anticancer studies due to their direct relevance to human diseases. Commonly used lines, such as HeLa (cervical cancer), MCF-7 (breast cancer), A549 (lung cancer), and PC3 (prostate cancer), allow researchers to evaluate compounds for cytotoxicity, apoptosis induction, anti-proliferative effects, and mechanisms of action.

These models employ cost-effective assays like MTT (measuring cell viability based on mitochondrial activity), SRB (assessing total protein content), and trypan blue exclusion (identifying non-viable cells). While these assays are relatively inexpensive, maintaining cancer cell lines requires specialized infrastructure, such as biosafety cabinets, CO_2 incubators, and sterile culture facilities, making these experiments costlier than microbial or plant-based *in vitro* models.

Ready-to-use media (e.g., DMEM or RPMI-1640) and disposable cell culture consumables can lower operational costs, allowing laboratories with modest budgets to undertake these studies. However, the absence of a tumor microenvironment in 2D cell cultures limits the biological relevance of findings.

Despite these challenges, cancer cell line models remain indispensable for early-stage anticancer drug discovery. They provide robust platforms to identify promising compounds before transitioning to more complex 3D cultures, animal models, or clinical studies.

17.2 Limitations of Animal and Human Models

Animal models, such as mice and rats, and human clinical trials are often employed in advanced phases of research for comprehensive toxicity and efficacy evaluation. However, these systems are expensive, require sophisticated facilities, and involve complex ethical considerations. Additionally, results from animal models may not always translate directly to humans. For these reasons, they are not suitable for preliminary cytotoxicity and anticancer activity studies, especially in resource-constrained settings.

Overall, cost-effective cytotoxicity and anticancer assays provide a robust foundation for early-phase drug discovery. Microbial models, chick embryo CAM assays, and cancer cell line studies offer affordable yet reliable platforms for screening novel compounds. By minimizing reliance on costly and ethically complex animal and human studies, these models enable researchers to make significant strides in anticancer research without the need for extensive resources.

In this chapter, we have explored the significance of various *in vitro* and *ex vivo* models for anticancer activity studies, highlighting their cost-effectiveness and relevance in resource-limited laboratory setups. These models, including the Onion Root Tip Model, Microbial Models (Bacterial, Yeast, and Fungal Systems), Chick Embryo Chorioallantoic Membrane (CAM) Assay, and Cancer Cell Line Models, provide versatile and ethical alternatives for early-stage drug discovery. Each model offers unique advantages for evaluating cytotoxicity, mitotic disruption, and anticancer potential. In the following sections, we will discuss detailed protocols for these models, enabling researchers to conduct effective and affordable anticancer activity assays.

Antimitotic Activity Assay Protocol

Onion Root Tip Model

Cancer is characterized by uncontrolled cell division, making mitotic regulation a critical target for anticancer therapies. The Onion Root Tip Model, utilizing the rapidly dividing meristematic cells in onion root tips, offers a simple, reliable, and cost-effective platform to assess the antimitotic potential of compounds. This model is especially valuable for resource-limited laboratories, as it does not require expensive cell culture facilities or complex ethical clearances. By evaluating the effects of test compounds on mitotic activity, this assay provides insights into their potential to disrupt cell division, a hallmark of effective anticancer agents.

Principle

The assay relies on observing the impact of test compounds on the mitotic process in onion root tip cells. Meristematic cells in the root tip exhibit high mitotic activity. When exposed to a potential anticancer compound, these cells may exhibit mitotic inhibition, chromosomal aberrations, or other abnormalities, reflecting the compound's antimitotic and cytotoxic potential. The extent of mitotic inhibition is quantified using the mitotic index, calculated as the percentage of cells undergoing mitosis. This simple approach allows researchers to screen compounds for cytotoxic and anticancer potential in an ethical and economical manner.

Requirements

1. **Biological Material**:
   - Onion bulbs (*Allium cepa*)
2. **Chemicals and Reagents**:
   - Test compound solution
   - Distilled water
   - Acetocarmine stain or Feulgen stain
   - Hydrochloric acid (1 N HCl)
3. **Glassware and Equipment**:
   - Beakers and glass slides
   - Coverslips
   - Forceps and scalpel
   - Compound microscope
   - Dropper
   - Filter paper
4. **Control Setup**:
   - ***Positive control:*** Known antimitotic agent (e.g., colchicine, methotrexate etc.)
   - ***Negative control:*** Distilled water

Methodology

1. **Preparation of Onion Root Tips**:
    - Place onion bulbs in beakers containing distilled water with the roots submerged.
    - Allow root tips to grow 2–3 cm in length at room temperature.
2. **Treatment with Test Compound**:
    - Replace the distilled water with a solution of the test compound at a desired concentration.
    - Incubate for 24 hours. Use distilled water for negative and colchicine or methotrexate or doxorubicin like standard drug for positive controls, respectively.
3. **Fixation**:
    - After treatment, cut approx. 5 to 8 mm length of root tips using a scalpel and fix them in 1 N HCl for 5 minutes to soften the tissues.
4. **Staining**:
    - Transfer the root tips to a watch glass containing acetocarmine stain.
    - Allow staining for 10–15 minutes.
5. **Slide Preparation**:
    - Place the stained root tip on a glass slide, add a drop of distilled water, and gently squash using a coverslip to spread the cells.
    - Remove excess stain using filter paper.
6. **Microscopic Analysis**:
    - Observe the slide under a compound microscope at 40× magnification.
    - Count dividing cells (prophase, metaphase, anaphase, telophase) and non-dividing cells (interphase) in multiple fields.
    - One can match the different stages of the cell division and arrangements of chromosomes with standard images from standard books or web sources.
    - Images of the cells can be taken either by built in camera of microspore or by any mobile phone.

Calculations

1. **Mitotic Index (MI)**:

$$\text{Mitotic Index}(\%) = \frac{\text{Number of dividing cells}}{\text{Total number of cells observed}} \times 100$$

2. Compare the MI of the test compound-treated root tips to controls.
    - A significant decrease in MI indicates antimitotic activity.

- Chromosomal abnormalities can be quantified and recorded for further analysis.

Result Interpretation

- Reduced MI or abnormal mitotic figures (e.g., sticky chromosomes, spindle defects) in treated samples suggest potential anticancer activity.
- The extent of mitotic inhibition can help infer the potency of the test compound.

This simple and cost-effective protocol provides valuable preliminary insights into a compound's antimitotic and anticancer potential, making it a practical choice for resource-limited labs, however, the experiment is tedious and requires skills to get optimum representable results.

Protocol for Growth Inhibition Assay on Bacterial Models

Introduction

Bacterial growth inhibition assays are widely used as an initial screen for cytotoxic effects of potential anticancer compounds. These assays evaluate the impact of test compounds on bacterial proliferation, offering insights into their general toxicity. While bacterial models like *Escherichia coli* (a Gram-negative bacterium) and *Bacillus subtilis* (a Gram-positive bacterium) are not directly representative of eukaryotic systems, they provide a cost-effective, rapid, and reproducible method for preliminary toxicity studies.

Principle

This assay measures the inhibitory effect of a test compound on the growth of bacterial cultures. Bacterial cells are grown in the presence and absence of the test compound, and the growth is monitored by measuring the optical density (OD) at 600 nm using a colorimeter of a spectrophotometer. A decrease in OD relative to the control indicates growth inhibition, reflecting the compound's cytotoxic effects.

Requirements

1. **Biological Material**:
   - *Escherichia coli* (Gram-negative)
   - *Bacillus subtilis* (Gram-positive)

   Bacterial cultures can be procured from reliable culture collections such as the American Type Culture Collection (ATCC), Microbial Type Culture Collection and Gene Bank (MTCC), or the National Collection of Industrial Microorganisms (NCIM). Ensure that the cultures are authenticated and free from contamination before use in experiments.
2. **Chemicals and Reagents**:
   - Test compound solution

- Luria-Bertani (LB) broth or Nutrient broth
- Sterile distilled water
- Antibiotic or standard cytotoxic compound (e.g., ampicillin, tetracycline, methotrexate or doxorubicin) as a positive control.
- 70% ethanol (for sanitization, wiping and maintaining aseptic environment)

3. **Equipment**:
   - Laminar air flow cabinet and other microbiology lab set ups
   - Colorimeter or Spectrophotometer (set at 600 nm)
   - Sterile test tubes
   - Micropipettes and sterile tips
   - Incubator (37°C)
4. **Control Setup**:
   - Positive control: Known cytotoxic compound or antibiotic
   - Negative control: Untreated bacterial culture

Methodology

1. **Preparation of Bacterial Cultures**:
   - Inoculate *E. coli* and *B. subtilis* in separate flasks containing LB broth.
   - Incubate overnight at 37°C with shaking (120–150 rpm) to achieve mid-log phase growth. One can do it without shaking if shaking incubator is not available.
2. **Dilution and Test Setup**:
   - Dilute the overnight cultures to an OD of 0.1 at 600 nm (approximately 10^6 CFU/ mL).
   - Aliquot 1 mL of the diluted culture into sterile test tubes.
3. **Addition of Test Compound**:
   - Add the test compound at different concentrations (e.g., 10, 50, 100 μg/mL) to the test tubes.
   - Include one tube with an antibiotic of cytotoxic compound as a positive control and another with no compound as a negative control.
4. **Incubation**:
   - Incubate all tubes at 37°C for 18–24 hours with shaking.
   - Intermittent shaking can be done in case if shaking incubator is not available.

5. **Growth Measurement**:
    - Measure the OD at 600 nm using a spectrophotometer after incubation.

Calculations

1. **Percent Growth Inhibition**:

$$\text{Growth Inhibition}(\%) = \frac{\text{OD of Control} - \text{OD of Treated}}{\text{OD of Control}} \times 100$$

2. **Interpretation**:
    - A high percentage of growth inhibition indicates strong cytotoxicity of the test compound.
    - Compare the effects on *E. coli* and *B. subtilis* to assess Gram-specific differences in cytotoxicity.

Result Interpretation

- Compounds showing significant growth inhibition in both *E. coli* and *B. subtilis* may exhibit broad-spectrum cytotoxicity.
- Differences in inhibition between the two models can indicate selectivity based on cell wall composition (Gram-positive vs. Gram-negative).

Aseptic Techniques and Cross-Contamination Prevention

It is essential to maintain strict aseptic techniques throughout the procedure to ensure the validity of results and prevent cross-contamination. All bacterial cultures and reagents should be handled in a sterile environment, ideally under a laminar air flow cabinet. Use sterile equipment such as pipettes, test tubes, and petri dishes, and always wear gloves and appropriate personal protective equipment (PPE). This minimizes the risk of contamination and ensures that the observed effects on bacterial growth are solely due to the test compound. Proper sterilization of media, culture vessels, and working surfaces is crucial to avoid external microbial interference.

This assay offers a straightforward and economical approach to initial cytotoxicity screening, making it a valuable tool for resource-limited labs focusing on anticancer drug discovery.

Yeast Proliferation Inhibition Assay Protocol

Introduction

The yeast *Saccharomyces cerevisiae* serves as a valuable model for anticancer studies due to its eukaryotic cellular structure, genetic similarity to human cells, and ease of cultivation. Anti-proliferation assays using yeast provide an inexpensive, ethical, and effective platform for determining compound toxicity before proceeding to complex systems.

Principle

The assay is based on the ability of a test compound to inhibit the growth of *S. cerevisiae*. The growth rate is assessed spectrophotometrically by measuring optical density (OD) at 600 nm. A decrease in OD compared to controls indicates inhibition of yeast proliferation, reflecting the cytotoxic or anti-proliferative effects of the compound.

Requirements

- **Biological material:**
  - *Saccharomyces cerevisiae* culture (procured from MTCC, NCIM, or ATCC)
- **Reagents and chemicals:**
  - YPD broth (Yeast extract, Peptone, Dextrose)
  - Phosphate-buffered saline (PBS, pH 7.4)
  - Test compound (dissolved in DMSO or water)
  - Sterile distilled water
  - Positive control (e.g., Amphotericin B or an established cytotoxic agent)
  - Negative control (untreated culture)
- **Equipment:**
  - Laminar airflow cabinet
  - Autoclave
  - Microplate reader or spectrophotometer (600 nm)
  - Incubator shaker (30°C)
  - Sterile culture tubes or 96-well plates
  - Pipettes and sterile tips

Methodology

1. **Preparation of Yeast Culture:**
   - Inoculate *S. cerevisiae* in YPD broth and incubate overnight at 30°C in a shaker incubator (150 rpm) until the culture reaches the exponential growth phase.
   - Adjust the culture to an OD_{600} of 0.1 using sterile PBS.
2. **Test Compound Preparation:**
   - Prepare serial dilutions of the test compound in sterile water or DMSO to obtain different concentrations. Ensure that the DMSO concentration does not exceed 1% in the final setup.

3. **Assay Setup:**
   - In a 96-well plate, add the following:
     - 100 μL of adjusted yeast culture to each well.
     - 100 μL of the test compound at various concentrations.
     - Include wells for the positive control, negative control, and solvent control.
   - Mix gently and incubate the plate at 30°C for 24–48 hours.
4. **Growth Measurement:**
   - Measure the OD_{600} at 0 hours (baseline reading).
   - After the incubation period, measure the OD600 again to assess growth inhibition.

Calculation:

Calculate the percentage inhibition of growth using the formula:

$$\text{Growth Inhibition}(\%) = \frac{\text{OD of Control} - \text{OD of Sample}}{\text{OD of Control}} \times 100$$

- OD Control is the optical density of the negative control (untreated).
- OD Sample is the optical density of the test sample.

Precautions:

- Ensure aseptic conditions by working under a laminar air flow cabinet.
- Verify the sterility of media and reagents to avoid contamination.
- Perform all experiments in triplicates for accuracy.

This assay provides an economical and straightforward method to screen potential anticancer compounds by evaluating their cytotoxic effects on yeast proliferation.

Yeast Cell Viability Assay Protocol

Introduction

Methylene blue staining of yeast cell is a quick, cost-effective, and reliable method for assessing cell viability. Viable yeast cells exclude the dye due to intact cell membranes, whereas non-viable cells take up the dye and appear blue under a microscope. This assay is useful for studying the cytotoxicity of potential anticancer agents.

Principle

When yeast cells are treated with methylene blue, only cells with damaged membranes (non-viable cells) absorb the dye and appear blue under a microscope. Viable cells, with intact membranes, remain unstained or faintly stained. This method differentiates between viable and non-viable yeast cells based on their ability to exclude the dye. This differential staining enables quantification of live and dead cells, providing insights into the cytotoxicity of test compounds.

Requirements

- **Biological Material:**
  - *Saccharomyces cerevisiae* culture (from MTCC, NCIM, or ATCC)
- **Reagents and Chemicals:**
  - YPD broth (Yeast extract, Peptone, Dextrose)
  - Phosphate-buffered saline (PBS, pH 7.4)
  - Methylene blue solution (0.01% w/v in PBS)
  - Test compound (dissolved in DMSO or water)
  - Positive control (e.g., Amphotericin B or an established cytotoxic agent)
  - Negative control (untreated culture)
- **Equipment:**
  - Laminar air flow cabinet
  - Autoclave
  - Incubator shaker (30°C)
  - Centrifuge
  - Hemocytometer or Neubauer chamber
  - Light microscope

Methodology

1. **Preparation of Yeast Culture:**
   - Inoculate *S. cerevisiae* in YPD broth and incubate overnight at 30°C in a shaker incubator (150 rpm).
   - Adjust the culture to an OD_{600} of 0.1 using sterile PBS.
2. **Test Compound Treatment:**
   - Divide the yeast culture into aliquots and treat with the test compound at different concentrations.

- Include controls:
    - Positive control (to induce cell death).
    - Negative control (untreated culture).
    - Solvent control (if DMSO is used for the test compound).
- Incubate the treated samples at 30°C for 24 hours.

3. **Centrifugation and Washing:**
    - Centrifuge the samples at 3000 rpm for 5 minutes and discard the supernatant.
    - Wash the cells twice with PBS to remove residual compounds.
4. **Staining with Methylene Blue:**
    - Resuspend the yeast pellet in 100 μL of 0.01% methylene blue solution.
    - Incubate at room temperature for 2 minutes.
5. **Observation and Counting:**
    - Place 10 μL of the stained suspension on a clean glass slide.
    - Cover with a coverslip and observe under a light microscope at 40x magnification.
    - Use a hemocytometer or Neubauer chamber for cell counting.
    - Count the number of blue-stained (non-viable) and unstained (viable) cells in multiple fields.
6. **Calculation:**
    - Calculate the percentage of non-viable cells using the formula:

$$\text{Non - viable cell}\,(\%) = \frac{\text{Number of blue stained cells}}{\text{Total cell counted}} \times 100$$

Precautions:

- Maintain aseptic conditions using a laminar air flow cabinet to avoid contamination.
- Prepare methylene blue solution fresh to ensure staining quality.
- Perform the assay in triplicates for reliable results.

This simple and economical assay provides a direct measure of yeast cell viability and cytotoxic effects of compounds, offering insights into their potential anticancer activity.

Protein Kinase Inhibition Assay Protocol

Introduction to *Aspergillus nidulans* Bald Colony Model

Protein kinases regulate critical signalling pathways in cell growth and division. Aberrant kinase activity is often implicated in cancer progression. *A. nidulans*, a filamentous fungus, serves as a convenient eukaryotic model for studying protein kinase inhibition. This model exploits the characteristic development of altered aerial mycelia or "bald" colonies when kinase signalling pathways involved in hyphal growth and conidiation are disrupted. Mutations or kinase inhibitors affecting conidiation pathways in *A. nidulans* result in bald colonies, making it a visual and functional system for preliminary screening of kinase inhibitors.

Principle

Kinase inhibitors disrupt signalling pathways controlling hyphal growth and sporulation in *A. nidulans*. In the presence of such inhibitors, colonies fail to develop normal aerial hyphae and conidiation structures, appearing bald. The extent of colony baldness can be quantified to infer the inhibitory effect of the compound.

Requirements

- **Biological Material:**
    - *Aspergillus nidulans* strain (mutant or wild type capable of showing bald phenotype under kinase inhibition, available from MTCC or other culture banks).
- **Reagents and Media:**
    - Glucose minimal medium (GMM) or complete medium (CM) agar plates.
    - Test compound (dissolved in DMSO or other suitable solvent).
    - Positive control (known kinase inhibitor, e.g., staurosporine).
    - Negative control (untreated fungal culture).
    - Solvent control (if DMSO is used).
- **Equipment:**
    - Laminar air flow cabinet.
    - Autoclave.
    - Incubator (28–30°C).
    - Sterile petri plates and pipettes.
    - Stereomicroscope (optional for detailed observation).

Methodology

1. **Preparation of Fungal Culture:**
   - Inoculate *A. nidulans* spores in liquid CM and incubate at 28°C for 16–24 hours to obtain active mycelia.
   - Prepare GMM or CM agar plates and allow them to solidify.
2. **Test Compound Preparation:**
   - Prepare serial dilutions of the test compound in suitable solvent (e.g., sterile distilled water or DMSO) to achieve desired concentrations.
3. **Plate Inoculation:**
   - Spot-inoculate *A. nidulans* spores (approximately 10^4 spores per spot) on the prepared agar plates.
   - Apply the test compound directly onto the agar or mix it into the medium before solidification.
4. **Controls:**
   - ***Positive control:*** Plates with known kinase inhibitor.
   - ***Negative control:*** Untreated spores on the medium.
   - ***Solvent control:*** Spores with solvent only (e.g., DMSO).
5. **Incubation:**
   - Incubate the plates at 28–30°C for 48–72 hours.
   - Observe colony morphology and the presence or absence of aerial mycelia and conidiation structures.
6. **Observation and Documentation:**
   - Record the development of bald colonies (absence of aerial mycelia and conidia).
   - Use a stereomicroscope for detailed observation, if necessary.
   - One can take the images of the colony morphology with camera or any mobile phone.
7. **Quantification:**
   - Measure the colony diameter and record the percentage of colonies showing bald phenotypes.
   - Score baldness severity (e.g., 0 = normal, 1 = partial baldness, 2 = complete baldness).

Calculations

- Calculate the percentage of bald colonies:

$$\text{Bald Colony (\%)} = \frac{\text{Number of bald colonies}}{\text{Total colonies observed}} \times 100$$

- Determine the inhibition concentration (IC_{50}) of the test compound if a dose-response curve is generated.

Precautions:

Maintain aseptic conditions throughout the experiment to prevent contamination, particularly during inoculation and preparation of media. Perform all steps in a laminar air flow cabinet to ensure sterility and reproducibility.

This assay provides a visual and quantitative approach to evaluate the kinase inhibition potential of compounds. The *A. nidulans* bald colony model is a cost-effective and ethical method, bridging basic research and drug discovery in anticancer studies.

Chorioallantoic Membrane (CAM) Assay Protocol

Introduction

The CAM assay is a widely used *ex vivo* model sometimes considered as *in vivo* model to study angiogenesis, tumour growth, and metastasis. Most precisely it is referred as *in ovo* model. The highly vascularized CAM provides a conducive environment to observe neovascularization and the effects of test compounds on vascular and tumour tissues. This method is cost-effective, rapid, and does not involve ethical concerns associated with mammalian models.

Principle

The CAM of a developing chick embryo supports angiogenesis, essential for embryonic development. A compound with anticancer properties may inhibit or disrupt blood vessel formation (anti-angiogenic effect) or reduce tumor size and proliferation. The assay evaluates these effects by treating the CAM with the test compound and analysing changes in vasculature or tumour tissue. This protocol is focused on anti- angiogenic activity of samples.

Requirements

- **Biological Material:**
    - Fertilized chicken eggs (preferably 8–10 days old).
    - Can be sourced from local villages or chicken farms
- **Reagents and Materials:**
    - Test compound (diluted in PBS, DMSO, or suitable solvent).
    - Positive control (e.g., known anti-angiogenic drug like thalidomide).
    - Negative control (PBS or solvent only).
- **Equipment:**
    - Incubator (37°C, with controlled humidity).

- Sterile forceps and scissors.
- Micropipette with sterile tips.
- Laminar air flow cabinet.
- Stereomicroscope or digital camera for observation and documentation.

Methodology

1. **Pre-Experimental Preparations**
    - Before setting up the experiment, all glassware must be thoroughly cleaned, dried, and sterilized by autoclaving following standard procedures. The working area was disinfected by wiping surfaces with 70% ethanol to maintain a contamination-free environment, essential for culturing chick embryos. Such precautions are crucial to minimize the risk of contamination-induced abnormalities or mortality in embryos, which could otherwise compromise experimental outcomes.
2. **Preparation of Fertilized Eggs:**
    - On Day 0, disinfect the eggshells with 70% ethanol to prevent
    - Incubate fertilized eggs at 37°C with 60–70% humidity for 48 hours
    - Placing the eggs horizontally for 15–20 minutes before the culturing process ensures the embryo's position is correctly aligned at the top. Sterile handling techniques, including wiping hands with 70% ethanol, were maintained throughout. Eggs were transferred to an incubator to continue development under sterile conditions.
    - On Day 8, clean the eggshell surface with 70% ethanol.
3. **Albumin Removal:**
    - After 48 hours, carefully pierce a small hole at the lower side of each egg using a sterile needle.
    - Remove approximately 2 mL of albumin gently using a sterile syringe to separate the CAM from the eggshell. Seal the pierced hole with sterile laboratory tape.
4. **Window Creation:**
    - On Day 3, create a small window (~1–2 cm) was on the blunt end of the eggshell by carefully removing a portion of the shell.
    - Confirm the viability and normal development of the embryo under sterile conditions.
5. **Application of Test Compound:**
    - Prepare serial dilutions of the test compound in PBS or DMSO.
    - Apply 10–20 μL or 100 μL (as per the requirement of your experimental design and dosing) of the test solution directly onto the CAM at a predefined spot using a micropipette.

1. **Controls:**
   - ***Positive control:*** Apply a known anti-angiogenic compound.
   - ***Negative control:*** Apply PBS or solvent only.
2. **Incubation:**
   - Seal the window after dosing with sterile parafilm or adhesive tape to maintain sterility.
   - Return the eggs to the incubator for an additional 24–72 hours for incubation.
3. **Observation and Documentation:**
   - After incubation, examine the CAM under a stereomicroscope to evaluate blood vessel branching points.
   - Record changes in vasculature (e.g., reduced vessel density, disrupted vessel morphology).
   - Reduction in the number of branch points compared to the control group would be recorded as evidence of antiangiogenic activity.

Calculations

1. **Angiogenesis Inhibition:**
   - Count the number of blood vessels in treated vs. control areas.

$$\text{Vessel Inhibition}(\%) = \frac{\text{Vessel count in control} - \text{Vessel count in treated}}{\text{Vessel count in control}} \times 100$$

Or

   - Count the number of branch points in treated vs. control areas.

$$\text{Inhibition}(\%) = \frac{\text{Branch points in control} - \text{Branch points in treated}}{\text{Branch points in control}} \times 100$$

2. **Statistical Analysis:**
   - Data from treated and control groups were compared using statistical software for significance testing (e.g., t-tests or ANOVA).

The CAM assay is an effective and ethical alternative to mammalian models for studying angiogenesis and anticancer effects. Its cost-effectiveness and simplicity make it a valuable tool for early-stage drug screening. However, it requires, precision skills in handling.

Anticancer Activity by MTT Assay Protocol

Introduction

The MTT assay is a colorimetric assay widely used to assess the viability and proliferation of cells. It evaluates the ability of viable cells to convert MTT (a yellow tetrazolium salt) into formazan crystals, which are purple in colour, via mitochondrial enzymes. This assay is a cost-effective, reliable method for determining the cytotoxic and anticancer potential of test compounds in cell line models.

Principle

MTT ([3-(4,5-dimethylthiazol-2-yl)-2,5-diphenyltetrazolium bromide]) is reduced by metabolically active cells into insoluble purple formazan crystals by the mitochondrial dehydrogenase enzyme. Dead or non-viable cells cannot perform this reduction. The intensity of the purple colour is proportional to the number of viable cells and can be quantified spectrophotometrically after dissolving the formazan crystals.

Requirements

Biological Material

- Cancer cell lines (e.g., HeLa, MCF-7, A549, PC3, etc.)

Reagents and Chemicals

- MTT reagent (5 mg/mL in PBS)
- Dimethyl sulfoxide (DMSO)
- Dulbecco's Modified Eagle Medium (DMEM) or other suitable media for the cell line
- Fetal Bovine Serum (FBS)
- Antibiotic solution (penicillin-streptomycin)
- Test compound (prepared at different concentrations)
- Phosphate-Buffered Saline (PBS)

Equipment

- CO_2 incubator (37°C, 5% CO_2)
- Biosafety cabinet (laminar air flow)
- 96-well flat-bottom culture plates
- Inverted phase-contrast microscope
- Microplate reader (570 nm wavelength)
- Sterile micropipettes and tips

Methodology

1. Pre-Experimental Preparations

- All procedures must be conducted aseptically under a laminar air flow cabinet to avoid contamination.

- Sterilize all equipment and ensure proper sterilization of the working environment by cleaning with 70% ethanol.

2. Cell Culture and Seeding

1. Thaw the cancer cell line and culture in DMEM supplemented with 10% FBS and 1% penicillin-streptomycin.
2. Incubate the cells at 37°C in a 5% CO_2 atmosphere until 70–80% confluency is reached.
3. Harvest the cells by trypsinization, centrifuge, and resuspend in fresh media.
4. Seed 1×10^4 cells/well into a 96-well plate in 100 μL of media.
5. Incubate the plate for 24 hours to allow cell attachment.

3. Treatment with Test Compounds

1. Prepare serial dilutions of the test compound in media (e.g., 10 μM, 25 μM, 50 μM, 100 μM).
2. Replace the old medium with 100 μL of medium containing the test compound in the respective wells.
3. Include controls:
   - ***Negative control:*** Media without the test compound.
   - ***Positive control:*** A known cytotoxic agent (e.g., doxorubicin).
4. Incubate the plate for 24–48 hours under the same conditions.

4. MTT Assay

1. After incubation, add 10 μL of MTT solution (5 mg/mL in PBS) to each well.
2. Incubate for 3–4 hours at 37°C in the dark to allow formazan formation.
3. Carefully remove the supernatant without disturbing the cells.
4. Add 100 μL of DMSO to each well to dissolve the formazan crystals.
5. Gently shake the plate for 10 minutes to ensure complete dissolution.

5. Measurement of Absorbance

1. Measure the absorbance at 570 nm using a microplate reader.
2. Record the values for all wells, including controls.

Calculations

1. Cell Viability (%):

$$\text{Cell Viability (\%)} = \frac{\text{Absorbance of Treated Cells}}{\text{Absorbance of Control Cells}} \times 100$$

2. Cytotoxicity (%):

$$\text{Cytotoxicity (\%)} = 100 - \text{Cell Viability (\%)}$$

3. **IC_{50} Determination**:
   - Plot the % cytotoxicity against the logarithmic concentration of the compound.
   - Determine the IC_{50} (concentration causing 50% inhibition) using non-linear regression or interpolation.

Anticancer Activity by SRB Assay Protocol

The SRB assay (Sulforhodamine B assay) is a colorimetric method to evaluate cell proliferation and cytotoxicity by measuring total cellular protein content. It is widely used to determine the anticancer potential of test compounds on cell lines.

Principle

SRB is a bright pink aminoxanthene dye that binds electrostatically to basic amino acid residues in cellular proteins under acidic conditions. The amount of dye retained by the cells after washing reflects the cellular protein content and is proportional to the number of viable cells. Absorbance measurement quantifies the effect of the test compound on cell proliferation or cytotoxicity.

Requirements

1. **Biological Materials**
   - Cell lines: Suitable cancer cell lines (e.g., MCF-7 for breast cancer, HT-29 for colorectal cancer).
   - Cell culture medium: DMEM or RPMI-1640 supplemented with 10% FBS.
   - Trypsin-EDTA for cell detachment.
2. **Reagents**
   - SRB dye (0.4% in 1% acetic acid).
   - 1% Acetic acid (for washing).
   - 10% Trichloroacetic acid (TCA) for protein precipitation.
   - 10 mM Tris base (pH 10.5) for dye solubilization.
3. **Equipment**
   - 96-well flat-bottom microplates.
   - CO_2 incubator.
   - Microplate reader (absorbance at 515 nm).
   - Pipettes and sterile tips.
   - Laminar airflow hood.
4. **Test Compounds**
   - Serial dilutions of the compound in DMSO or culture medium.

Methodology

1. **Cell Seeding**
   - Seed 5,000–10,000 cells/well in 96-well plates with 100 μL of complete growth medium.
   - Incubate overnight at 37°C in a CO_2 incubator for cell adherence.
2. **Treatment**
   - Replace medium with 100 μL of fresh medium containing serial dilutions of the test compound.
   - Include control wells (untreated cells, vehicle control, and blank medium).
   - Incubate for 48–72 hours at 37°C in a CO_2 incubator.
3. **Fixation**
   - After incubation, add 50 μL of ice-cold 10% TCA to each well.
   - Incubate at 4°C for 1 hour to precipitate proteins.
4. **Washing**
   - Wash wells 3–5 times with 1% acetic acid to remove unbound compounds and medium.
   - Air dry the plate at room temperature.
5. **Staining**
   - Add 100 μL of 0.4% SRB solution to each well.
   - Incubate at room temperature for 30 minutes.
6. **Washing and Dye Solubilization**
   - Wash wells with 1% acetic acid to remove unbound dye.
   - Air dry the plate completely.
   - Add 200 μL of 10 mM Tris base to each well to solubilize the protein-bound dye.
   - Shake the plate gently for 5–10 minutes.
7. **Measurement**
   - Measure absorbance at 515 nm using a microplate reader.

Calculations

Percentage Cell Viability:

$$\%\text{Cell Viability} = \frac{\text{OD of Treated Wells}}{\text{OD of Control Wells}} \times 100$$

- **Percentage Growth Inhibition**:

$$\% \text{ Inhibition} = 100 - \%\text{Cell Viability}$$

- **IC_{50} Determination**:
- Plot the % cytotoxicity against the logarithmic concentration of the compound.
- Determine the IC_{50} (concentration causing 50% inhibition) using non-linear regression or interpolation.

The SRB assay is a cost-effective and highly sensitive method for screening potential anticancer agents that provides reliable data on cell proliferation and cytotoxicity.

Trypan Blue Exclusion Assay Protocol

The Trypan Blue exclusion assay is a simple and widely used method to evaluate cell viability, based on the principle that live cells with intact cell membranes exclude the dye, whereas dead cells with compromised membranes absorb the dye. This assay is commonly used to determine the cytotoxicity of test compounds in cell line models for anticancer studies.

Principle

Trypan Blue is a vital stain that is excluded by viable cells but is absorbed by cells with damaged membranes (i.e., non-viable cells). The number of viable cells can be quantified by counting the unstained cells, while dead cells can be identified by the blue staining. The ratio of viable to total cells indicates the cytotoxic effect of a compound.

Requirements

1. **Biological Materials**
    - Cell lines: Cancer cell lines (e.g., MCF-7, HT-29, A549).
    - Cell culture medium: DMEM or RPMI-1640 supplemented with 10% FBS.
    - Trypsin-EDTA for cell detachment.
2. **Reagents**
    - Trypan Blue solution (0.4% in PBS or saline).
    - Phosphate-buffered saline (PBS) or saline for cell washing.
3. **Equipment**
    - Hemocytometer or automated cell counter.
    - 96-well plate or culture flask.
    - Pipettes and sterile tips.

- Laminar airflow hood.
- Centrifuge (optional, for cell pellet).
- Incubator at 37°C with 5% CO_2.

4. **Test Compound**
   - Serial dilutions of the test compound dissolved in appropriate solvent (e.g., DMSO, PBS, or culture medium).

Methodology

1. **Cell Seeding**
   - Seed 1–2 × 10^5 cells in a 6-well plate or a suitable culture flask in 2 mL of complete growth medium.
   - Incubate the cells overnight at 37°C in a CO_2 incubator to allow them to adhere.
2. **Treatment**
   - Replace the medium with fresh medium containing serial dilutions of the test compound.
   - Include control wells with untreated cells and vehicle control.
   - Incubate for 24–72 hours, depending on the compound's expected effect.
3. **Cell Harvesting**
   - After incubation, collect the cells by trypsinization (use 0.25% trypsin-EDTA) and neutralize with culture medium containing FBS.
   - Centrifuge the cells at 1500 rpm for 5 minutes, if necessary, to form a pellet.
   - Resuspend the cell pellet in PBS or culture medium.
4. **Trypan Blue Staining**
   - Mix an equal volume of the cell suspension (100 μL) with 100 μL of 0.4% Trypan Blue solution.
   - Incubate for 2–5 minutes at room temperature.
5. **Cell Counting**
   - Load 10 μL of the stained cell suspension onto a hemocytometer or use an automated cell counter.
   - Count both the blue-stained (dead) and unstained (live) cells under a microscope.
   - Count cells in at least 4 quadrants for accuracy.

Calculations

1. **Cell Viability Percentage**:

$$\% \text{ Viability} = \frac{\text{Total number of live cells}}{\text{Total number of cells (live + dead)}} \times 100$$

2. **Cytotoxicity (Inhibition) Percentage**:

$$\% \text{ Cytotoxicity} = 100 - \% \text{ Viability}$$

Alternatively, the cytotoxicity can also be calculated as:

$$\% \text{ Cytotoxicity} = \frac{\text{Number of dead cells in treated group}}{\text{Number of dead cells in control group}} \times 100$$

The Trypan Blue exclusion assay is a reliable and simple method for evaluating cell viability and cytotoxicity in response to a potential anticancer compound. It is particularly useful for testing low-cost compounds or crude extracts.

Endnote

Cell Line Protocols and Anticancer and Cytotoxicity Assays Considerations

- ✓ All experiments were conducted under aseptic conditions in a biosafety cabinet to maintain the sterility of cell cultures, reagents, and media, ensuring the reliability of the results and minimizing the risk of contamination.
- ✓ Various cancer cell lines, including MCF-7 (breast cancer), A549 (lung cancer), HeLa (cervical cancer), HCT-116 (colorectal cancer), and SCC-9 (oral fibroblast), were cultured in DMEM supplemented with 10% FBS and 1% antibiotics. Cells were seeded at 1×10^4 cells/well, maintained at 37°C in 5% CO_2, and the media was refreshed every 48 hours. These cell lines serve as representative models to evaluate anticancer activity across different cancer types.
- ✓ Normal cell lines, such as L929 (mouse fibroblasts), HEK-293 (human embryonic kidney cells), and WI-38 (human lung fibroblasts), were cultured in DMEM supplemented with 10% FBS and 1% antibiotics. Cells were seeded at 1×10^4 cells/well, maintained at 37°C in 5% CO_2, with media changes every 48 hours. These normal cell lines are used to evaluate the cytotoxicity of compounds, ensuring that the compounds are safe for healthy cells while showing efficacy against cancer cells.
- ✓ The MTT, SRB, and Trypan Blue exclusion assays provide effective, reproducible, and non-invasive methods for assessing cell viability and cytotoxicity.
- ✓ Cell line experiments are highly efficient for evaluating the anticancer and cytotoxic potential of extracts or compounds, providing accurate and reproducible results that closely mimic human cellular responses. Unlike animal models, these studies do not pose ethical challenges, making them a preferred choice. However, the experimental procedures and laboratory setups, including cell culture facilities, specialized equipment, and reagents, are relatively costlier compared to alternative methods discussed.

Chapter 18

Basic Toxicological and Safety Screening Techniques

Toxicological and safety screening techniques are pivotal in the early stages of product development to ensure safety for humans, animals, and the environment. This chapter explores fundamental methodologies for conducting toxicological evaluations while adhering to ethical principles and minimizing reliance on mammalian models.

A cornerstone of safety evaluation is the **dose-response study** using non-mammalian models, such as *Drosophila melanogaster*, zebrafish embryos, or *Caenorhabditis elegans*. These models provide cost-effective, rapid, and ethically sound insights into toxicological thresholds and potential risks associated with various substances.

Ethical toxicology also emphasizes **genotoxicity and mutagenicity assessments**, employing innovative *in vitro* techniques like the Ames test, comet assay, and micronucleus test. These methods avoid animal use and provide reliable data on genetic stability impacts.

The chapter further advocates for **safety screening using harmless models**, such as plant bioassays or yeast systems, to identify potential toxic agents early in research. Such models align with the principles of the 3Rs (Replacement, Reduction, Refinement) in toxicological research.

Finally, the chapter outlines **guidelines for preliminary safety evaluation**, emphasizing regulatory requirements, risk assessment protocols, and ethical practices. This framework aids researchers in conducting robust, reproducible, and ethically compliant toxicological studies, ensuring safety without compromising scientific integrity.

18.1 Simple Dose-Response Studies Using Non-Mammalian Models

Dose-response studies are essential in pharmacology to evaluate the biological activity and toxicity of test substances. These studies establish the relationship between the dose of a substance and its corresponding effect on a biological system. Non-mammalian models are increasingly used as ethically sound and cost-effective alternatives to traditional mammalian systems, making them ideal for resource-limited laboratories.

18.1.1 Significance of Non-Mammalian Models

Non-mammalian models, such as *Drosophila melanogaster* (fruit fly), zebrafish (*Danio rerio*), and *Caenorhabditis elegans* (nematode), provide several advantages. They are inexpensive to maintain, have short life cycles, and are genetically tractable, enabling high-throughput screening. These models are well-accepted for toxicological studies due to their physiological and genetic similarities with higher organisms.

Methodology for Dose-Response Studies

1. **Selection of Model Organism:**

   Choose a non-mammalian model based on the research objective. For example, zebrafish embryos are ideal for studying developmental toxicity, while *C. elegans* is suitable for neurotoxicity assays.

2. **Preparation of Test Solutions:**

   Prepare serial dilutions of the test substance to create a range of concentrations. Ensure proper solubility and pH adjustment to maintain the viability of the model organism.

3. **Exposure Protocol:**

   Expose the organisms to the test solutions under controlled environmental conditions, such as temperature, light, and aeration. Include appropriate controls (positive and negative) for comparison.

4. **Endpoints for Measurement:**

   Common endpoints include mortality, developmental abnormalities, behavioural changes, or enzyme activity modulation. Quantitative endpoints, like LC_{50} (lethal concentration for 50% of the population) or EC_{50} (effective concentration for 50% of the population), provide valuable dose-response data.

18.1.2 Ethical and Regulatory Considerations

Using non-mammalian models aligns with ethical principles and global regulations, such as the 3Rs (Replacement, Reduction, Refinement) framework. These models reduce the need for vertebrate testing, ensuring minimal ethical concerns while maintaining scientific rigor.

Applications and Benefits

Non-mammalian dose-response studies are particularly beneficial for resource-limited laboratories. They offer a rapid, reproducible, and economical means to screen compounds for pharmacological activity or toxicity. Moreover, these studies provide a solid foundation for further *in vitro* or *in silico* analyses, minimizing the need for animal experimentation.

Simple dose-response studies using non-mammalian models represent a transformative approach in pharmacological research. They bridge the gap between ethical practices and scientific discovery, enabling laboratories with limited resources to contribute significantly to the fields of toxicology and drug development.

18.2 Techniques to Assess Genotoxicity and Mutagenicity Ethically

Genotoxicity and mutagenicity studies are vital in evaluating the safety of pharmaceuticals, chemicals, and natural compounds. These tests detect the potential of substances to cause genetic damage, including DNA mutations, chromosomal aberrations, or changes in genetic material integrity. Ethically sound and cost-effective techniques are particularly important for resource-limited laboratories, enabling researchers to adhere to global standards while minimizing the use of animals.

18.2.1 Ethical Considerations in Genotoxicity Testing

The use of non-animal and *in vitro* methods aligns with the principles of the 3Rs (Replacement, Reduction, Refinement), promoting ethical research. These techniques provide reliable data while circumventing ethical concerns associated with mammalian models. Regulatory agencies, including OECD and FDA, endorse several *in vitro* genotoxicity assays as part of safety evaluations.

Key Techniques for Genotoxicity and Mutagenicity Assessment

1. **Ames Test (Bacterial Reverse Mutation Test):**
    - **Overview:** This is a widely accepted, cost-effective method to detect mutagenicity. It employs strains of *Salmonella typhimurium* or *Escherichia coli* with mutations in histidine or tryptophan biosynthesis pathways.
    - **Procedure:** The test substance is applied to bacteria in the presence or absence of a metabolic activation system (S9 mix). Reversion of mutations allows bacteria to grow on selective media, indicating mutagenic activity.
    - **Advantages:** Simple, rapid, and inexpensive. It minimizes animal use by employing microorganisms.
2. **Comet Assay (Single-Cell Gel Electrophoresis):**
    - **Overview:** The comet assay evaluates DNA strand breaks in individual cells, providing insights into genotoxic potential. It is adaptable to a variety of cell types, including plant, yeast, and human cells.
    - **Procedure:** Cells are exposed to the test compound, embedded in agarose, lysed, and subjected to electrophoresis. Damaged DNA migrates, forming a "comet" shape under a fluorescence microscope.
    - **Advantages:** Sensitive, versatile, and capable of detecting low levels of DNA damage.
3. **Micronucleus Assay:**
    - **Overview:** This assay identifies chromosomal damage by detecting micronuclei, which are small DNA-containing structures formed during cell division. It is often performed in human lymphocytes or cultured mammalian cells.
    - **Procedure:** Cells are exposed to the test substance, and micronuclei are visualized using staining techniques or fluorescent dyes.
    - **Advantages:** Reliable for detecting chromosomal damage and relatively simple to perform.
4. **Yeast-Based Genotoxicity Tests:**
    - **Overview:** Yeast strains, such as *Saccharomyces cerevisiae*, are genetically modified to detect genotoxicity. These systems monitor DNA repair mechanisms or mutation frequencies.
    - **Advantages:** Cost-effective and free from ethical concerns associated with animal use.

5. **High-Throughput Screening (HTS) Methods:**
   - **Overview:** Automated platforms integrating assays like γ-H2AX phosphorylation or p53 activation provide rapid and efficient genotoxicity screening.
   - **Advantages:** HTS minimizes resource use and accelerates data collection.

18.2.2 Practical Applications for Resource-Limited Laboratories

Resource-limited laboratories can prioritize low-cost methods like the Ames test and comet assay while gradually integrating advanced techniques as resources permit. Yeast-based and bacterial systems are particularly suitable due to their affordability and ease of handling.

Ethically sound genotoxicity and mutagenicity assessment techniques empower researchers to conduct meaningful safety evaluations without compromising on ethics or quality. By leveraging *in vitro* and non-animal models, laboratories with limited resources can contribute significantly to pharmacological and toxicological research. These techniques not only ensure compliance with ethical standards but also align with global regulatory frameworks, fostering innovation in a responsible and cost-effective manner.

18.3 Safety Screening Using Harmless and Ethically Sound Models

Safety screening is a fundamental step in evaluating the potential risks associated with pharmaceuticals, chemicals, and natural products. Traditional approaches often rely on animal testing, raising ethical concerns and incurring high costs. Harmless and ethically sound models provide viable alternatives, particularly for resource-limited laboratories. These models not only reduce reliance on animal testing but also offer cost-effective, reliable, and reproducible results in early safety assessments.

18.3.1 Significance of Ethical and Harmless Models

Ethically sound models minimize harm to living organisms and align with global regulations promoting humane research practices. Harmless models such as *in vitro* systems, microbial assays, and plant-based tests are increasingly recognized for their ability to provide valuable safety data while adhering to the principles of Replacement, Reduction, and Refinement (3Rs).

Common Harmless Models for Safety Screening

1. **Plant Bioassays:**
   - **Overview:** Plants such as *Allium cepa* (onion root tips) and *Lemna minor* (duckweed) are commonly used for toxicity testing. These bioassays evaluate cytotoxicity, genotoxicity, and phytotoxicity.
   - **Procedure:** The test compound is applied to plant roots or growth media, and parameters such as root length, mitotic index, and chromosomal aberrations are measured.
   - **Advantages:** Cost-effective, simple to perform, and free from animal use.

2. **Microbial Models:**
    - **Overview:** Microorganisms like *Escherichia coli* and *Saccharomyces cerevisiae* are excellent tools for safety screening. They are widely used in assays such as the Ames test and yeast-based genotoxicity tests.
    - **Applications:** Assess mutagenicity, genotoxicity, and cytotoxicity using well-established protocols.
    - **Advantages:** Highly affordable, reproducible, and ethically sound.
3. **Cell Culture Systems:**
    - **Overview:** Human or animal-derived cell lines provide a robust platform for *in vitro* safety screening. Tests such as cytotoxicity (MTT or resazurin assay), oxidative stress (DPPH or ROS assays), and membrane integrity (LDH assay) are commonly performed.
    - **Advantages:** High relevance to human biology, scalable, and suitable for high-throughput screening.
4. **Invertebrate Models:**
    - **Overview:** Invertebrates like *Caenorhabditis elegans* and *Artemia salina* (brine shrimp) offer an intermediate option between *in vitro* and vertebrate models. These organisms are used to study developmental toxicity, neurotoxicity, and general cytotoxicity.
    - **Procedure:** Involve exposing the test organism to the compound under controlled conditions, followed by evaluation of survival rates or physiological changes.
    - **Advantages:** Simple handling, cost-effective, and fewer ethical concerns compared to vertebrate models.
5. **Zebrafish Embryo Assays:**
    - **Overview:** Zebrafish embryos are gaining popularity as a non-mammalian vertebrate model for safety assessments. They are particularly useful for assessing developmental toxicity and teratogenicity.
    - **Advantages:** Transparent embryos enable real-time observation, and testing is considered ethically sound due to their non-protected status in early development.

18.3.2 Guidelines for Effective Safety Screening

- **Selection of Model:** Choose models that align with the nature of the compound and research objectives.
- **Validation of Methods:** Ensure that the chosen assays are validated and recognized by regulatory authorities.
- **Incorporation of Controls:** Include positive and negative controls for reliable data interpretation.
- **Scalability and Feasibility:** Opt for methods that are practical for resource-limited settings and adaptable to high-throughput formats if needed.

Key Insights

Safety screening using harmless and ethically sound models bridges the gap between scientific rigor and ethical responsibility. By leveraging plant bioassays, microbial systems, and simple invertebrate models, resource-limited laboratories can conduct high-quality safety evaluations. These techniques align with modern regulatory frameworks and provide a sustainable, humane approach to early-stage screening. As research progresses, integrating these models with advanced *in vitro* and computational methods can further enhance their utility and global acceptance.

18.4 Guidelines for Preliminary Safety Evaluation

Preliminary safety evaluation is a crucial step in pharmacological research, providing foundational data on the potential toxicity and risk profile of compounds. By adopting ethical and cost-effective methods, researchers in resource-limited laboratories can effectively perform safety screenings without compromising quality or compliance with regulatory standards. This chapter outlines practical guidelines for conducting such evaluations, emphasizing ethical considerations and resource efficiency.

Step-by-Step Guidelines

1. **Define the Objective and Scope:**
   - Clearly outline the purpose of the safety evaluation. Determine whether the focus is on general cytotoxicity, genotoxicity, mutagenicity, or specific toxic effects like hepatotoxicity or neurotoxicity.
   - Choose appropriate assays and models that align with the study's goals.
2. **Selection of Ethical and Cost-Effective Models:**
   - ***In Vitro* Models:** Utilize cultured human or animal cells for cytotoxicity assays, genotoxicity studies (e.g., comet assay), or enzyme-based activity tests.
   - **Non-Mammalian Models:** Employ microorganisms (e.g., *E. coli*, yeast), plant bioassays (e.g., *Allium cepa*), or simple invertebrates like *C. elegans* for initial toxicity screening.
   - **Avoid High-Cost Systems:** Focus on models that require minimal infrastructure, such as bacterial systems or plant-based assays.
3. **Prepare Test Solutions and Controls:**
   - Prepare serial dilutions of the test compound to cover a range of concentrations.
   - Include appropriate controls:
     - **Negative Control:** Without the test substance to account for baseline effects.
     - **Positive Control:** A known toxic agent to validate the assay's performance.

4. **Perform Key Assays for Safety Screening:**
   - **Cytotoxicity Tests:** Use assays like MTT, neutral red uptake, or resazurin to assess cell viability and metabolic activity.
   - **Genotoxicity Tests:** Employ the comet assay, Ames test, or micronucleus assay to detect DNA damage or chromosomal alterations.
   - **Oxidative Stress Tests:** Measure reactive oxygen species (ROS) production or antioxidant activity using DPPH or ABTS assays.
5. **Data Collection and Analysis:**
   - Record quantitative and qualitative data meticulously. For instance, in cytotoxicity assays, calculate IC_{50} values (the concentration at which 50% inhibition occurs).
   - Analyze dose-response relationships to identify potential hazards.
6. **Adhere to Ethical Standards:**
   - Prioritize non-animal and minimally invasive techniques to align with ethical frameworks.
   - Follow global guidelines like OECD Test Guidelines for *in vitro* and alternative models, and align with the ICH (International Council for Harmonisation) Guidelines on safety pharmacology and toxicity studies.
   - **Indian Guidelines:**
     - **Good Laboratory Practices (GLP) by the National GLP Compliance Monitoring Authority (NGCMA):** Ensure adherence to GLP standards for non-clinical studies as outlined by the Department of Science and Technology (DST), India. These standards are critical for maintaining the reliability and reproducibility of safety studies.
     - **ICMR Guidelines:** Follow the **Indian Council of Medical Research (ICMR) Ethical Guidelines for Biomedical Research on Human Participants**, which emphasize the ethical use of human-derived samples and the necessity of obtaining informed consent for such studies.
     - **CPCSEA Guidelines:** For any *in vivo* preliminary work involving animals, comply with the **Committee for the Purpose of Control and Supervision of Experiments on Animals (CPCSEA)**, which mandates humane treatment and ethical practices in animal research.
     - **Biosafety Regulations by DBT:** Adhere to the **Department of Biotechnology (DBT) Biosafety Guidelines** when working with genetically modified organisms or hazardous materials to ensure safety for researchers and the environment.
   - By integrating these Indian standards alongside global guidelines, laboratories can ensure their research is not only ethical and compliant with local regulations but also aligned with

international norms. This dual compliance enhances the credibility of research outputs and facilitates their acceptance on a global platform.

Best Practices for Resource-Limited Laboratories

- **Maximize Resource Utilization:** Share laboratory resources or collaborate with nearby institutions for access to advanced equipment.
- **Validate Low-Cost Assays:** Validate less expensive methods with standard reference compounds to ensure reliability.
- **Document Procedures Rigorously:** Maintain comprehensive records to ensure reproducibility and credibility of the data.

Insights and Implications

Preliminary safety evaluation using ethically sound and cost-effective methods is essential for early-stage pharmacological research. By adhering to these guidelines, laboratories with limited resources can contribute to scientific discovery while upholding ethical standards. These practices not only ensure compliance with global regulatory norms but also foster innovation in sustainable and humane research methods.

Chapter 19

Data Analysis, Statistical Models, and Interpretation

The chapter "Data Analysis, Statistical Models, and Interpretation" serves as a cornerstone for transforming raw data into meaningful insights. In the realm of scientific research, data analysis forms the critical bridge between hypothesis formulation and conclusion, enabling researchers to unravel patterns, relationships, and trends within the data. This chapter outlines the fundamental and advanced statistical techniques employed to ensure robust and accurate results.

It begins with an overview of the essential principles of data analysis, highlighting the significance of organizing, summarizing, and visualizing data. Key statistical models are explored, focusing on their applications, assumptions, and limitations. These models range from descriptive statistics to inferential techniques, including regression analysis, hypothesis testing, and multivariate methods, tailored to the specific research objectives.

Interpretation, the final step in the analytical pipeline, is emphasized as a vital process of contextualizing numerical findings within the scope of the research problem. The chapter underscores the importance of critical thinking and scientific rigor in drawing conclusions, addressing variability, and mitigating biases.

By the end of this chapter, readers will gain a comprehensive understanding of how to systematically analyze data, apply appropriate statistical models, and derive meaningful interpretations to support evidence-based decision-making in their research.

19.1 Statistical Tools for Easy Data Analysis

Statistical tools are indispensable in modern research, providing a streamlined approach to data analysis. They simplify complex calculations, enhance data interpretation, and allow researchers to focus on the implications of their findings rather than the mechanics of analysis. This section explores various statistical tools, their applications, and their significance in making data analysis accessible and efficient.

19.1.1 Overview of Statistical Tools

Statistical tools refer to software, platforms, or frameworks designed to handle data processing, analysis, and visualization. Their purpose is to automate repetitive tasks, reduce computational errors, and offer insightful outputs. Popular tools include:

- **Spreadsheet Software:** Microsoft Excel and Google Sheets, known for their ease of use in basic analysis.
- **Statistical Packages:** SPSS, SAS, and Minitab, which offer user-friendly interfaces for both beginners and professionals.

- **Programming Platforms:** R and Python, equipped with libraries like NumPy, Pandas, and SciPy, suitable for advanced users.
- **Visualization Tools:** Tableau and Power BI for dynamic data representation.

19.1.2 Simplifying Descriptive Statistics

Descriptive statistics summarize large datasets into comprehensible metrics. Key tools like Excel, SPSS, and Python provide features to calculate:

- **Measures of Central Tendency:** Mean, median, and mode.
- **Measures of Dispersion:** Range, variance, and standard deviation.
- **Data Distribution Insights:** Tools can generate histograms, box plots, and frequency tables to visualize data spread.

These tools ensure that even non-specialists can understand the overall characteristics of data.

19.1.3 Conducting Inferential Statistics

Inferential statistics help researchers draw conclusions about populations based on sample data. Statistical tools simplify methods such as:

- **Hypothesis Testing:** T-tests, chi-square tests, and ANOVA for comparing groups.
- **Confidence Intervals:** Estimating population parameters with a margin of error.
- **Probability Models:** Tools like R and SPSS automate the application of statistical tests and display results with comprehensive interpretations.

Such functionalities save time and improve accuracy in decision-making.

19.1.4 Regression and Correlation Techniques

Regression and correlation analyses are critical for identifying relationships between variables. Tools like Minitab, SPSS, and Python's statsmodels library enable:

- **Correlation Analysis:** Calculating Pearson or Spearman coefficients to measure the strength and direction of relationships.
- **Regression Models:** Building linear, logistic, or multiple regression models to predict outcomes.
- **Trend Analysis:** Tools visualize relationships through scatter plots with regression lines.

These techniques provide insights into predictive patterns within datasets.

19.1.5 Advanced Statistical Analyses

For complex data problems, tools offer advanced features such as:

- **Multivariate Analysis:** Principal Component Analysis (PCA), factor analysis, and cluster analysis for high-dimensional data.
- **Machine Learning Models:** Libraries in Python like scikit-learn and TensorFlow extend statistical analysis to predictive modelling and classification tasks.
- **Time-Series Analysis:** Specialized packages like R's forecast and Python's statsmodels handle temporal data efficiently.

These capabilities make it possible to tackle intricate research questions with ease.

19.1.6 Data Visualization for Enhanced Understanding

Visual representation is vital for interpreting and presenting data effectively. Tools like Tableau, Power BI, and Python's Matplotlib or Seaborn libraries provide customizable:

- Charts: Bar graphs, pie charts, and line graphs.
- Dashboards: Interactive visuals for real-time exploration.
- Heatmaps: Detailed representations of correlations and patterns.

Visualization bridges the gap between raw data and actionable insights.

19.1.7 Selecting the Right Statistical Tool

Choosing the right tool depends on factors such as:

- **Nature of Data:** Size, type, and complexity.
- **Level of Expertise:** Beginners may prefer SPSS or Excel, while experienced users can utilize R or Python.
- **Research Goals:** Advanced techniques may require specialized tools like MATLAB or machine learning libraries.

Understanding these factors ensures an optimal match between tools and analysis requirements.

By incorporating these statistical tools into research workflows, data analysis becomes more accessible, reliable, and insightful. These tools not only democratize the analytical process but also empower researchers to focus on deriving meaningful conclusions from their data.

19.2 Curve Fitting, IC_{50}, EC_{50}, and Other Dose-Response Metrics

Curve fitting and dose-response metrics such as IC_{50} (half-maximal inhibitory concentration) and EC_{50} (half-maximal effective concentration) are crucial tools in pharmacological, toxicological, and biological studies. They help quantify the effects of substances like drugs, chemicals, or bioactive compounds on a biological system. This section delves into the principles, requirements, methodologies, and calculations involved in determining these metrics.

19.2.1 Principles of Dose-Response Analysis and Curve Fitting

Dose-response analysis examines the relationship between the concentration of a substance and the magnitude of its effect on a biological system. The principle of dose-response analysis rests on two key ideas:

- **Threshold Effect:** There is a minimum dose required to elicit a measurable response.
- **Sigmoidal Response Curve:** The relationship between dose and response often follows a sigmoidal pattern, characterized by an initial lag phase, a linear increase, and a plateau.

Curve fitting is used to model this relationship mathematically, enabling precise determination of dose-response parameters like $IC_{50}$and EC_{50}.

19.2.2 Requirements for Dose-Response Studies

To perform dose-response studies and curve fitting, the following are essential:

- **Experimental Data:** Accurate measurements of responses (e.g., enzymatic activity, cell viability, or inhibition percentage) at varying concentrations of the test substance.
- **Biological Relevance:** The system or assay should be sensitive and specific to the substance under study.
- **Software Tools:** Programs like GraphPad Prism, OriginPro, R (using packages like drc), or Python (using SciPy or NumPy) are widely used for fitting dose-response curves.
- **Standard Models:** Commonly used models include Hill's equation, sigmoidal, and logistic regression.
- Proper experimental design and reliable data collection are fundamental to obtaining meaningful results.

19.2.3 Methodology for Curve Fitting and Metric Estimation

18.2.3.1 Data Preparation

1. Perform experiments at different concentrations of the substance.
2. Record responses (e.g., percent inhibition or stimulation) for each dose.
3. Normalize the response data if required, setting the control response as 0% or 100%.

19.2.3.2 Choosing a Model

The most common model for dose-response studies is the **Hill Equation**:

$$E = E_{\text{min}} + \frac{(E_{\text{max}} - E_{\text{min}})}{1 + \left(\frac{EC_{50}}{C}\right)^n}$$

Where:

- E is the effect at concentration C.
- E_{min} and E_{max} are the minimum and maximum effects.
- EC_{50} is the concentration producing 50% of the maximum effect.
- n is the Hill slope, indicating the steepness of the curve.

For IC_{50}, the same equation is applied to measure inhibition instead of stimulation.

19.2.3.3 Curve Fitting

1. Input the dose-response data into software.
2. Fit the data to the chosen model using nonlinear regression.
3. Assess goodness-of-fit using metrics like R-squared, residual plots, or Akaike Information Criterion (AIC).

19.2.4 Calculations of IC_{50}, EC_{50}, and Other Metrics

After fitting the curve, dose-response metrics are calculated as follows:

- **IC_{50}:** The concentration at which the response is reduced by 50% relative to the maximum inhibition. Derived directly from the fitted curve.
- **EC_{50}:** The concentration at which 50% of the maximum effect is observed.
- **Hill Slope (n):** Indicates the steepness of the dose-response curve. A higher slope suggests a more abrupt response near the midpoint.
- **LOEC (Lowest Observed Effect Concentration):** The smallest dose where a statistically significant effect is observed.

Software automates these calculations, but manual checks, such as interpolation, may be employed for validation.

19.2.5 Applications and Interpretation

These metrics provide quantitative insight into the potency and efficacy of substances. For example:

- **IC_{50}** is commonly used in drug development to evaluate inhibitor strength.
- **EC_{50}** helps measure agonist activity in receptor-ligand studies.
- **Dose-response curves** aid in comparing the effects of different substances under identical conditions.

The accurate interpretation of these metrics requires an understanding of the biological system and experimental conditions.

Key Insight

Curve fitting and dose-response metrics are invaluable for understanding the effects of bioactive compounds. Proper experimental design, model selection, and careful interpretation ensure reliable and reproducible outcomes. These tools provide the foundation for advancing research in pharmacology, toxicology, and related fields.

19.3 Interpretation of *In Vitro* Pharmacological Data

Interpreting *in vitro* pharmacological data is a vital step in evaluating the biological activity, efficacy, and safety of compounds. This involves analyzing results from laboratory experiments to assess how substances interact with biological systems under controlled conditions. Proper interpretation ensures that experimental findings contribute meaningfully to drug discovery, toxicology, or natural product research. This section discusses the principles, requirements, methodology, and calculations associated with interpreting *in vitro* data.

19.3.1 Principles of *In Vitro* Pharmacological Data Interpretation

In vitro studies are conducted in a controlled environment, such as cell cultures, enzyme assays, or isolated tissues. The interpretation of data from these studies relies on several principles:

- **Concentration-Response Relationship:** Understanding how varying concentrations of a compound influence the magnitude of the observed effect.
- **Specificity:** Ensuring that the response is directly attributable to the compound being tested.
- **Reproducibility:** Data should be consistent across replicates and independent experiments.
- **Comparative Analysis:** Comparing the effects of the test compound to known standards, controls, or untreated conditions.

These principles guide the accurate extraction of pharmacological insights from raw experimental data.

19.3.2 Requirements for Interpreting *In Vitro* Data

Proper interpretation of *in vitro* pharmacological data requires:

- **High-Quality Data:** Accurate and reproducible measurements obtained using validated protocols.
- **Appropriate Controls:** Positive and negative controls to validate the assay system.
- **Analytical Tools:** Software such as GraphPad Prism, R, or Python for data analysis.
- **Standard Metrics:** Metrics like IC_{50}, EC_{50}, or percentage inhibition provide quantifiable insights.

These elements form the foundation for reliable and meaningful data interpretation.

19.3.3 Methodology for Data Interpretation

19.3.3.1 Data Cleaning and Preparation

1. **Data Validation:** Remove outliers and ensure consistency across replicates.
2. **Normalization:** Convert raw data into percentage responses relative to controls (e.g., 0% for untreated control and 100% for maximal effect).

19.3.3.2 Data Visualization

Graphical representation of data, such as dose-response curves or bar plots, provides a clear overview of trends and patterns. Tools like Excel or specialized software are used for creating these visuals.

19.3.3.3 Analysis of Key Parameters

Analyze essential metrics such as:

- **IC_{50}/EC_{50}:** Determine the concentration required to achieve 50% of maximum inhibition or effect.
- **Maximum Effect (Emax):** Identify the highest observable response.
- **Hill Slope (n):** Assess the steepness of the dose-response relationship.

19.3.4 Calculations and Metrics Interpretation

- **Percent Response Calculation:**

$$\%\ \text{Response} = \frac{R_{\text{sample}} - R_{negative\,control}}{R_{\text{positive control}} - R_{negative\,control}} \times 100$$

  Where R represents the response (e.g., absorbance, luminescence).

  - **IC_{50}/EC_{50} Estimation:**

    Use curve-fitting models, such as the Hill equation, for nonlinear regression to calculate these values.

  - **Selectivity Index (SI):**

    To assess compound safety, calculate:

  A higher SI indicates a safer compound.

19.3.5 Applications and Contextualization

In vitro pharmacological data interpretation helps:

- Identify lead compounds for drug development.
- Understand mechanisms of action by comparing effects across concentrations.

- Evaluate therapeutic windows by contrasting effective and toxic concentrations.
- Inform further *in vivo* studies by selecting the most promising candidates.

Key Insight

Interpreting *in vitro* pharmacological data bridges experimental findings and their practical implications. Following systematic methodologies and leveraging standardized metrics ensure that results are both accurate and actionable. Proper interpretation not only enhances the credibility of research but also accelerates the translation of laboratory discoveries into real-world applications.

19.4 Practical Tips for Interpreting Results with Minimal Resources

Interpreting experimental results effectively on a limited budget requires creativity, resource optimization, and reliance on cost-effective tools. Practical tips outlined in this section help researchers derive meaningful conclusions from their data, even in resource-constrained environments. This includes understanding core principles, fulfilling minimal requirements, following simplified methodologies, and performing essential calculations.

19.4.1 Principles of Resource-Efficient Data Interpretation

When working with minimal resources, the following principles guide effective result interpretation:

- **Focus on Core Objectives:** Prioritize key outcomes that directly address the research questions.
- **Simplify Data Analysis:** Use straightforward statistical tools and minimize computational complexity.
- **Repurpose Available Tools:** Leverage open-source software and multipurpose instruments.
- **Validate Data with Replicates:** Even with limited resources, ensure reproducibility by conducting replicates instead of relying on single measurements.

These principles ensure that resource constraints do not compromise the reliability of the findings.

19.4.2 Requirements for Minimal Resource Interpretation

Efficient interpretation requires:

- **Accurate Raw Data:** Well-documented and verified experimental observations are critical.
- **Open-Source Software:** Tools like R, Python, or free Excel add-ons for basic statistical analysis.
- **Simple Graphing Tools:** Low-cost or free platforms such as Google Sheets for visualizing trends.
- **Standard Reference Data:** Publicly available datasets or literature values for benchmarking results.
- **Critical Thinking:** A focus on data relevance and logical deductions to draw insights.

Meeting these basic needs allows for meaningful analysis without expensive resources.

19.4.3 Methodology for Result Interpretation with Minimal Resources

19.4.3.1 Data Organization

- Collect and record data systematically in spreadsheets or notebooks.
- Organize data by grouping replicates, controls, and treatments for easy comparison.

19.4.3.2 Visualization and Trend Analysis

- Use simple line graphs, bar plots, or scatter plots to visualize results.
- Identify patterns and trends that indicate potential relationships or anomalies.

19.4.3.3 Basic Statistical Analysis

- Calculate means, standard deviations, and percentages to summarize findings.
- Perform basic tests like t-tests or ANOVA using free tools like R or online calculators to evaluate statistical significance.

19.4.3.4 Qualitative Interpretation

Where quantitative analysis is not feasible, qualitative assessment (e.g., relative inhibition or stimulation) can provide meaningful insights.

19.4.4 Calculations and Low-Cost Metrics

- **Percentage Response:**

$$\%\ \text{Response} = \frac{\textit{Test Value} - \textit{Control Value}}{\textit{Maximum Value} - \textit{Minimum Value}} \times 100$$

- **Fold Change:**

$$\text{Fold Change} = \frac{\text{Test Response}}{\text{Control Response}} \times 100$$

  Fold change highlights the magnitude of difference between treatments and controls.

- **Normalized Data:**

  Normalize responses to facilitate comparison across experiments:

$$\text{Normalized Response} = \frac{\text{Raw Value}}{\text{Maximum Control Value}} \times 100$$

- **Statistical Significance:**

  Use open-source tools or simple calculators for p-value estimation to determine if observed differences are significant.

19.4.5 Practical Tips for Efficiency

- **Leverage Public Tools:** Use freely available databases or software for calculations and data visualization.
- **Share Resources:** Collaborate with peers or institutions to access shared equipment or expertise.
- **Document Thoroughly:** Maintain meticulous records of experiments to avoid data redundancy or errors.
- **DIY Approaches:** Build simple, makeshift lab setups for common assays using local or recycled materials.

Key Insight

Interpreting experimental results with minimal resources is achievable through strategic planning, resource optimization, and reliance on cost-effective tools. By adhering to simplified methodologies and focusing on essential metrics, researchers can extract meaningful insights while maintaining the integrity of their studies. This approach empowers research in resource-constrained environments, fostering innovation and progress.

19.5 Standardized Documentation Methods for Reproducibility

Reproducibility is a cornerstone of scientific research, ensuring that experimental results can be consistently duplicated under the same conditions by other researchers. Standardized documentation methods play a vital role in achieving this goal. Below is a detailed discussion of these methods.

19.5.1 Importance of Standardized Documentation

Standardized documentation serves as the foundation for:

- **Transparency**: Clearly outlining the methodology allows others to understand and replicate the process.
- **Accuracy**: Prevents errors in recording experimental details.
- **Collaboration**: Facilitates effective knowledge sharing among researchers.
- **Credibility**: Enhances trust in the research findings.

19.5.2 Core Elements of Standardized Documentation

A well-structured documentation protocol typically includes the following elements:

1. **Experimental Design**:
   - A clear description of hypotheses, objectives, and the experimental framework.

   - Inclusion of detailed protocols, controls, and variables.

2. **Materials and Methods**:
   - Comprehensive list of reagents, instruments, and software used.
   - Step-by-step procedures with appropriate references to standard operating procedures (SOPs).
3. **Data Collection**:
   - Precise data recording formats, including units of measurement and calibration details.
   - Maintenance of raw data in an organized and accessible manner.
4. **Analysis and Interpretation**:
   - Documentation of data processing methods and statistical analyses performed.
   - Proper attribution to tools or scripts used for computational studies.
5. **Version Control**:
   - Use of software like Git for tracking changes in protocols, datasets, or analysis scripts over time.

19.5.3 Tools for Standardized Documentation

Modern research employs a variety of tools to maintain consistency in documentation:

- **Electronic Lab Notebooks (ELNs)**: Digital alternatives to traditional lab notebooks, offering features like time stamps and version histories.
- **Protocol Repositories**: Platforms like *Protocols.io* that allow for sharing and archiving experimental methods.
- **Data Management Plans (DMPs)**: Formalized strategies for data storage, sharing, and preservation.
- **Metadata Standards**: Use of standard formats like MIAME (Minimum Information About a Microarray Experiment) for specific research domains.

19.5.4 Guidelines for Effective Documentation

Researchers should follow these best practices:

- **Clarity**: Use simple, unambiguous language to describe procedures and observations.
- **Consistency**: Adhere to institutional or domain-specific guidelines for documentation formats.
- **Traceability**: Maintain records in a way that allows easy backtracking of steps.
- **Automation**: Integrate automated data logging tools where possible to reduce manual errors.

19.5.5 Challenges in Standardization

Despite its importance, implementing standardized documentation faces hurdles:

- Lack of training on proper documentation practices.
- Resistance to adopting new technologies like ELNs.
- Variability in standards across disciplines and institutions.

19.5.6 Future Directions

Efforts to improve reproducibility through documentation are continuously evolving:

- Development of universal documentation standards.
- Increased use of Artificial Intelligence for automated and error-free record-keeping.
- Integration of FAIR (Findable, Accessible, Interoperable, and Reusable) data principles in scientific workflows.

Key Insight

Standardized documentation methods are indispensable for enhancing reproducibility in research. By fostering transparency, consistency, and collaboration, they ensure that scientific discoveries stand the test of time and scrutiny, laying a robust foundation for future innovations.

Bibliography

Ahmed, H. Y., Gazzar, E. M. E., Safwat, N., & Badawy, M. M. M. (2023). Dual anticancer activity of *Aspergillus nidulans* pigment and ionizing γ-radiation on human larynx carcinoma cell line. *BMC Complementary Medicine and Therapies, 23*, 327.

Akshatha, N., & Kamble, S. (2021). Anti-angiogenic activity of *Calotropis gigantea* leaf extract by chick chorioallantoic membrane (CAM) assay method. *RGUHS Journal of Medical Sciences, 11*(1), 43-48.

Amin, M., Anwar, F., Naz, F., Mehmood, T., & Saari, N. (2013). Anti-Helicobacter pylori and urease inhibition activities of some traditional medicinal plants. *Molecules, 18*(2), 2135-2149.

Aranjani, J. M., Manuel, A., Mallikarjuna Rao, C., Udupa, N., Rao, J. V., Joy, A. M., Radhakrishnan, E. K., & Radhakrishnan, M. (2013). Preliminary evaluation of *in vitro* cytotoxicity and *in vivo* antitumor activity of *Xanthium strumarium* in transplantable tumors in mice. *The American Journal of Chinese Medicine, 41*(1), 145–162.

Benzie, I. F. F., & Strain, J. J. (1996). The ferric reducing ability of plasma (FRAP) as a measure of "antioxidant power": The FRAP assay. *Analytical Biochemistry, 239*(1), 70–76.

Bhattacharya, S. (2024). Evaluation of anthelmintic activity of medicinal plants: Why earthworm? *Indian Journal of Pharmacology, 56*(1), 64–65.

Blois, M. S. (1958). Antioxidant determinations by the use of a stable free radical. *Nature, 181*(4617), 1199–1200.

Bundy, G. L., Peterson, D. C., Cornette, J. C., Miller, W. L., Spilman, C. H., & Wilks, J. W. (1983). Synthesis and biological activity of prostaglandin lactones. *Journal of Medicinal Chemistry, 26*(8), 1089–1099.

Cappuccino, J. G., & Sherman, N. (2014). *Microbiology: A laboratory manual* (10th ed.). Pearson.

Capula, M., Corno, C., El Hassouni, B., Li Petri, G., & Aranđelović, S. (2019). A brief guide to performing pharmacological studies *in vitro*: Reflections from the EORTC-PAMM course "Preclinical and early-phase clinical pharmacology." *Anticancer Research, 39*(7), 3413–3418.

Das, S. R., Saili, K. S., & Tanguay, R. L. (2014). Nonmammalian models in toxicology screening. In *Encyclopedia of Toxicology* (pp. 609–613).

Das, S. S., Dey, M., & Ghosh, A. K. (2011). Determination of anthelmintic activity of the leaf and bark extract of *Tamarindus indica* Linn. *Indian Journal of Pharmaceutical Sciences, 73*(1), 104–107.

Díaz, L., Zambrano, E., Flores, M. E., Contreras, M., Crispín, J. C., Alemán, G., Bravo, C., Armenta, A., Valdés, V. J., Tovar, A., Gamba, G., Barrios-Payán, J., & Bobadilla, N. A. (2021). Ethical considerations in animal research: The principle of 3Rs. *Revista de Investigación Clínica*, 73(4), 199–209.

Ellman, G. L., Courtney, K. D., Andres, V., & Featherstone, R. M. (1961). A new and rapid colorimetric determination of acetylcholinesterase activity. *Biochemical Pharmacology, 7*(2), 88–95.

Field, A. (2013). *Discovering statistics using IBM SPSS statistics* (4th ed.). SAGE Publications.

Fox, J. (2016). *Applied regression analysis and generalized linear models* (3rd ed.). SAGE Publications.

Gaziano, T., Reddy, K. S., Paccaud, F., Horton, S., Chaturvedi, V., Jamison, D. T., Breman, J. G., Measham, A. R., & et al. (2006). Cardiovascular disease. In D. T. Jamison, J. G. Breman, A. R. Measham, et al. (Eds.), *Disease control priorities in developing countries* (2nd ed., Chapter 33). The International Bank for Reconstruction and Development / The World Bank. Available from https://www.ncbi.nlm.nih.gov/books/NBK11767/ Co-published by Oxford University Press, New York.

Gelman, A., & Hill, J. (2007). *Data analysis using regression and multilevel/hierarchical models*. Cambridge University Press.

Gore, M. G. (Ed.). (2000). *Spectrophotometry and Spectrofluorometry: A Practical Approach*. Oxford University Press. ISBN: 978-0199638111

Gunathilake, K., Ranaweera, K., & Rupasinghe, H. (2018). *In vitro* anti-inflammatory properties of selected green leafy vegetables. *Biomedicines, 6*(4), 107.

Hameed, I., Masoodi, S. R., Mir, S. A., Nabi, M., Ghazanfar, K., & Ganai, B. A. (2015). Type 2 diabetes mellitus: From a metabolic disorder to an inflammatory condition. *World Journal of Diabetes, 6*(4), 598.

Handa, S. S., Khanuja, S. P. S., Longo, G., & Rakesh, D. D. (2008). *Extraction technologies for medicinal and aromatic plants*. United Nations Industrial Development Organization and the International Centre for Science and High Technology.

Harborne, J. B. (1973). *Methods of plant analysis*. In *Phytochemical methods* (pp. 1–10). Chapman and Hall.

Harborne, J. B. (1998). *Phytochemical methods: A guide to modern techniques of plant analysis*. Springer Science & Business Media.

Hughes, J., Rees, S., Kalindjian, S., & Philpott, K. (2011). Principles of early drug discovery. *British Journal of Pharmacology, 162*(6), 1239–1249.

Hussain, F., Islam, A., Bulbul, L., Moghal, M. R., & Hossain, M. S. (2014). *In vitro* thrombolytic potential of root extracts of four medicinal plants available in Bangladesh. *Ancient Science of Life, 33*(3), 162–164.

Ingraham, J. L., & Ingraham, C. A. (1996). *Introduction to microbiology* (6th ed.). Wadsworth Publishing Company.

Jiratchayamaethasakul, C., Ding, Y., Hwang, O., Park, S., Kim, Y., & Lee, H. (2020). *In vitro* screening of elastase, collagenase, hyaluronidase, and tyrosinase inhibitory and antioxidant activities of 22 halophyte plant extracts for novel cosmeceuticals. *Fish Aquatic Sciences, 23*, 6.

John, J., Mathew, A. J., Shreedhara, C. S., & Setty, M. M. (2010). *In vitro* anticancer study of *Clerodendron paniculatum*. *Pharmacologyonline, 3*, 384–391.

Kalra, A., Yetiskul, E., Wehrle, T., & Tuma, F. (2023). Physiology, liver. In *StatPearls*. StatPearls Publishing. Retrieved from https://www.ncbi.nlm.nih.gov/books/NBK535438/

Kaur, C., & Kapoor, H. C. (2002). Anti-oxidant activity and total phenolic content of some Asian vegetables. *International Journal of Food Science and Technology, 37*(2), 153–161.

Kavitake, D., Veerabhadrappa, B., Sudharshan, S. J., Kandasamy, S., Bruntha Devi, P., Dyavaiash, M., & Shetty, P. H. (2022). Oxidative stress alleviating potential of galactan exopolysaccharide from *Weissella confusa* KR780676 in yeast model system. *Scientific Reports, 12*, 1089.

Lobo, V., Patil, A., Phatak, A., & Chandra, N. (2010). Free radicals, antioxidants, and functional foods: Impact on human health. *Pharmacognosy Reviews, 4*(8), 118.

Longo, V. D., Gralla, E. B., & Valentine, J. S. (1996). Superoxide dismutase activity is essential for stationary phase survival in *Saccharomyces cerevisiae*. *Journal of Biological Chemistry, 271*(21), 12275–12280.

Marklund, S., & Marklund, G. (1974). Involvement of the superoxide anion radical in the autoxidation of pyrogallol and a convenient assay for superoxide dismutase. *European Journal of Biochemistry, 47*(3), 469–474.

Mishra, A., Siddiqui, S., & Tiwari, S. (2021). Evaluation on *in vitro* blood clot dissolving potential of aqueous extract of *Sida acuta* Burm. F. leaves. *Journal of Drug Delivery & Therapeutics, 11*(5), 96–99.

Polshettiwar, S. A., & Ganjiwale, R. O. (2007). Spectrophotometric estimation of total tannin in some Ayurvedic eye drops. *Indian Journal of Pharmaceutical Sciences, 69*(4), 574–576.

Prakoso, N. I., & Nita, M. T. (2023). Exploring anticancer activity of the Indonesian guava leaf (*Psidium guajava* L.) fraction on various human cancer cell lines in an *in vitro* cell-based approach. *Open Chemistry, 21*(1), 20230101.

Raheel, R., Saddiqe, Z., Iram, M., & Afzal, S. (2017). *In vitro* antimitotic, antiproliferative and antioxidant activity of stem bark extracts of *Ficus benghalensis* L. *South African Journal of Botany, 111*, 248–257.

Rahman, H., Eswaraiah, M. C., & Dutta, A. M. (2015). *In-vitro* anti-inflammatory and anti-arthritic activity of *Oriza sativa* Var. Joha rice (An aromatic indigenous rice of Assam). *American-Eurasian Journal of Agricultural and Environmental Sciences, 15*(1), 115–121.

Ravindran, R., Chakrapani, G., Mitra, K., & Doble, M. (2020). *Inhibitory activity of traditional plants against Mycobacterium smegmatis and their action on Filamenting temperature sensitive mutant Z (FtsZ)—A cell division protein. PLOS ONE, 15(5), e0232482.* doi:10.1371/journal.pone.0232482

Re, R., Pellegrini, N., Proteggente, A., Pannala, A., Yang, M., & Rice-Evans, C. (1999). Antioxidant activity applying an improved ABTS radical cation decolorization assay. *Free Radical Biology and Medicine, 26*(9-10), 1231–1237.

Riaz, Z., Ali, M. N., Qureshi, Z., & Mohsin, M. (2020). *In vitro* investigation and evaluation of novel drug based on polyherbal extract against type 2 diabetes. *Journal of Diabetes Research, 2020*, 1–9.

Ricciotti, E., & FitzGerald, G. A. (2011). Prostaglandins and inflammation. *Arteriosclerosis, Thrombosis, and Vascular Biology, 31*(5), 986–1000.

Saeedi, P., Petersohn, I., Salpea, P., Malanda, B., Karuranga, S., Unwin, N., Colagiuri, S., Shaw, J., Zimmet, P., & Williams, R. (2019). Global and regional diabetes prevalence estimates for 2019 and projections for 2030 and 2045: Results from the International Diabetes Federation Diabetes Atlas, 9th edition. *Diabetes Research and Clinical Practice, 107843.*

Shamsa, F., Monsef, H., Ghamooshi, R., & Verdian-rizi, M. (2008). Spectrophotometric determination of total alkaloids in some Iranian medicinal plants. *Thai Journal of Pharmaceutical Sciences, 32*, 17–20.

Shih, Y.-E., Lin, Y.-C., Chung, T., Liu, M.-C., Chen, G.-H., Wu, C.-C., & Tzen, J. T. C. (2017). *In vitro* assay to estimate tea astringency via observing flotation of artificial oil bodies sheltered by caleosin fused with histatin 3. *Journal of Food and Drug Analysis, 25*(4), 828–836.

Singleton, V. L., Orthofer, R., & Lamuela-Raventos, R. M. (1999). Analysis of total phenols and other oxidation substrates and antioxidants by means of Folin-Ciocalteu reagent. *Methods in Enzymology, 299*, 152–179.

Smith, W. L., Garavito, R. M., & DeWitt, D. L. (1996). Prostaglandin endoperoxide H synthases (cyclooxygenases)-1 and −2. *Journal of Biological Chemistry, 271*(52), 33157–33160.

Sofowora, A. (1993). *Medicinal plants and traditional medicine in Africa* (2nd ed.). Spectrum Books.

Solich, P., Sedliakova, V., & Karlicek, R. (1992). Spectrophotometric determination of cardiac glycosides by flow-injection analysis. *Analytica Chimica Acta, 269*(2), 199-203.

Svane, S., Sigurdarson, J. J., Finkenwirth, F., Eitinger, T., & Karring, H. (2020). Inhibition of urease activity by different compounds provides insight into the modulation and association of bacterial nickel import and ureolysis. *Scientific Reports, 10*(1).

Tenguria, M., Chand, P., & Upadhyay, R. (2012). Estimation of total polyphenolic content in aqueous and methanolic extracts from the bark of *Acacia nilotica*. *International Journal of Pharmaceutical Science and Research, 3*(9), 3458–3461.

Valko, M., Leibfritz, D., Moncol, J., Cronin, M. T. D., Mazur, M., & Telser, J. (2007). Free radicals and antioxidants in normal physiological functions and human disease. *The International Journal of Biochemistry & Cell Biology, 39*(1), 44–84.

VanderWeele, T. J. (2016). Mediation analysis: A practitioner's guide. *Annual Review of Public Health, 37*(1), 17–32.

Wilson, K., & Walker, J. (Eds.). (2018). *Principles and Techniques of Biochemistry and Molecular Biology* (8th ed.). Cambridge University Press. ISBN: 978-1107162273

Winter, C. A., Risley, E. A., & Nuss, G. W. (1962). Carrageenin-induced edema in hind paw of the rat as an assay for antiinflammatory drugs. *Experimental Biology and Medicine, 111*(3), 544–547.

Yedgar, S., Cohen, Y., & Shoseyov, D. (2006). Control of phospholipase A2 activities for the treatment of inflammatory conditions. *Biochimica et Biophysica Acta (BBA) - Molecular and Cell Biology of Lipids, 1761*(11), 1373–1382.

Youdim, M. B. H., Edmondson, D., & Tipton, K. F. (2006). The therapeutic potential of monoamine oxidase inhibitors. *Nature Reviews Neuroscience, 7*(4), 295–309.

www.ingramcontent.com/pod-product-compliance
Ingram Content Group UK Ltd.
Pitfield, Milton Keynes, MK11 3LW, UK
UKHW062007290726
14090UKWH00022B/1441